A LITMUS TEST CASE OF MODERNITY

INTERDISCIPLINARY STUDIES
ON CENTRAL AND EASTERN EUROPE

Vol. 5

Edited by
Christian Giordano, Nicolas Hayoz & Jens Herlth

PETER LANG
Bern · Berlin · Bruxelles · Frankfurt am Main · New York · Oxford · Wien

LEONIDAS DONSKIS (ED.)

A LITMUS TEST CASE OF MODERNITY

Examining Modern Sensibilities and the Public Domain in the Baltic States at the Turn of the Century

PETER LANG
Bern · Berlin · Bruxelles · Frankfurt am Main · New York · Oxford · Wien

Bibliographic information published by Die Deutsche Nationalbibliothek
Die Deutsche Nationalbibliothek lists this publication in the Deutsche Nationalbibliografie; detailed bibliographic data is available on the Internet at ‹http://dnb.d-nb.de›.

British Library and Library of Congress Cataloguing-in-Publication Data:
A catalogue record for this book is available from The British Library, Great Britain

Library of Congress Cataloging-in-Publication Data

A litmus test case of modernity : examining modern sensibilities and the public domain in the Baltic states at the turn of the century / Leonidas Donskis (ed.).
p. cm. -- (Interdisciplinary studies on Central and Eastern Europe ; v. 5)
ISBN 978-3-0343-0335-4 (alk. paper)
1. Baltic States--Social conditions. 2. Baltic States--Politics and government--1991-
3. Baltic States--Economic conditions. I. Donskis, Leonidas.
HN539.6.L58 2010
306.09485'09049--dc22

2009036001

Cover image by Saulius Bajorinas

ISSN 1661-1349
ISBN 978-3-0343-0335-4

Hochfeldstrasse 32, CH-3012 Bern, Switzerland
info@peterlang.com, www.peterlang.com, www.peterlang.net

Printed in Germany

Table of Contents

Introduction

Lithuania cherishes her historical memories of once having been a multi-ethnic, multi-religious and multi-cultural country. It also cherishes the most generous and noble-spirited traditions of the Romantic ethos of liberal nationalism, and quite justifiably so. In the late 1980s, Lithuania's national movement of rebirth, *Sajudis*, and its 'singing revolution' not only revived the spirit of the nineteenth century epoch of the springtime of the peoples (whose slogan – 'For your and our freedom!' – was raised as the banner), but also became a litmus test of the Soviet policy of glasnost and perestroika. The first breakaway republic in the former Soviet Union, Lithuania came to embody the historic triumph of East-Central Europe's time-honored struggle for freedom.

It was with good reason that the great Polish Romantic poet Adam Mickiewicz, who was born in Lithuania and who regarded Lithuania as his motherland, depicted Lithuania as a mysterious country, which, repeatedly, disappears from history and then returns to it. In 1990, Lithuania restored her independence after fifty years of political and cultural isolation from the rest of the world. In 1918, Lithuania declared her independence after one hundred and twenty-three years as a part of Tsarist Russia. Each time, Lithuania came back into existence through the revival of her historical memory and culture, rather than through the exercise of power. Culture is what led Lithuania from a political non-entity to a political presence. Her culture paved the way to politics, and not the other way around.

Lithuania had long had at least two visions of how to fulfill herself as a modern historical actor. One of them, as mentioned, dealt with Lithuania as a multi-ethnic, multi-religious and multi-cultural country deeply grounded in the political and cultural realities of the Renaissance and Baroque eras. The other sees Lithuania as a culture that is rooted in Romanticism – the Lithuania of mystical influences, spirituality and an organic community. Both visions and interpretations of Lithuanian culture can be richly supported by historical evidence.

The vision of Renaissance and Baroque Lithuania is inseparable from the Polish-Lithuanian Commonwealth, a unique political entity that preceded the EU in more than one way. That of neo-Romantic Lithuania is deeply permeated with archaic and pagan layers of culture and Roman Catholicism - a blend of archaic religious artwork and a modern, more or less neo-Romantic mythology of history and culture. It represents a combination of wooden sculpture and architecture, profoundly archaic in its form and character, and modern mysticism, the latter best represented by the composer and painter Mikalojus Konstantinas Ciurlionis.

In the first half of the twentieth century, Lithuania's self-image came into existence in the form of a moderate messianic construct, casting this small nation as an important bridge between East and West, the former often reduced to Slavic civilization or Russia. The concept of a synthesis of civilizations - East and West - was elaborated by the Lithuanian philosopher Stasys Salkauskis, particularly in *Sur les confins de deux mondes* [On the Boundary of Two Worlds, 1919], a book on Lithuania he wrote in French at the University of Fribourg in Switzerland. So, history claimed that the Republic of Lithuania became an actor on the inter-war European political stage for a short period of time, from 1918 to 1940 when it was occupied and annexed by the Soviet Union. This concept of Lithuania's being on the boundary of two worlds and bridging the civilizations of East and West, further elaborated in other works of Salkauskis, was instrumental in an effort to reflect on the new state's place in the world and also in its cultural and educational policies.

Interestingly enough, Salkauskis argued that Lithuania should never confine herself to one particular pattern of culture. Instead, he insisted that Lithuania should reconcile and embrace - within the limits of her identity and trajectories of consciousness - Germanic, Romance and Slavic influences. The more cultures and influences Lithuania embraces, the more conscious of her complex history and culture she becomes.

Much ink has been spilt since then on the discussion whether it makes sense to take this vision seriously - particularly now that Lithuania has become a member of the EU and NATO, qualifying for membership in clubs that were supposed to be beyond reach for such a long time. Yet we should not forget that Salkauskis's concept of Lithuania as a bridge between the civilizations of East and West stressed the importance of culture, conceived of as a concert of nations and their educational processes rather than political domination or power.

Lithuania's accession to the European Union, and also becoming a member of NATO, are arguably two of the pivotal events in Lithuanian history. This invites reconsideration of what happened to Lithuania over the past sixteen years. There is little doubt that Lithuania has already achieved a turning point in her history, which might be compared only to her baptism in the fourteenth century. A latecomer to Christianity and modernity, a country with several planes of cultural and civilizational identity, Lithuania seems finally to be on her way to integrate herself into the Western system of trade and security.

Historically speaking, Lithuania is an old polity, which dates back to the early Middle Ages. It has an ancient language and an old culture both recalled and revived during the national rebirth movement in the nineteenth century. One of the greatest powers in medieval Europe whose territory stretched from the Baltic Sea to the Black Sea, she eventually crumbled and lost her influence in modern Europe. Bearing in mind the fact that the country was part of Tsarist Russia from 1795 to 1918, that the Lithuanian elite adopted the Polish language and, finally, that Lithuania underwent considerable Russification in the nineteenth century, the emergence of the Republic of Lithuania in 1918 was nothing short of miraculous. Yet Lithuania enjoyed parliamentary democracy for just eight years: in the coup of 1926, the democratic regime was replaced by mild authoritarian rule until 1940. Incidentally, this was the case in all three Baltic states.

At the same time, Lithuania would be unthinkable without her magnificent Jewish legacy. Prior to the Second World War, Lithuania was famous for her very large Jewish community. About 240,000 Jews lived in Lithuania; only 20,000 survived the Holocaust. The Lithuanian capital, Vilnius - occupied by Poland from 1920 to 1939 - was known around the world as the Jerusalem of the North, and many internationally eminent Jews lived in or were from Lithuania. Needless to say, the history of Jewish civilization would be unthinkable without Lithuania's Jews - the Litvaks.

It suffices to recall those who inscribed the names of the Litvaks and Lithuania on the cultural map of the twentieth-century world – the philosophers Emmanuel Lévinas and Aron Gurwitsch, the painters Chaïm Soutine (a close friend of Amedeo Modigliani in Paris), Pinkus Krémègne, Michel Kikoine, Marc Chagall (all these painters were related to Belarus and, in one way or another, to Lithuania – most importantly, all were Litvaks) and Neemija Arbitblatas, the sculptor Jacques Lipchitz, the violinist Jascha Heifetz and the art critic Bernard Berenson.

To cut a long story short, Lithuanian cultural history reads like an exciting novel, if not an adventure story. Much of it remains to be discovered by our fellow Europeans. The same applies to us – only now does Lithuania appear to be capable of truly challenging herself and offering new interpretations of her complex historical past.

What happened in 1940 was a tragedy for the Baltic region: the Baltic states were occupied and annexed by the Soviet Union. Having experienced the worst nightmares of both totalitarian ideologies and regimes during the Second World War, Lithuania was again occupied by the Soviets in 1945, condemning the country to five decades of isolation from the Western world. Lithuania lost considerable groups from her society: as mentioned, hundreds of thousands of Lithuanian Jews perished in the Holocaust, the most educated and prosperous part of Lithuanian society was either exterminated or exiled to Siberia. Tens of thousands of Lithuanians fled to Germany after the Second World War. Having spent several years in DP camps in West Germany, some of them moved to the US, Great Britain, Canada, and Australia; others found their shelter in continental Europe.

Modern Lithuania has emerged as a characteristically East-Central European nation with an emphasis on a strong sense of history and also on the critical role of culture and language in the process of political emancipation. Lithuania can quite legitimately be described as a nation of language, culture, and historical memory. Having been confined to a world of total control, severe censorship, violent politics, cynical lies, sinister ideological indoctrination, and brutal violation of all basic human rights, Lithuania, like other nations of Central and Eastern Europe, knows the taste and value of freedom better than any Western European country. Torn away and isolated from the family of free nations for half a century, Lithuania had finally made her return to where it belonged for centuries, namely, the Western world as a shared space of values.

Since the nineteenth century, literature in Lithuania has become something incomparably more than a sheer matter of fiction and aesthetic experience. For a small people - whose native language and Latin alphabet was banned by Tsarist Russia's administration for forty years (1864–1904), and whose book smugglers were engaged in what was regarded as illegal activities, becoming legendary as heroes of national rebirth and political rebels - literature was bound to become a form of self-assertion and self-discovery.

Czeslaw Milosz, himself born and brought up in Lithuania, once wittily remarked that modern Lithuania was created by a bunch of philologists. If we can assert that culture precedes and anticipates politics, Lithuania would exemplify this better than anything else. The struggle for the survival of the Lithuanian language unavoidably led to its modernization and also to the political mobilization of the intelligentsia.

Modern Lithuanian literature has experienced a number of important influences - Polish, Russian and Scandinavian literature should be mentioned first. Interestingly enough, two fine writers in pre-war Lithuania, Ignas Seinius and Jurgis Savickis, had much to do with the Nordic countries - the master of Lithuanian impressionist prose Ignas Seinius served as the Lithuanian Ambassador to Sweden, whereas Jurgis Savickis, a skilled writer of political memoirs acted as a diplomat in Denmark and Finland before he was appointed the Lithuanian representative to the League of Nations in Geneva.

One of the most enigmatic traits of Lithuanian literature was formed during the Soviet period. Lithuanian poets ceased being merely poets. Instead, they were perceived as the very embodiments of truth, honor and conscience. Their readership and the audience of the poetry reading nights would engage in a form of covert action; a conspiracy of souls against the totalitarian regime's cynical lies and contempt for human individuals, peoples and their freedom. The emergence of poetry readings and theatre performances as a sort of silent conspiracy against brutal oppression, evil and cynical lies sheds new light on the elusive side of existence in Soviet Lithuania, particularly during the early 1970s.

At the same time, Lithuania has a sensitive grasp of political and cultural pluralism by virtue of once having been a multi-ethnic, multi-religious and multi-cultural country. Although political, linguistic and cultural nationalism has considerably changed the character of modern political existence in Lithuania and beyond, Lithuania still has much to say about a peaceful co-existence of religions, cultures and ethnic groups. This is undoubtedly one of the assets and sources of strength of Lithuanian political culture, which reaffirms its roots in Central European tradition of cultural diversity.

Lithuania is a country of emigrants, and it has always been so. Despite the country's relatively small size, Lithuanian culture is disseminated all over the world. Throughout the twentieth century, Lithuanians were a nation of emigrants, settling in Western Europe, North America, South America and Australia, and forming a particularly active and influential Diaspora in the United States of America. It is therefore worth mentioning some émigré scholars who were and continue to be active in Lithuanian culture.

To name just a few: the archaeologist and student of mythology Marija Gimbutas in the USA, the civilization theorist and sociologist of culture Vytautas Kavolis in the USA, the semiotician and literary scholar Algirdas Julius Greimas in France, the art historian Jurgis Baltrusaitis in France (whose father Jurgis Baltrusaitis, a Lithuanian diplomat in Moscow, established himself as a Russian poet writing in Russian and joined the great Russian symbolists), and the political theorist Aleksandras Shtromas in the UK and the USA. All of them had a great impact on Lithuanian culture.

Lithuanian émigrés played a critical role in twentieth-century Lithuanian politics and culture. If they had not championed the Lithuanian cause in the West, Lithuania would have had difficulty restoring her independence. Probably even more important was their role in creating an alternative vision for the future of the country or 'yet another Lithuania.' They made a major contribution to what has been termed by Tomas Venclova, a great poet and literary scholar who teaches literature at Yale University, the second voice of culture, the voice which acquires crucial significance when the first voice either remains silent or sings the wrong or imposed melody.

What is the relationship between Lithuania and the other two Baltic nations? In more than one way, Lithuania differs from Latvia and Estonia. No matter how rich of her historically formed religious communities and minorities, the Roman Catholic Lithuania, due to her historic liaisons with Poland and other Central/East European nations, is much more of an East-Central European nation than the Lutheran Latvia and Estonia. It would be quite misleading to assume that the seemingly identical paths of the Baltic states means that their roles and places in modern history are the same. Lithuania's history and its understanding would be unthinkable without taking into account such countries as Poland, Belarus and Ukraine, among others, whereas Latvia is inseparable from major German and Swedish influences, and Estonia from Swedish and Danish, not to mention her close cultural ties with Finland. As mentioned already, Lithuania is an old polity with her strong presence in Mediaeval and Renaissance Europe, whilst Latvia and Estonia emerged as new political actors in the twentieth century.

It was with sound reason, then, that after 1990, when Lithuania and other two Baltic nations became independent, politicians and media people started making jokes about the unity of three Baltic sisters, which was achieved by them through their common experience of once having been three inmates in the same cell of the same prison. This led the former foreign minister (now president) Toomas Hendrik Ilves of Estonia to go so far as to describe Estonia as a Nordic country, rather as a Baltic nation. In fact, the Baltic states, having come into existence, underwent considerable political change in the twentieth century. It is worth recalling that Finland, before World War II, was considered a Baltic State as well. This is to say that the four Baltic states existed in interwar Europe – the fact that only three entered the twenty-first century, is an oddity of recent history.

Yet some similarities and affinities of the Baltic states are too obvious to need emphasis. All three nations stood at the same historic crossroads after World War I; all were linked to the fate of Russia in terms of (in)dependence and emancipation; all three existed as independent states from 1918 to 1940; at that time, all three introduced liberal minority policies granting a sort of personal, non-territorial cultural autonomy to their large minorities – Lithuania to her Jewish, Latvia to her German, and Estonia to her German and Russian minorities; all three sought the source of strength and inspiration in their ancient languages and cultures; all have a strong

Romantic element in their historical memory and self-perception; and last but not least, all benefited from émigrés and their role in politics and culture.

Suffice it to mention that presidents of all three Baltic states were or continue to be émigrés who spent much of their time abroad and who returned to their respective countries when independence was restored after 1990 – Valdas Adamkus of Lithuania, Vaira Vyke-Freiberga of Latvia, and Toomas Hendrik Ilves of Estonia. Most importantly, the trajectories of Lithuanian and Baltic identity allow us to understand the history of the twentieth century better than anything else.

This volume offers the insights of Baltic and Western European scholars into present socio-economic, migration, identity, diaspora, gender, race, media, and historical memory issues in the Baltic states. The book attempts to show the intensity and depth of social, economic and cultural change in the Baltic region, which enables us to understand why and how three small countries have become a litmus test case of modernity and its sensibilities, stretching from authoritarian and totalitarian past to their liberal-democratic present with its promises to keep fidelity to freedom of conscience and expression, civil liberties, rule of law, and diversity. An historic jump from the Soviet Union to the European Union was accompanied by a dramatic struggle of the Baltic states for their inalienable right to return to the political map of the world.

The Baltic states allow us a better glimpse of the twentieth century history than anything else. If we seek to understand the horrible political and mental legacies of totalitarianism, a painful withdrawal from Europe's public space and value system followed by a gradual return to it, or the transformation from the planned economy to the nearly libertarian free-market zeal so characteristic of the Baltic region now, then, as Arnold J. Toynbee would have it, we have to study the modern saga of the withdrawal and return of the Baltic states.

Leonidas Donskis

Part I:
Socio-Economic Issues

Tatjana Muravska

The EU Approach to Socio-Economic Democracy and the Post EU Accession Latvia

The economic development of the new member states after the UE enlargements of 2004 and 2007 can be characterized in many ways. However, one of them was of particular importance: the new member states need to increase economic efficiency and productivity. The task of bringing the economies of the new members up to par with the economies of the old member states has proven to be a formidable one. As has been noted in the Lisbon strategy, a framework for further development of the EU - highlighting a strategy for social policy implementation, increasing employment and productivity in the member states - was set up.

The discussion about which particular model of development Latvia should follow after attaining membership to the EU - in the implementation of different aspects of social policy, social partnership and social dialog - is still not concluded. It has also gained particular attention at the time of the current crisis. This paper will examine the case of Latvia for the years 2004–2008, when high economic growth was combined with natural population decline and emigration that called for policies to promote human capital development in the country.

Economic Democracy and the European Union

Economic democracy is a concept that was developed in the 19th and 20th centuries, with the main idea of applying democratic principles to an economic system. This concept aims to minimize potential conflict in the decision-making process on the subject of the wealth distribution in society, and focuses on such issues as concentration of wealth and on democratic principles. A macro-level approach to this dilemma requires involvement of a government to develop a mechanism for the harmonization of interests of different social groups. Besides, this approach needs certain strategies for the transformation of power and property by the promotion of further democratization of a welfare state and public sector, corporative management, cooperatives and self-management.

The implementation of the concept of socio-economic democracy is foreseen through the implementation of social policy and social protection. The European Social Charter articulates a number of fundamental rights in such areas as collective bargaining, protection from unjustified dismissal, safety at work etc.[1] It also involves regulation of employer-employee relations in a form of financial participation, which is regarded in the EU as a pillar of European social model.[2]

The idea of financial participation originates in the notion of the conflicting nature of laissez-faire capitalism, when wealth is generated only by labor with appropriate skills and knowledge. A number of schemes have been discussed and implemented with different degrees of achievement in different countries and continents since the first International Congresses on profit-sharing[3] in Paris in 1889[4] that also adopted the definition of the profit sharing. It is remarkable that the economic crisis in the US steel industry in the late 1930s resulted in the labor-management cooperation known as the Scanlon plan[5], which focused on financial participation. In 1956, Louis Kelso

1 European Social Charter, Council of Europe Treaty, adopted in 1961, revised in 1996, http://www.hrcr.org/docs/Social_Charter/soccharter.wpd.

2 Jens Lowitzsch et al.(2007) 'Financial Participation for a New Social Europe. A Building Block Approach,' Free University Berlin, p. 5.

3 Profit sharing refers to definite arrangements under which workers regularly receive, in addition to their wages and salaries, a share on some predetermined basis, in the profits of the undertaking, the sum allocated to workers varying with the level of profits.

4 T.W. Cynog-Jones (OECD, 1956), 'Workers Investments in Industry,' OECD Employment Outlook, July 1995, Chapter 4, 'Profit-sharing in OECD countries,' pp. 139–166.

5 Kenneth W. Thornicroft (1991), 'Promises Kept, Promises Broken: Reciprocity and the Scanlon Plan,' *Journal: Employee Relations*, 1991, vol. 13, no. 5, pp. 12–21.

invented the Employee Stock Ownership Plan (ESOP)[6] which in the beginning was implemented in many companies in the US, UK ,and Ireland, and later spread into other European countries.

One of the most conceptual debates in Western Europe in modern times has been on economic democracy and the transition from the capitalist welfare state to democratic socialism. The major themes considered have focused on the free market, market socialism and socialization of the market. The major question remains whether market forces should play a central role in the economy or whether they should function under the pressure of democratic decision making. These debates have been determined to great extend by the 'Swedish Model' of socialism and by the theories of Gösta Rehn, one of the fathers of the that model, and Rudolf Meidner. The most influential economic wage earner fund model of the twentieth century is known as the 'Rehn-Meidner Model.'[7] As the result of the economic crises in the 1970s and 1980s, the Rehn-Meidner model became one of the most widely used financial participation schemes in Europe. It argues that financial participation is essential for economic democracy and is a basis for employee motivation. However, financial participation schemes in different societies have varied considerably and have clearly reflected very different traditions and regulations.

European initiatives have, since the early 1990s, encouraged moves to boost profit-sharing, employee share ownership and employee stock options throughout the European Union.

In past decades modern welfare states were confronted with major economic, technological, and demographic challenges. The social dimension of the Lisbon Strategy, which aims at the modernization of the European social model, can thus contribute to the economic dynamism of the EU rather than impairing it. The Lisbon

6 Louis O. Kelso, Patricia Hetter Kelso (1986), 'Democracy and Economic Power: Extending the ESOP Revolution Through Binary Economics,' Cambridge, Massachusetts: Ballinger Publishing Co., pp. 15–54.

7 Brian Burkitt, Phillip Whyman (1994). 'Employee Investment Funds in Sweden: Their Past, Present and Future,' *Journal: European Business Review*, vol. 94, no. 4, pp. 22–29; Lennart Erixon (2008), 'The Rehn-Meidner Model in Sweden: Its Rise, Challenges and Survival,' Department of Economics, Stockholm University (http://www.ne.su.se/paper/wp08_02.pdf).

Strategy also seeks to strengthen the EU'ssocial cohesion by improving its economic structures and efficiency.

Social policy is increasingly accepted in the European Union as being a productive factor. Building the sustained economic growth is necessary for long-term employment creation and social protection schemes in all European states, but it is of special importance in the new member states. This task will require an unprecedented level of political, economic, and social cooperation between governments, business, social partners and individuals in every member state throughout Europe.

The most common approach is to consider social policy of the EU or social dimension of European integration, as actions carried out under the social policy chapter of the EC Treaties. The subsidiarity principle enshrined by the EU Single European Act (1986), the Maastricht Social Agreement (1992), Amsterdam (1997), and Nice (2001)[8] means that the competence of the EU is restricted to areas where national governments cannot meet policy objectives through their own actions. The social policy is the responsibility of the member states and they set common goals and promote cooperation, as well as exchanging information and experience with the Open Method of Coordination (OMC). European level regular debates on the national employment policy have a harmonizing effect on the social policies of Europe.[9]

Consequently the national policies in Europe can no longer be analyzed without reference to the EU.

8 Consolidated version of the Treaty, *Official Journal C 321 E* of 29 December 2009; Single European Act (1986), *Official Journal L 169* of 29 June 1987; Treaty on European Union (1992), *Official Journal C 191* of 29 July 1992; Treaty of Amsterdam, *Official Journal C 340* of 10 November 1997; Treaty of Nice (2001), *Official Journal C 80* of 10 March 2001.

9 The EU implemented an Open Method of Coordination (OMC) at the Essen European Council of 1994. The OMC is an EU level approach that is an alternative to regulation. It is based on European guidelines for national action plans, and national reports based on common indicators and EU level evaluations. Since the Amsterdam Treaty has formalized employment policy of the EU, the EU has adopted employment policy guidelines. Their specification and implementation is left to the national level so that the domestic situation can be taken into considerations.

The EU policy makers are confronted by conflicting social and economic goals, i.e., high levels of productivity and growth and maximization of social protection, inclusion and cohesion. However, the EU social policy and the Lisbon Strategy can be tools for EU member states in the process of adapting to the more competitive environment brought by globalization. This is critically important for the further reform of the European social model. Given the diversity that exists, reform can only be addressed at the national level. The definition of European social model was adopted by the Barcelona European Council in March 2002 and it states 'the European social model is based on good economic performance and high levels of social protection, education, and social dialogue.'[10] Most specifically, the Commission hopes to modernize the 'European social model.' This definition stresses the necessity to combine social cohesion with good economic performance. Interest in financial participation has been growing in the European Union. There has been a series of initiatives at EU level in this area since 1990 and began with the PEPPER (Promotion of Employee Participation in Profits and Enterprise Results Report).Reports commissioned by the European Commission. The European Council[11]_recommendations for the promotion of employees' financial participation[12] encourage the European Commission, the member states and social partners to promote the concept of the financial participation of employees. In

10 Presidency Conclusions, Barcelona European Council, 15–16 March 2002, paragraph 22, (http://ue.eu.int/ueDocs/cms_Data/docs/pressData/en/ec/71025.pdf).

11 The Promotion of Participation by Employed Persons in Profits and Enterprise Results (including equity participation) (92/443/EEC). European Council Recommendation of 27 July 1992. (http://eurlex.europa.eu/smartapi/cgi/ sga_doc?smartapi!celexapi!prod!CELEXnumdoc&lg=en&numdoc=31992H0443 & model=guichett).

12 PEPPER Reports. EC (http://www.eurofound.europa.eu/areas/participationatwork/pepperreports.htm), P5_TA (2003) 0253 Employee Financial Participation. European Parliament resolution on the Commission communication to the Council, the European Parliament, the Economic and Social Committee and the Committee of the Regions on a framework for the promotion of employee financial participation (COM(2002) 364 – 2002/2243(INI)) (http://www.europarl.europa.eu/registre/seance_pleniere/textes_adoptes/definitif/2003/ 06-05/0253/P5_TA(2003)0253_EN.pdf).

2002 the Commission issued a Communication on the topic, calling on member states to take steps to assist the development of financial participation. Most of the member states have taken initiatives to promote financial participation.[13] France and the UK have a long tradition of encouraging financial participation. Ireland, Finland, and the Netherlands focus on achieving greater employee involvement, improved productivity, competitiveness, and wage flexibility on labor markets. The governments of Germany, Spain and Italy encouraged social partners to promote financial participation schemes in the course of their negotiations. However, there are differing traditions and practice concerning financial participation schemes in the countries of the European Union. For example as a study by Andrew Pendleton and Erik Poutsma[14] shows, Belgium has adopted a law on profit-sharing and share ownership; France has implemented a new law to promote financial participation in SMEs; Germany has taken measures to promote employee share ownership as well as reforming its company law to facilitate the use of stock options. Italy has also made changes in company law, providing new opportunities for financial participation schemes, and has advocated a more coherent framework for employee share ownership. In the European Commission's documentation, financial participation is divided into the following main forms: *profit-sharing, employee share ownership* and *employee stock options*.[15] Participation in profits means sharing of profits between those providing the capital and those providing the labor by giving employees a variable income, in addition to their fixed pay, that is linked with the profits or another measure of the enterprise's results. Employee's shareholding offers employees indirect participation in the enterprise's performance in the form of

13 A Commission Report links employee financial participation and productivity. European Industrial Relations Observatory online (http://www.eurofound.europa.eu/eiro/1997/02/inbrief/eu9702106n.htm).

14 Andrew Pendleton and Erik Poutsma (2004), Nijmegen: Manchester Metropolitan University and Radboud University, 'Financial Participation: The Role of Governments and Social Partners,' Luxembourg: Office for Official Publications of the European Communities, European Foundation for the Improvement of Living and Working Conditions, pp. 9–17.

15 EC Working Paper on Employee Financial Participation, July 2001(EU0108232F) (http://www.eurofound.europa.eu/eiro/2001/08/feature/eu0108232f.htm).

dividends and/or appreciation of the value of the capital they hold.[16] Employee stock options grant employees a right to acquire shares at some future point at a fixed price that is set when the right is granted. There is also a range of hybrid schemes, including convertible bonds, phantom stock, and stock appreciation rights.[17]

The challenge to balance the economic and social policies agenda is a challenge in particularly for the new EU member states struggling for economic convergence, as is the case for Latvia. Following the streamlining of the social policy, member states are now charged with translating the common objectives into National Development Plans.

The European Approach to the Social Model

There is not one European social model, as European countries have diverse approaches to social policy. However, in the context of the European experience of social policy implementation, four major models can be distinguished.

The Anglo-Saxon model, consisting of liberal Anglo-American market capitalism with the domination of the free market, is followed by the UK and Ireland and is based on a more limited collective provision of social protection and more flexible labor markets. This model is more oriented towards individual responsibility and market solutions to social issues. The Rhineland or Continental model (a corporatist-conservative one) of social welfare is supported

16 The Council, the European Parliament, the Economic and Social Committee and the Committee of the Regions – 'On a framework for the promotion of employee financial participation COM/2002/0364 final' (http://eurlex.europa.eu/smartapi/cgi/sga_doc?smartapi!celexplus!prod!DocNumber&lg=en&type_doc=COMfinal&an_doc=2002&nu_doc=364).

17 Andrew Pendleton and Erik Poutsma (2204), Nijmegen: Manchester Metropolitan University and Radboud University, Financial Participation: The Role of Governments and Social Partners. Luxembourg: Office for Official Publications of the European Communities, 2004 ISBN 92-897-0887-5, European Foundation for the Improvement of Living and Working Conditions, p. 2–3.

by France and Germany, as well as some other Central European countries. All of them share several communalities - such as equality, solidarity, non-discrimination, redistribution of resources - and are very distinct from the Anglo-Saxon model. The Continental model entails the provision of social assistance through public insurance-based systems in the Bismarckian tradition. In these countries, the role of the market in the provision of social assistance is limited and employment protection is high. The Mediterranean model (a post-authoritarian model) combines high legal employment protection with lower levels of unemployment benefits. The Nordic or Scandinavian model - social-democratic - is characterized by a high level of social protection, high taxes and includes a labor market that emphasizes significant investment into social welfare.[18] The models influence the levels of productivity and efficiency of a national economy. According to Esping-Andersen, the structure of the various welfare states has been historically influenced also by the social balance of power and the shifting patterns of political alliances and co-operation between various social forces.[19]

Table 1. Social Models in the EU

	Efficiency (social policy as a productive factor)		
	Low		High
Equity	High	Rhineland/Continentals	Nordic
	Low	Mediterranean	Anglo-Saxon

As many of the studies in this area show, the process did and does produce mixed results, as well as controversy, reflected in both economic policies and social policy implementation. All models involve government interventions to achieve a fairer distribution of income,

18 Sapir, Andre.(2006), 'Globalisation and the Reform of the European Social Models,' *Journal of Common Market Studies*, vol. 44, no. 2, pp. 369–390..

19 Gosta Esping-Andersen (2004), UK: Blackwell Publishing Ltd. pp. 144–221.

provide social protection, impact on employment as well as promoting equality of opportunity. The new member states are in the process of developing their own model for social policy development but they may also have their own contribution to the European social model.

Social policy was not one of the major issues in the EU initially; however, the Treaty of Rome established the European Social Fund (ESF)[20] and the Economic and Social Committee. Moreover, in the 1970s and 1980s there were some steps towards the implementation of social policy as one of the tasks of the European Community. The crises in the 1970s and 1980s influenced certain civil society movements to launch a campaign to develop social policy at the EU-level. This trend came to a stop when the subsidiarity principle was formally enshrined in the Maastricht Treaty.

Currently all member states of the European Union are showing the same, or at least very similar, symptoms of crisis. They are experiencing the same problem situations (weak growth, unemployment, negative demographic trends, overloading of the social welfare systems), to which the reform process is a reaction.

European Union social policy now has a broad scope of action plans that range from establishing Europe-wide legislation to promoting non-binding exchanges of information and opinions related to the European social model.

The fundamental components of European social policy are the OMC with exchanges of best practice as well as an orientation of the European Social Fund to encourage social inclusion. The ESF and OMC are two instruments for supporting social inclusion efforts by member states. The OMC formulates common objectives which all member states are expected to implement through national measures in the areas of social protection, social inclusion, pensions, health, long-term care, and poverty prevention. The overarching objectives of the OMC for social protection and social inclusion are to promote:

- social cohesion, equality between men and women and equal opportunities for all through adequate, accessible, financially

20 The ESF was created in 1957 to ensure the solidarity between the member states. (http://ec.europa.eu/employment_social/esf/index_en.htm).

sustainable, adaptable and efficient social protection systems and social inclusion policies;
- effective and mutual interaction between the Lisbon objectives of greater economic growth, more and better jobs and greater social cohesion, and the EU's Sustainable Development Strategy;
- good governance, transparency and the involvement of stakeholders in the design, implementation and monitoring of policy.[21]

Social policy in the European Union incorporates labor law, occupational health and safety as well as gender mainstreaming. It is also sets standards and objectives in these areas, as well as laying down the principles of anti-discrimination policy. The European Union has no powers to harmonize the numerous, in some cases very different systems of social protection in the member states. Instead, its role is to coordinate these systems in order to protect the main principles of the Common market. The European Employment Strategy was launched in 1997 to encourage exchange of information and joint discussions by all member states with involvement to the social dialog social partners, the European Parliament, European Economic and Social Committee, and the Committee of Regions.

A principle of 'flexicurity' was established to conciliate both employers' and workers' needs, flexibility and security, by ensuring the worker safe transitions inside the labor market, while maintaining and improving competitiveness of the companies and also preserving the European social model. Based on consultations with the member states, international organizations, social partners and academic community, the European Commission has suggested 'pathways' and 'common principles' in order to achieve flexicurity.[22] In the Integrated Guidelines (IG) member states are asked to promote flexibility combined with employment security - flexicurity - and

21 European Commission. The communication 'Working together, working better: proposals for a new framework for the open co-ordination of social protection and inclusion policies' (http://ec.europa.eu/employment_social/spsi/docs/social_inclusion/2006/objectives_en.pdf).

22 'Flexicurity Pathways. Turning hurdles into stepping stones,' June 2007, Report by the European Expert Group on Flexicurity. (http://ec.europa.eu/social/main.jsp?catId=117&langId=en).

reduce labor market segmentation with due regard to the role of the social partners.

The Legacy of Social Policy Development in Latvia 2004-2008

The requirements for social policy development in Latvia are determined by the EU common aims in relation to social protection and employment policies. This helps to create the overall domestic system for social policy implementation. social policy system development process in Latvia before the accession was significantly influenced by programs and projects implemented by international organizations such as the World Bank, the United Nations Development Programme, International Labor Organization and the European Union. This provides sustainability of the main principles and measures of social policy set up already before accession.

The legal framework development for the social policy implementation in Latvia was a long process that coincided with the transition to a market economy, structural reforms, requirements to fulfill the Copenhagen criteria for the accession to the EU, and the urgent need to provide a social safety net system.

These conflicting trends in the development of the socio-economic system are reflected in the legislative process. Latvian legislation does not give an explicit definition of the term 'social protection.'[23] Nevertheless Latvia has signed several international agreements on human rights and welfare as well as social protection. The most important of these documents are the Universal Declaration on Human Rights (UN)[24] and the European Social Charter (ESC)[25].

23 EC Regulation Nr. 322/97 art. 2.

24 The Universal Declaration of Human Rights, United Nations General Assembly resolution 217 A (III) from 10 December 1948.

25 European Social Charter, Council of Europe Treaty, adopted in 1961, revised in 1996. (http://www.hrcr.org/docs/Social_Charter/soccharter.wpd).

The Constitution of Latvia (article 109)[26] assures everyone the right to social security when old or in the case of work inability or unemployment.

An accession period was required to design and implement the National Employment Plan[27] launched in 2004 and a National Action Plan for Reduction of Poverty and Social Exclusion (2004)[28] that was in line with the Single National Economy Strategy (2004-2006)[29], Joint Memorandum on Social Inclusion (2003).[30] The Ministry of Welfare in Latvia has issued two important strategy documents: the 'Conception of the Development of Labor Protection from 2007–2013' and 'The Program for Development of Labor Protection from 2007–2010.'

It is important to stress that major legislative steps to develop the social protection system were taken in the pre-accession period. However this process was not always systematic because it was frequently demand-driven, as in the case of pensions. This increases a risk of diminishing public confidence towards the stability and sustainability not only to the pension system but to the safety net system in general.

Social policy administration is a complex process and requires the active involvement of number of government institutions and agencies such as the Ministry of Welfare, Ministry of Health, State Employment Agency and others. It also requires an ensuring social dialog with the stakeholders. While the economic development aspect and its various components are fully recognized, the social dimension is more diffuse and not always fully integrated in the development process. Understandably, often different interests promote economic growth and social development:

26 Constitution of the Republic of Latvia (1992), as amended, (www.likumi.lv).

27 European Foundation for the Improvement of Living and Working Conditions. (http://www.eurofound.europa.eu/areas/qualityoflife/eurlife/index.php?template=3&radioindic=158&idDomain=3).

28 Latvian National Action Plan for Reduction of Poverty and Social Exclusion (2004–2006) (accepted on July 23, 2004).

29 Tautsaimniecibas vienota strategija, 2004. (http://www.likumi.lv/doc.php?id=72377).

30 Joint Memorandum on Social Inclusion prepared by Latvia together with European Commission (JIM), signed on December 18, 2003.

The social benefit system among the others includes unemployment, benefits. The basic structure of the benefits has been continued in the after-accession period. The general policy direction has been employment centered, i.e., the social risks are compensated taking into account earlier earnings for which social insurance payments have been made. The individual is seen as responsible for his own protection. The means-tested benefit allocation is secondary.

The percentage of GDP spent on social protection in Latvia and in the other Baltic States is very significantly lower that in the rest of the European Union.

In Latvia, social protection expenditure[31] accounted for 12.2% of GDP in 2006. This ratio of social protection expenditures to GDP has furthermore been decreasing: it was 12.9% and 12.4% of GDP in 2004 and 2005, respectively. Similarly, the ratio has been declining in the other Baltic countries as well, while it remains stable between 27% and 28% of GDP in EU25.

The EU27 average continues to mask major disparities between member states. Social protection expenditure as a percentage of GDP was around 30% in 2006 in Belgium (30.1%), Denmark (29.1%), Germany (28.7%), France (31.1%), the Netherlands (29.3%), Austria (28.5%) and Sweden (30.7%), and below 15% in Latvia (12.2%), Estonia (12.4%) and Lithuania (13.2%). These disparities reflect differences in living standards, but are also indicative of the diversity of national social protection systems and of the demographic, economic, social and institutional structures specific to each member state.

Expenditure on social protection has been steadily increasing since 2000, but at a slower rate then the overall state budget (see Table 2), reaching almost two billion Euro in 2006 (and increasing further thereafter; the precise data was inaccessible at the moment of writing). Unemployment benefits have been increasing at the same rated as the increase in the total budget for social security. Since

31 Social protection expenditure and receipts are calculated in line with the methodology of the 1996 version of the ESSPROS (European System of Integrated Social Protection Statistics) Manual. Expenditure includes social benefits, administration costs and other expenditure linked to social protection schemes. Social benefits are recorded without deduction of taxes or other compulsory levies payable by recipients. 'Tax benefits' (tax reductions granted to households as part of social protection) are generally excluded.

mid-2008, with rising unemployment (see Table 3), expenditures for unemployment benefits have been rising rapidly.

Table 2. Social Security Expenditures in Latvia 2000–2006, Million Euro (according to ESSPROS classification)

	2000	2001	2002	2003	2004	2005	2006
Total expenditure for social security	1,032.4	1,062.9	1,141.2	1,253.2	1,367.6	1,120.2	1,368.2
Unemployment expenditures	38.0	33.7	33.9	37.4	45.5	58.9	70.01

Source: Central Statistical Bureau, Latvia electronic databases (tables 12–15)

The Baltic States had shown positive and strong economic development until mid-2008. The most impressive growth rate among the Baltic States was experienced by Latvia, which was also the highest in the EU until recently. Latvia's GDP growth was more than 10% per year during 2004–2007 (2004 - 10.4%; 2006 - 11.9%; end of 2007 - 10.2%). In Estonia the GDP growth in the same period was 4.5% and in Lithuania 8.1%.[32]

However, experts had repeatedly warned Latvia during 2007 for the need to have a strategy to avoid a 'hard landing' for its economy. That in general refers also to the sister states in the Baltics[33].

In 2008, real GDP contracted by 4.6% after the economy had accumulated major imbalances in 2005–2007, when rapid expansion was based on domestic demand fuelled by easy credit conditions and an expansionary fiscal stance. The recession, which started in the

32 Eurostat. *Flash Estimate* 14 February 2008.

33 'Worrying about a Crash,' *the Economist*: July 5th 2007. (http://www.economist.com/world/europe/displaystory.cfm?story_id=9443551). Statement by IMF Mission to Latvia on 2007, article IV Consultation Discussions *Press Release* no. 07/87, May 4, 2007. (http://www.imf.org/external/np/sec/pr/2007/pr0787.htm).

first half of 2008 and originated in the reversal of the domestic real estate boom, worsened rapidly when risk aversion became extreme on the global financial markets.[34]

Table 3. The Economic Forecast for Latvia in the Spring of 2009 by the European Commission

	2007	2008	2009	2010
GDP growth (%, yoy)	10.0	-4.6	-13.1	3.2
Inflation (%, yoy)	10.1	15.3	4.6	-0.7
Unemployment (%)	6.0	7.5	15.7	16.0
Public budget balance (% of GDP)	-0.4	-4.0	-11.1	-13.6
Current account balance (% of GDP)	-22.5	-13.6	-1.5	-1.9

Source: European Commission

Between 2003 and 2007 there has been surplus in the social budget (see Table 4) as opposed to the general budget and a debate in the society accelerated as to whether it should be invested in the financial markets to save for the future to prepare for the future accelerating social payment that would come with the aging of society, or alternatively if it should be used for increasing pensions for the current pensioners and social benefit recipients. The increase of the social insurance budget depends directly on social insurance payments made from earned income. As seen in Table 4, the social insurance budget from 2004 to 2007 had a positive balance at the end of the year and increased from 60.8 million Euro to 458.6 million Euro in that time.

34 EC European Economy no 32009, May 4, 2009.(http://ec.europa.eu/economy_finance/pdf/2009/springforecasts/lv.html).

Table 4. State Social Insurance Budget Trends in Latvia 2003–2007 in Million Euro

Year	2003	2004	2005	2006	2007
Income - total	800.1	929.6	1049.1	1396.4	1777.3
Expenses - total	801.8	868.8	980.1	1137.4	1318.5
Fiscal balance	-1.7	60.8	48.5	258.9	458.6

Source: Central Statistical Bureau, Latvia

Evidence suggests that in Europe there is a general tendency for countries with relatively high levels of GDP per head to have a more equal distribution of income (as measured by Gini index), whereas with rapid economic development also the Gini index increases, i.e., the gap between the rich and the poor increases. In Latvia the Gini coefficient has been increasing by about 1% every year since 2004, thus widening social gap in Latvian society. Income is more equally distributed in most EU member states than in Latvia. The Gini coefficient in 2004 in EU was 32.7[35], while in Latvia it was 35.5, comparable to the US coefficient of 35.7.

Regional analysis of Latvia's per capita GDP reveals another cause for concern: increasing regional disparities in personal disposable income. The Gini index measuring inequality in the distribution of per capita disposable income in 2006 was 0.36, compared to the level of 0.30 in 1996.[36] To radically change regional disparities in the country requires efficient implementation of the Cohesion Funds and

35 The social situation in the European Union 2007; Social Cohesion through Equal Opportunities, European Commission, DG for Employment, Social Affairs and Equal opportunities, April 2008; the Gini coefficient is defined as the relationship of cumulative shares of the population arranged according to the level of income, to the cumulative share of the equalized total net income received by them.

36 European Foundation for the Improvement of Living and Working Conditions. (http://www.eurofound.europa.eu/areas/qualityoflife/eurlife/index.php?template=3&radioindic=158&idDomain=3).

especially ESF in the retraining of human resources and business environment development with particular attention to small and medium enterprises.(SMEs).

However, efforts are also needed to improve existing and imminent enterprise performance in the area of health and safety at work. As it is stated in the European Single Act (Article 118A), member states should pay particular attention to encouraging improvement especially in the working environment as regards the health and safety of workers. EC adopted a large number of Directives that covers many elements of safety at work.[37] The EU accession has promoted discussion on health and safety issues at the workplaces as the accession of new member states has reopened inherent tensions in the EU policymaking in health and safety at the workplace as a result of two incompatible objectives: the need to ensure broad member state compliance with regulation around agreed minimum standards through active regulatory enforcement and the promotion of voluntary initiatives in the management of work place risks and hazards in order to create 'a culture of prevention.'

Table 5 summarizes the accident situation at the work place in Latvia according to the governmaent labor inspectorate.

Table 5. Health and Safety at Work: Work Place Accidents in Latvia

	2004	2005	2006	2007
Number of workers (millions)	1.018	1.036	1.088	1.119
Workplace accidents	1402	1568	1772	1870
Fatalities	61	56	53	58
Serious injuries	244	275	293	268

Source: State Work Inspection, 2007 report

37 Council Directive on 89/391/EEC/ of 12 June 89 on the 'Introduction of Measures to Encourage Improvements in the Safety and Health of Workers at Work.' *Official Journal of the EU L* 183 of 29 June, 1989, p. 1–8.

It is important to note that while the number of fatalities and serious injuries have remained constant between 2004 and 2007, the number of workplace accidents has shown a significant increase (Table 5), considerably in excess to the increasing size of the workforce. It is to be hoped that the implementation of the EU twinning project to further the occupational health and safety strategy will lead to the expected results.

According to the European Agency for Safety and Health at Work and estimating the EU labor forces to be about 220 million, the fatalities rate per million workers in the EU is 25 as compared with over 50 in Latvia. Taking into account the cost estimations by the Agency of work place accidents in the EU (20 bln Euro per year – this would represent for Latvia approximately 100 million Euros per ml workers on the average). However, in view in the more than double workplace accident rates in Latvia using fatalities as an indicator, the cost of workplace accidents in Latvia may exceed 200 million Euros. Thus workplace accidents represent not only a human tragedy, but are also a major economic burden that must be urgently addressed.

Preconditions for the Financial Motivation of Manpower

The demographic imbalance in the future can be linked to potential fiscal crises in many European countries, including Latvia. The society will experience important changes and will never be the same as today. The economically active population will fall, and the inactive population will grow, so the working people will have to work more productively and more to provide for the leaving conditions of the elderly; at least at the current level. It may also turn out to be the case that not the young care for the old, but rather the old care for the even older. In itself, the demographic development implies increasing social budget requirements and brings with itself need for more healthcare, social houses, care work, as well as important social policy decisions – potentially increasing the age of retirement etc.[38]

It is also important to create a basis for capital formation in the country, one of the trends of which is the establishment of pensions funds.

In Latvia the most dramatic reforms of the pension system were carried out before the EU accession, i.e., the transition to the three tier pension system. Following accession Latvia has continued the improvements and adjustments of the pension system, however without major changes. Size of all pensions have increased during the previous years and the average old age pension has increased by more than 40 percent in the after-accession period, the invalidity and survivors pensions have increased by almost the same percentage. However, the living costs have also increased significantly due to inflation and the minimum wage has increased from 141 Euro in 2004 to 189 Euro in 2007 and 229 Euro in 2008. [39]

The old age pensions comprise the majority of all pension payments. Comparing the old age pensions with subsistence minimum in Latvia, we see that the welfare of the elderly has effectively not improved, a worrying situation. Slightly over 80% of pensioners in Latvia received pensions which are below the subsistence minimum defined by the state[40].

Pension indexation is performed according to the Law 'On State Pensions'[41] considering the actual inflation and actual increase in average insurance contributions wage. The system of pension indexation made by the Ministry of Welfare attempts to protect the pensions from the rapid increase of inflation in Latvia because the applied rates are higher than official inflation. However, the indexation system has not managed to improve the welfare level of pensioners and it does not solve the problem connected with current low pensions.

To ensure the stability of the pension system over the long term, in accordance with conception on pension reform and the Law On State

38 Cunska Z. Muravska T. (2009) 'Social Policy Implementation in Latvia: Post EU Accession' in Promotion of Social Policies – an Investment in the Future, Riga: EC Representation in Latvia and the University of Latvia, p.293–294.

39 Central Statistical Bureau, Latvia.

40 Volskis E. (2008), Pensiju sistemas pilnveidosanas problemas Latvija, promocijas darbs ekonomikas doktora grada iegusanai, Riga: Latvijas Universitate.

41 LR Law On Pensions. Latvijas Vestnesis, 182 (465), 23.11.1995, as amended.

Pensions, the pensioning age for women was gradually increased from 55 to 62 years. The pensioning age for men has already been 62 years since January 2003. If the social insurance period exceeds 30 years, i.e., if the person has been working and paid social insurance tax for at least 30 years, he/she can benefit of early pensioning option and retire two years before the stated pensioning age, i.e., at the age of 60 years. Early pensioning will be possible for only three more years, until 2012.

A controversial issue in the pension system development was the complete transfer of administrative rights of the state's funded pension funds to the private sector. It has led to a high concentration of financial resources within the private pension plans and investments of these resources abroad, especially the US bonds. As a consequence, these resources are not facilitating the development of the Latvian national economy, but rather working against the intervention policy of the Bank of Latvia.[42]

Accession to the EU has brought rapid and fundamental changes for Central and East European countries (CEEC). The CEEC have enlarged the internal market of the EU and, as many of the studies in this area show, the process has produced mixed results: free movement of people has introduced difficulties with regard to cross-national border migration of labor. The Latvian experience shows significant outflow of manpower, thus creating labor shortages in crucial economic sectors. The human capital drain via emigration is aggravated by Latvia's natural population decline; this translates into a low number of young labor market entrants, which is expected to prevail for the coming decade. In the last decade the total population has declined by 8% of the entire Latvian population due to emigration and natural decline. Part of the documented population decline is due to the falling birth rates. In Latvia, for example, the natural[43] reduction in population in the period from 1995 to 2006 amounts to

42 Cunska Z. Muravska T.(2009) 'Social Policy Implementation in Latvia: Post EU Accession,' in *Promotion of Social Policies – an Investment in the Future,* EC Representation in Latvia and the University of Latvia, p. 293–294.

43 The difference between the number of live births and the number of deaths during the year. The natural increase (or natural decrease) is negative when the number of deaths exceeds the number of births.

about 6% of the population in Latvia of 2006. This alone is already a worrisome development, as it confronts the country with a shrinking labor force in a time of needed long-term economic development.[44]

This trend confirms that serious problems have resulted for the small and fast growing economy from its integration into the European internal market. This is a cause for concern, as the Latvian economy relies on sustained economic growth in order to catch up to average EU levels of per capita GDP and living standards. In addition, internal regional disparities aggravate the residents' dissatisfaction with the status quo and provide incentives for emigration. This requires effective policy choices for sustainable development and Cohesion policy implementation; given that the country's human resources for successful economic restructuring are limited.

It is obvious that, in order to prevent further significant population outflows, attention should be focused upon making Latvia a more hospitable place for its own people to live and work. This brings us to the domain of Latvia's economic and social policy in the wider sense.

Financial Participation in Latvia: Legal and Fiscal Framework

Latvia, as the other EU member states, is aiming to maintain its economic growth and to transform its national economy into a knowledge-based economy. The demographic situation in the country leads to labor shortages and negatively influences the availability for knowledgeable and skilled labor. Under such circumstances new human resource management approaches are required to promote sustained economic development. One of them is financial participation that not only helps to attract and retain employees, but also

44 Muravska T. King R. (2008),'Policy Choices for Latvia: A Hard or a Soft Lending?' in EU 50 year: Challenges for the Future, *Termas De Integracao*, Portugal: G.C.-GRAFICA DE COIMBRA, LDA, p. 90.

provides confidence for the employees that while working they are making adequate provisions for their retirement. The development and accumulation of pension funds is furthermore badly needed for the development of capital formation in the country.

There is also a strong push within SMEs on the European scale to increase private equity companies. As the result companies could facilitate financial participation that is based upon democratic principles and aims at increasing productivity of labor and involvement of employees in the decision-making process. To address these questions, a program of empirical and analytical research was undertaken in Latvia within the framework of the EU, mainly in the PEPPER III Report. The results of this research showed that financial participation has had a relatively short history in Latvia and followed the legacy of the privatization process. The initial stage of privatization in 1991–1995 gave employee ownership an important role in allowing for employee involvement in managerial decision making, forming financial incentives to increase their contribution into major changes in the enterprise governance system. Privatization shaped the environment for employees' financial participation and influenced the current state of employee share ownership and profit-sharing.

A number of legislative acts and regulations which have been implemented before the accession to the EU can and do influence the approach to financial participation.[45] There are no legal limitations regarding profit-sharing; however; there are also no exact regulations regarding such profit-sharing. It is possible to declare that salaries are to be dependent upon the profit of the company and it is also possible to provide benefits in the form of premiums as well as other benefits directly connected with the profit of a particular company. However, all those benefits are subject to personal income tax of 25%.[46] Thus the incentive to provide additional benefits is

45 Law on Privatization (1991), the Law on Cooperatives (1998), The Law of the Reorganization of State and Municipal enterprises in Corporations (1996), Commercial Law, the Law on Financial Instruments Market (2003) the Law on Taxation.

46 The Law 'On Individual Income Tax,' adopted in 1993, sets out the basis of taxation of individuals' personal income. The basic rate of taxable personal

reduced since the benefits of profit-sharing are 25% less than they would be in the case of stocks that pay out dividends to shareholders, because dividend payments are not subject to tax. Employee share ownership and profit-sharing are used in Latvian companies and are directly or indirectly regulated by legislation affecting the effectiveness of such forms of financial participation. Whereas no special legal regulation on profit-sharing exists, there are several pieces of legislation that touch upon employee share ownership and which should be interpreted in correlation with each other. Such joint-stock companies can issue special employee stock without voting rights corresponding to up to 10% of the equity capital in the course of a capital increase. For employee stock of state and municipal companies, there is an additional provision that employees cannot alienate such stock away from the company when leaving, but that the company is also obliged to transfer these shares to other employees and cannot use them for other purposes. However, regulation of employee share ownership has not been developed systematically, so that the legislation partly creates incentives and partly inhibits the development of such schemes.[47] There is no legal basis for involving worker representatives in the executive bodies of companies. Latvian company legislation by and large provides for a two-tier structure, with a management board and a supervisory board. The conclusion of collective agreements is mainly limited to the enterprise level. There is still hardly any dialogue at the sectoral and none at the regional level. The number of collective agreements concluded at enterprise level remains low: only approximately 20% of Latvian employees are covered by them. Although the direct election of 'authorized employee representatives' by the workforce has been possible since 2002, the main channel for employee interest representation at the workplace remains the trade unions.[48] After

income is 25% which is withheld at source and remitted to the tax authorities (http://www.lowtax.net/lowtax/html/latvia/jlvpetx.html#income).

47 PEPPER III Report. (2006)'Promotion of Employees Participation in the Profits and Enterprise Results in the New Member and Candidate Countries of the European Union (Latvia),' Rome/Berlin: European Foundation for the Improvement of Living and Working Conditions, p. 186.

48 LR Law 'On Trade Unions' 1990.13/12. (http://www.ilo.org/dyn/natlex/docs/WEBTEXT/41291/64965/E90LVA01.htm).

Latvia's independence in 1991, however, trade unions experienced a sharp fall in influence and membership: today they represent roughly 30% of the workforce. In practice, workplace social dialogue mainly takes place where unions are strongly represented, which de facto leaves a large proportion of Latvian employees without any representation at all.[49]

Financial participation schemes are likely to be used in new, human capital intensive sectors, e.g. information technologies (IT)[50]. The same trend exists in service industries, especially in real estate industry, law firms and consulting and real estate companies. IT is one of the most competitive and profitable sectors. Despite the fact that employees' participation is presently low, there are factors that may influence the development of the financial participation of employees in these sectors in the future. Most employees are young and highly qualified, have knowledge of economic issues and are not necessarily bound to one company, so that employers have to create incentives to keep them, e.g. by introducing profit-sharing, and taking into account their high profits; in IT firms, employers are in a position to do so. The real estate sector was also generating high profits; it is typical for real estate companies to enable realtors to participate in the profit made from the price of objects sold by them. In Latvia, realtors receive 3–5% of the profit. However, such participation should be considered as a means of motivation, not as typical profit-sharing, since it usually means that the basic salary of realtors is very low.[51] Nevertheless, some companies consider profit-sharing to be a motivation scheme and use it in their management systems.

49 The European Company - Prospects for worker board-level participation in the enlarged EU, edited by. Norbert Kluge and Michael Stoll, Brussels, 2006, pp. 95–96 (http://www.seeuropenetwork.org/homepages/seeurope/file_uploads/booklet2006.pdf).

50 PEPPER III Report (2006), 'Promotion of Employees Participation in the Profits and Enterprise Results in the New Member and Candidate Countries of the European Union (Latvia),' Rome/Berlin: European Foundation for the Improvement of Living and Working Conditions, p. 186.

51 The European Company - Prospects for worker board-level participation in the enlarged EU (edited by Norbert Kluge and Michael Stoll). Brussels, 2006 pp. 95–96. (http://www.seeurope-network.org/homepages/seeurope/file_uploads/booklet2006.pdf).

A recent survey in on financial participation in SMEs[52] included over 100 companies. Most of the companies that were surveyed are in Riga or in the Riga region where most of labor and economic structures of Latvia are concentrated. Over forty per cent of the population lives in the capital city of Riga and around sixty per cent of domestic GDP are produced there.[53] A sectoral analysis of the selected enterprises and their comparative advantages in Latvia's economy were revealed by companies in the food processing industries, in textiles and clothing, as well as in services. An industry that has been developing very rapidly in the last 10 years is building and construction.[54] Agriculture and metal manufacturing are relatively small, which also reflects development changes in the structure of a national economy in transition period. The result of the survey repeated the conclusions of the PEPPER III Report that employee share ownership emerged in the course of privatization, but was not sufficiently supported after 1994 and has been steadily decreasing since. There is a tendency to use alternatives to paying salaries to employees, not by offering shareholdings in the company but rather by registering employees as self-employed persons and entering into service with these persons.[55]

52 Muravska T. Survey on Latvia for the project 'Assessing and Benchmarking Financial Participation of Employees in the EU 27,' VS/2006/770, EC (DG Employment, Social Affairs), Berlin, 2007

53 The relatively low labor participation rate and high unemployment rate in the regions are due to structural features of the labor market, notably skills mismatches, insufficient labor mobility, weak demand for labor in eastern regions, and disincentives to employment due to the high labor tax rate.

54 The structure of Latvian economy in sectoral profile has changed in favor of service sectors in the last years. The share of service sectors in the value added has increased to 74.8% in 2005 from 71.8% in 2000. Construction, trade services, transport and communications have grown faster than other sectors of the economy in terms of both the value added and the number of employees. According to the RL Ministry of Economics,' Economic Development of Latvia,' *Report*, July 2007, p. 15–45.

55 PEPPER III Report (2006),'Promotion of Employees Participation in the Profits and Enterprise Results in the New Member and Candidate Countries of the European Union (Latvia),' Rome/Berlin: European Foundation for the Improvement of Living and Working Conditions, p. 178–179.

The Role of the National Government

The role of governments in promoting, or impeding, a financial participation measure is of increasing importance. Likewise, the role of the social partners, either in influencing government thinking or blocking government initiatives in this domain, cannot be underestimated. Governments should promote the development of employment partnership and social dialogue at the local and regional government level.

Governments are important facilitators for the development of any financial participation regulation. Active exchange of information and possible promotion campaigns by governments may enhance the development of employee financial participation.

There are a variety of objectives and reasons for promoting financial participation and it is important to examine the nature of governmental aims to fully understand the specific provisions of legislation. These may include promoting such objectives as wage substitution, wage flexibility, income and wealth re-distribution, medium and long-term savings, better corporate performance and greater employee involvement in company affairs.

Governmental objectives are likely to influence corporate practice in three ways:

1. Via legislation and associated statutory instruments that are backed up by fiscal initiatives. Yet specific legislation on financial participation is not the only instrument by which governments may affect financial participation practice: securities law, company law, employment law and the overall taxation regime also contribute to the framework of financial participation. Amendments to these may be necessary in some cases if financial participation is to be encouraged.
2. Via the influence of government ideologies and views on the prevailing national attitude towards financial participation.
3. Via implementation strategies. Do governments simply set the legislative framework and leave the rest up to companies, or do they take a more active role in promoting the use of legislation?

However, regulation of financial participation schemes is not the only statutory and governmental influence on financial participation. Wider company law can also influence the incidence and character of financial participation, while legislative changes in this area also have an effect on the use of financial participation. [56]

Governments should also work in cooperation with non-governmental organizations in promoting financial participation. Programs of social and economic development have certain elements which are complementary but which may also come into conflict. Nevertheless, the following questions arise: how can substantial levels of social dialog, cohesion and development be balanced with economic growth and labor market needs; where is there is conflict, how can it be resolved and through what mechanisms?

The need to implement the aims of Lisbon strategy, principles of flexsecurity in Latvia will influence social dialogue between the Employers' Confederation of Latvia, the Free Trade Union Federation of Latvia and the Government. The development of such trends is still not included in the national programs on a large scale and does not have strong government support. Neither the government nor the social partners presently promote or are planning to promote financial participation schemes. Trade unions and other political forces which could support such schemes lack knowledge about methods and advantages of financial participation and thus do not even address this issue. The government is not concerned with the financial participation of employees, as the reduction of unemployment is considered to be the priority. The Ministry of Social Affairs concentrates its activities on solving problems related to the increase of minimum wages and allowances for the unemployed. Participation of employees has not been on the political agenda of the Saiema (parliament). Political parties and other policy makers have not given any attention to the issue of employees' financial participation. Financial participation as a component of a social model

56 Andrew Pendleton and Erik Poutsma (2004), Nijmegen: Manchester Metropolitan University and Radboud University, 'Financial Participation: The Role of Governments and Social Partners,' Luxembourg: Office for Official Publications of the European Communities, European Foundation for the Improvement of Living and Working Conditions, p 1–3.

development is not included in the economic sections of parties' programs. As individual interviews with policy makers have shown, there is no knowledge of the concept and no awareness of the possible positive economic impact of financial participation. There is also no dialogue between those representing the interests of employees and those of employers about the idea of financial participation.[57]

At the same time the position of the government in relation to social dialogue is clear: 'Social dialogue is important for achieving the goals of the National Lisbon Programme of Latvia. Measures are foreseen for improvement of the social dialogue both at the national and the regional levels. Among institutions involved in the employment partnership are the Employers' Confederation of Latvia and the Free Trade Union Confederation of Latvia.'[58]

There is awareness that the EU membership might have positive impact on the development of employee participation, including financial participation in the future.

Concluding Remarks

In the last decades modern welfare states were confronted with major economic, technological, and demographic challenges. Building sustained economic growth is necessary for long-term employment creation and social protection schemes in all European states and is of special importance in the new member states. The EU policy makers are confronted by conflicting social and economic goals, i.e., high levels of productivity and growth and maximization of social protection, inclusion and cohesion. However the EU social policy and the Lisbon Strategy can be a tools for EU member states in the

57 PEPPER III Report (2006),'Promotion of Employees Participation in the Profits and Enterprise Results in the New Member and Candidate Countries of the European Union (Latvia),' Rome/Berlin: European Foundation for the Improvement of Living and Working Conditions, p. 180.

58 Ministry of Economics, Republic of Latvia, Economic Development of Latvia, Report, July 2007, p. 43.

process of adapting to the more competitive environment brought by globalization and current crisis; this is critically important for the further reform of the European social model. The basic question is whether economic democracy, as a concept that was developed in the 19th and 20th centuries and strengthened at times of economic crises, should be also implemented in the new member states according to the same principles as in the other European countries. Will it contribute to the new social European model? The challenge to balance economic and social policies agendas is a challenge in particularly for the new EU member states struggling for economic convergence with the rest of the EU, as is the case for Latvia.

Latvia, as the other EU member states, is aiming to maintain economic growth and to transform its national economy into a knowledge-based economy. The demographic situation in the country leads not only to labor shortages but also negatively influences the availability for knowledgeable and skilled labor. Under such circumstances new human resource management approaches are required to promote sustained economic development. One of them is financial participation that helps to attract and retain employees, and also provides confidence for the employees that while working they prepare adequately their retirement. Financial participation is essential for economic democracy and is a basis for employee motivation. However, financial participation schemes in different societies have varied considerably as they reflect very different cultural traditions and legal regulations. On the European scale the transfer of financial participation plans across Europe is important to ensure employee mobility.

The results of this research showed that financial participation has a relatively short history in Latvia and followed the legacy of the privatization process. Employee share ownership as well as the other financial participation schemes emerged in the times of privatization (1991–1994), but were not supported and as the result have only been implemented in a very small number of domestic companies. Important facilitators for the development of any financial participation regulation are governments. The dramatic current economic situation requires fulfilling a dual task: to maintain the long-term goals of the social policies and to respond to economic and social challenges. The decision-making process should include the willingness of the governments in the new member states to learn from the experiences of other countries that have undergone economic crises and successfully reformed their social models.

Improved governance, transparency and involvement of stakeholders in the social dialogue are essential to strengthen the links between economic development and the development of a new social model.

Bibliography

Burkitt, Brian, and Phillip Whyman (1994). 'Employee Investment Funds in Sweden: Their Past, Present and Future,' *Journal: European Business Review*, vol. 94, no. 4, pp. 22–29.

Commission Report links employee financial participation and productivity. *European Industrial Relations Observatory on –line (*http://www.eurofound.europa.eu/eiro/1997/02/inbrief/eu9702106n.htm).

Consolidated version of the Treaty, *Official Journal C* 321 E of 29 December 2009; Single European Act (1986), Official Journal L 169 of 29 June 1987; Treaty on European Union (1992*), Official Journal C* 191 of 29 July 1992; Treaty of Amsterdam, *Official Journal C* 340 of 10 November 1997; Treaty of Nice (2001), *Official Journal C* 80 of 10 March 2001.

Constitution of the Republic of Latvia (1992), www.likumi.lv.

Council Directive on 89/391/EEC/of 12 June 89 on the Introduction of measures to encourage improvements in the safety and health of workers at work. Official journal of the EU L183 of 29 June 1989, pp. 1–8.

The Council, the European Parliament, the Economic and Social Committee and the Committee of the Regions - On a framework for the promotion of employee financial participation COM/2002/0364 final (http://eurlex.europa.eu/smartapi/cgi/sga_doc?smartapi!celexplus!prod!DocNumber&lg=en&type_doc=COMfinal&an_doc=2002&nu_doc=364).

Cunska, Z., and T. Muravska (2009), *Social Policy Implementation in Latvia: Post EU Accession in promotion of social Policies – an Investment in the Future, EC Representation in Latvia*, 2009, pp. 293–294.

Cynog-Jones, T.W., OECD (1956), 'Workers Investments in Industry,' *OECD Employment Outlook*, July 1995, Chapter Profit-sharing in OECD countries, pp. 139–166.

EC European Economy n° 32009, 4 May 2009 http://ec.europa.eu/economy_finance/pdf/2009/springforecasts/lv.html (retrieved 05.05.2009).

EC Regulation Nr. 322/97 art.2.

EC Working Paper on Employee Financial Participation, July 2001(EU0108232F) (http://www.eurofound.europa.eu/eiro/2001/08/feature/eu0108232f.htm).
The Economist: Worrying about a Crash, Jul 5th 2007 http://www.economist.com/world/europe/displaystory.cfm?story_id=9443551 (retrieved 05.05.2009).
Erixon, Lennart (2008), 'The Rehn-Meidner Model in Sweden: Its Rise, Challenges and Survival,' Department of Economics, Stockholm University (http://www.ne.su.se/paper/wp08_02.pdf).
Esping-Andersen, Gosta (2004), UK:Blackwell Publishing Ltd. pp. 144–221.
European Commission. The communication 'Working together, working better: proposals for a new framework for the open co-ordination of social protection and inclusion policies' (http://ec.europa.eu/employment_social/spsi/docs/social_inclusion/2006/objectives_en.pdf).
European Foundation for the Improvement of Living and Working Conditions. http://www.eurofound.europa.eu/areas/qualityoflife/eurlife/index.php?template=3&radioindic=158&idDomain=3 (retrieved 05.05.2009).
European Social Charter, Council of Europe Treaty, adopted in 1961, revised in 1996, (http://www.hrcr.org/docs/Social_Charter/soccharter.wpd).
Eurostat Flash Estimate 14 February 2008.
Flexicurity Pathways. 'Turning hurdles into stepping stones.' June 2007. *Report by the European Expert Group on Flexicurity* (http://ec.europa.eu/social/main.jsp?catId=117&langId=en).
Joint Memorandum on Social Inclusion prepared by Latvia together with European Commission (JIM), signed on December 18, 2003.
Kelso, Louis O., and Patricia Hetter Kelso (1986), 'Democracy and Economic Power: Extending the ESOP Revolution through Binary Economics,' Cambridge/Massachusetts: Ballinger Publishing Co., pp. 15–54.
King, R., and T. Muravska (2008), 'Policy Choices for Latvia: A Hard or a Soft Lending?' in EU 50 year: Challenges for the Future, *Termas De Integracao*, Portugal: G.C.-GRAFICA DE COIMBRA, LDA, p. 90.
Latvian National Action Plan for Reduction of Poverty and Social Exclusion (2004–2006) (accepted on July 23, 2004).
Lowitzsch, Jens, et al. (2007), 'Financial Participation for a New Social Europe. A Building Block Approach,' Berlin: Free University Berlin, 115 p.
LR Law On Pensions. Latvijas Vestnesis, 182 (465), 23.11.1995, as amended.
P5_TA (2003) 0253 'Employee Financial Participation.' *European Parliament Resolution* on the Commission communication to the Council, the European Parliament, the Economic and Social Committee and the Committee of the Regions on a framework for the promotion of employee financial participation (COM(2002) 364 - 2002/2243(INI)) (http://www.europarl.europa.eu/registre/seance_pleniere/textes_adoptes/definitif/2003/06-05/0253/P5_TA(2003)0253_EN.pdf).
Pendleton, Andrew, and Erik Poutsma (2004), 'Financial Participation: The Role of Governments and Social Partners,' Luxembourg: Office for Official Publications of the European Communities, European Foundation for the Improvement of Living and Working Conditions, 64 p.

PEPPER III Report (2006), 'Promotion of Employees Participation in the Profits and Enterprise Results in the New Member and Candidate Countries of the European Union (Latvia (pp. 178–190).' Rome/Berlin: European Foundation for the Improvement of Living and Working Conditions, 319 p.

Presidency Conclusions, Barcelona European Council, 15–16 March 2002, paragraph 22, http://ue.eu.int/ueDocs/cms_Data/docs/pressData/en/ec/71025.pdf.

The Promotion of Participation by Employed Persons in Profits and Enterprise Results (including equity participation) (92/443/EEC). *European Council Recommendation* of 27 July 1992. (http://eurlex.europa.eu/smartapi/cgi/sga_doc?smartapi!celexapi!prod!CELEXnumdoc&lg=en&numdoc=31992H0443&model=guichett).

Sapir, Andre (200), Globalisation and the Reform of the European Social Models. *Journal of Common Market Studies*, vol. 44, no. 2, pp. 369–390.

Statement by IMF Mission to Latvia on 2007 Article IV Consultation Discussions Press Release no. 07/87; May 4, 2007 http://www.imf.org/external/np/sec/pr/2007/pr0787.htm (retrieved 05.05.2009).

Tautsaimniecibas vienota strategija, 2004. http://www.likumi.lv/doc.php?id=72377(retrieved 05.05.2009).

Thornicroft, Kenneth W. (1991), 'Promises Kept, Promises Broken: Reciprocity and the Scanlon Plan.' *Journal: Employee Relations*, 1991, vol. 13, no. 5, pp. 12–21.

The Universal Declaration of Human Rights, United Nations General Assembly resolution 217 A (III) from 10 December 1948.

Uvalić, M. (1991), 'Promotion of Employee Participation in Profits and Enterprise Results in the Member States of the European', the PEPPER Report no. 3/91, Luxembourg: Office for Official Publications of the European Communities. 216 p.

Volskis, E. (2008), Pensiju sistemas pilnveidosanas problemas Latvija, promocijas darbs ekonomikas doktora grada iegusanai, Riga: Latvijas Universitate.

Kaarel Kilvits

Delocalization of Production: Threats and Opportunities for Estonia

Introduction

Enterprises operate increasingly more in international networks and value chains. They locate procurement, production, distribution, marketing, sales and servicing in different countries across the world. They perform every operation where the price-quality ratio is the best.

Manufacturing is a key area of economic and social development in Estonia. In 2008, 135,000 people, or 20.6% of the employed population, were employed in this branch of national economy (Statistics Estonia 2009).

After the drastic structural changes in the early 1990s and the Russian crisis provoked a slowing down of the growth in 1998–1999, the Estonian manufacturing enjoyed eight years of stable and fast growth. Structural changes in this period were quite slow, insignificant and painless. Entrepreneurs became accustomed to this and believed that it is the way it has to be and will be. But notwithstanding all sorts of regulations, cycles are inevitable in a market economy. Early in 2008 it was clear that the economic environment had significantly changed in recent years: unemployment was replaced by scarcity of labor; wages and salaries had risen; prices of many production inputs had risen; credit had grown more difficult to access and more expensive; economic openness had increased still further; the external environment was more unstable and restless - and old business plans didn't work any more. The Estonian manufacturing had reached the stage of faster, more radical and painful structural changes again. It was realized that further development in Estonia would largely be determined by external factors.

The following paper seeks to cover the restructuring of manufacture in Estonia - as a small EU member state with a very open economy - under the influence of the global economic crises. The general situation and tendencies in the world economy influencing restructuring of manufacturing in a small open economy will be discussed. The main goal of this paper is to summarize the objectives and experiences of knowledge applied by different agents and to study alternatives and opportunities for Estonia in this process.

Main Tendencies of World Manufacturing

Delocalization is a term referring to the spatial restructuring of production at a national, regional or global scale. Delocalization is difficult to quantify statistically since it takes different forms.

Foreign Direct Investment (FDI) is a category of international investment made by a resident entity in one country (direct investor) with the objective of establishing a lasting interest in an enterprise resident in another country (direct investment enterprise). Conventionally, a FDI enterprise is an incorporated enterprise in which a foreign investor owns 10% or more of the ordinary shares or voting power, or an unincorporated enterprise in which a foreign investor has equivalent ownership. Financial FDI data may be geographically based on the extent that MNEs use strategically located holding companies to intermediate their investments (Nicoletti et al. 2003, p. 12). Delocalization with capital contributions, i.e. creation of a subsidiary company or fusion-acquisition is very important. The company acquires a factory in other state and that factory starts to produce all or part of its production. The delocalization with capital contributions is the riskiest by far.

Outsourcing is delegation of tasks or jobs from internal production to an external entity (such as subcontractor). Most recently, it has come to mean the elimination of native staff to overseas staff (offshore outsourcing) where salaries are markedly lower. This is despite the fact that the majority of outsourcing that occurs today still occurs within country boundaries.

Subcontracting is defined as the manufacture of goods by one firm (the subcontractor) for another (the lead firm) based on the specifications of the latter. Often there can be several layers of firms or intermediaries mediating the relationship between the actual production workers and the end product market. The lead firms normally exercise considerable control over their subcontractors in terms of price, quality and timing of the products they supply. Companies are driven to subcontract to take advantage of national, regional or international differences in factor costs, notably low wages or materials. For developed countries, production or purchasing abroad is cheaper in many countries than domestic production or domestic buying. Ultimately, this enables companies to reduce the cost of final product and thereby to offer competitive prices (UNIDO 2003, p. 8).

There are two main types of subcontracting (UNIDO 2003, pp. 4–5):

- Capacity subcontracting. The main reason causing the subcontracting relationship to take place is the fact that the main contractor does not have enough capacity to undertake the fabrication of the specific component, part or material (Cuny and de Crombrugghe 2000, p. 16). In other words, the main contractor has reached a capacity limit in his production process and, in order to meet market demand for its product, is required to refer to a subcontracting specialist at least for a temporary period of time. This usually represents a complementary horizontal disintegration of production (Taymaz and Kilicaslan 2002, pp. 2–3).
- Specialist subcontracting. The main contractor relies upon the services of a subcontractor or set of subcontractors who has specialized equipment or machinery and skilled labor to undertake complex and precision tasks (Cuny and de Crombrugghe 2000, p. 16). This may involve either finished products or specialized components or supplies that require a higher level of technical expertize, which the main contractor does not possess or cannot meet. In such a situation, both firms have vertically related complementary assets and/or technologies (Taymaz, and Kilicaslan 2002, p. 3).

Subcontracting is classified also as follows (Johnson 1997, p. 4):

- Finding the most practical, productive and favorable subcontractor for performing the task, production or development of an idea (subcontracting).
- A product of one producer is input for another producer (industrial subcontracting).
- The subcontractor makes the whole product; the contractor's tasks are mostly marketing, logistics and sale of the product (commercial subcontracting).

Offshoring can be defined as relocation of business processes (including production/manufacturing) to an overseas lower cost location.

Offshore outsourcing is the practice of hiring an external organization to perform some or all business functions in a country other than the one where the product will be sold or consumed.

The main trends are internationalization, multinationalization and globalization. Economic, technological, political etc. processes change the world into an integral whole. Processes of globalization are increasingly making diverse and distant places, processes and people more interdependent. Geographical identities are becoming blurred and competitiveness is taking on a global dimension.

The economic unions, countries, regions, enterprises and also individuals have lost any kind of true option whether to participate in globalization or evade it. There are increasingly less real possibilities for isolated existence and development in the contemporary world. Global economic integration, international competition and technological development are key drivers of structural change. Delocalization of industries is by-product of a process of longer-term structural change.

The physical separation of different parts of a production process (fragmentation) allows production in different countries to be formed into cross-border production networks that can be within or between firms (Gereffi et al. 2005). Space is not homogenous. Different economic activities take place in different locations. The type of business that dominates today's global economic system operates on the basis of finding the cheapest production (in particular labor) cost.

Convergence theories that tell of the harmonization of development levels of different countries and regions have been extremely popular in recent decades. As the movement of goods, services, capital and labor across countries and regions is growing freer and freer, the law of connected vessels should at least theoretically work here. Differences between rich and poor countries and regions should rather decrease (Sachs 2000; Kilvits 2004). Removal of trade barriers will make the world more equal (Brakman and Garretsen 2005, p. ix).

However, contrary to the expectations, differences between rich and poor countries are often increasing. The statistics of recent years indicate that the technological convergence between countries and regions has not been very successful and rapid in the EU, either. The situation became even more complicated after the EU enlargement of 2004.

The opponents of the theory of convergence follow Myrdal's (1957) thesis, which is based on the understanding that growth is a process which leads to cumulating spatial economic differences. They suggested a reconsideration of the conclusions for convergence processes in the EU because these were formulated without including countries from EU South, mainly less developed countries (LDCs) for which the convergence process is not typical (Armstrong 1995).

Many economists (Totev and Sariiski 2007) share the understanding of the dualistic nature of development in the EU (differences in the economic development of the core and the periphery). Mack and Jacobson (1996) sustain the vision that these processes depend on the spatial specialization, which concerns the degree of technological processing - the centrally located EU regions (core regions) have a tendency to specialize and export to the periphery highly technologically processed manufactured goods, while the periphery specializes in the production of low technology goods. Going further it is maintained that the location of the industries with constant return of scale (mainly low technological processing industries, labor intensive industries) is a result of the distribution of those which have an increasing return of scale (high technology processing industries). The location of the labor-intensive industries finds its expression mainly through the delocalization process.

An effect of agglomeration is dominating in the world economy. Economic activities of a common kind show a strong tendency to agglomerate in certain locations, giving rise to patterns of national and regional specialization. Such agglomerations owe their self-perpetuation in large part to social and economic factors. The growing cluster attracts sellers, merchant intermediaries, and labor from afar. Firms of different types will cluster together in an urban region and will form an inter-reliance as the size of the region becomes large.

The economic effect created with territorial concentration of capital is much bigger than in the case of its dispersed location. In the former case it is cheaper for enterprises to organize subcontracting, buy services, strengthen infrastructure, exchange knowledge. It is also easier for enterprises in larger and more compact economies to specialize. It is difficult if not quite impossible in small and dispersed economies to organize high-technology enterprises that require larger fixed costs. High-technology enterprises in large and compact economies have clear competitive advantages (Sachs 2000; Kilvits 2004).

The world can be perceived as a core / periphery / semiperiphery dichotomy where core countries are characterized by high levels of development and a capacity of innovation. High value-added, high-technology and science-intensive production has been concentrated into the core, and low value-added, low-technology, labor- and land-intensive production into the periphery. The core has a level of dominance over the periphery.

The advantages of the core (clusters) are very important for decisions of location. But if the advantages of a new region are bigger (low production cost, good future prospects etc.), the firm will relocate to the 'new growth periphery.' High-technology enterprises in the core try to take up mainly R&D, product development, logistics and marketing that enable a higher profit (however involving higher risks). Production processes are transferred to the periphery ('cheap countries').

The advantage of the old industrialized economies is currently shifting from the factory to the office, distribution network and trading desk. The result would be a Nike-style industry, designing, importing and distributing the goods that are no longer the manufacturer's (Boulhol and Fontagne 2006; CEPII 2004). Firms reorganize themselves on a global level to take advantage of international cost differentials, specialising their overseas subsidiaries in different segments of the production process.

The economic performance of such offices ('producers without factories') is often quite excellent. But the workplaces are usually highly investment intensive and provide employment only to top specialists and qualified professionals in (major) towns. Not all people are fit for such manufacturing. Therefore the financial and regional stratification of people is increasing in the developed countries. A wide-spread opinion is that this is not socially acceptable. We need also low-technology production for uneducated and not so highly skilled people.

The economic effect of capital concentrated into the core would be remarkably higher if the same capital were dispersed. Owing to this, the developed industrial countries can levy higher tax rates on enterprises and physical persons than developing countries can. And they needn't be afraid that most of the high-technology production would escape from the country. Such production is ineffective if not impossible (despite the low wages, taxes, prices) to organize in the periphery. The periphery lacks a suitable economic environment for that – there is no skilled labor, it is difficult to organize subcontracting, buy services, guarantee security of production etc. Only low-technology production which the core is not interested in and wishes to get rid of can operate in the periphery.

Due to high taxes and enormous tax revenue collected from large income-turnover-property, the core countries can mitigate their social problems and thereby keep the society stable and sustainable. A core country also can sufficiently finance R & D and education (incl. advanced training) and in this way reinforce even more its position as a core.

Fast economic restructuring in the periphery (where state tax revenue and internal accumulation is low) is possible only with sufficient FDI. Peripheral countries therefore try to be attractive and draw mobile production resources. The periphery fighting for FDI usually does all it can to keep taxes and wages low. However, it is therefore hard to mitigate social problems and finance R & D and product development. The worst is that FDI tends to bring in mainly low-technology (primarily interested in low wages and taxes) production.

Estonia as a semiperiphery acts in respect to the periphery as a core and is at the same time exploited by the core countries. During the economic depressions, economic crises and in the periods of fast changes in general, it is just the semiperiphery that by way of delocalization of industries might sharply improve the structure of economy and achieve fast economic growth.

Most of the manufacturing enterprises today take part in international competition. They are active in global networks and value chains, locate procurement, production, distribution, marketing and services in different countries over the world. Each operation is performed wherever the best price-quality ratio exists. Transnational relocation of production - mainly through direct foreign investment and subcontracting - is growing at an increasingly faster rate (Labrianidis et al. 2007).

The wealth distribution scheme is contradictory in the contemporary globalized world. The success of advanced industrial economies is based on specialization in useful, high-value-added activities. They themselves produce very few simple products and buy them cheap from poor countries. Incomes of the participators in the world economy are most influenced by whether and how they can find a niche in a high-value-added branch and value chain (Sachs 2000; Rodrik 2004; Kilvits 2004).

Advanced industrial economies can force this kind of international division of labor upon poor countries because they have the contemporary technologies, machinery, capital and market relations the poor do not have. And also poor countries benefit from the international division of labor. If they were not 'exploited,' they would be even poorer.

Large firms in developed industrial countries dream of dedicating themselves only to product development, logistics and marketing. They try to administer trademarks, product portfolios and value chains. Production is organized in some 'cheap' country. There are increasingly more 'producers without a factory' (Labrianidis et al. 2007).

The situation in the EU is worrisome. In the market of high-technology goods, European firms cannot compete any more with the USA, in the market of cheap goods they cannot compete with China. They are internationally competitive only in the market of 'intermediate products.' However, this intermediate is drying up. European Union manufacturing industries participating in international competition keep relocating to regions where the production costs are lower. Productions with higher and higher technological level are delocating. Still, there are no completely dying branches of industry but there are dying activities in branches of industry. Under assault are first of all the routine-based activities, the others hope to survive in international competition (EU 2009; Labrianidis et al. 2007; Sikkut 2008).

The General Situation and Main Developments in Estonia

The Estonian economy is very small and open. Its foreign trade (export + import) to GDP ratio (1.23 in 2008) is one of the highest in the world (Statistics Estonia 2009; Eurostat 2009). Therefore Estonia is extremely sensitive to all influences of the global economic environment. Estonia has not apprehended all the sharpness of transnational relocation of production simply because until recently more production (jobs) have come in than have gone out.

By the end of 2008 Estonia had received more than 11.6 billion Euro worth of FDI (Bank of Estonia 2009). 14.0% of the total amount of FDI was made directly in manufacturing; however, based on expert estimates, quite large FDI reached Estonian manufacturing through financial intermediation (34.6% of all FDI) and other fields of activity as well. In many, if not in most of the cases these, with the help of FDI, involved delocalization of manufacturing industries from the donor countries to Estonia. Moreover, manufacturing industries of the same donor countries have been relocated to Estonia by way of ordering various subcontracting works. In some commodity groups (in particular manufacture of metals, machinery, equipment and apparatus) importation for inward processing and re-exportation after inward processing account for 50–90% of all Estonian imports and exports (Statistics Estonia 2009).

Also, the FDI made by Estonia (mostly foreign capital owned enterprises located in Estonia) into other countries have increased. By the end of 2008, the amount of such FDI was in excess of 4.8 billion Euros (Bank of Estonia 2009). Only 4.0% of the FDI outflow from Estonia went into manufacturing. However, based on expert estimates, FDI reached manufacturing and hence caused its delocalization from Estonia to other countries through financial intermediation (37.2% of all FDI) and other fields of activity as well. Moreover, Estonian enterprises are increasingly ordering subcontracting from foreign countries.

However, several industries with long historical traditions such as the cotton industry, for example, have already disappeared or are disappearing. Some of the foreign investments made in Estonia in the 1990s were primarily focused on cost advantage (cheap labor, electricity, water etc., partly also cheap resources and materials bought from Russia) and were not interested in operating here for long. Many low-technology, labor-intensive and low-capital-intensive productions that came to Estonia during this period have by now moved on to CIS or Asia. Entrepreneurs whose principal business idea was to profit from low wages and taxes in Estonia now face big difficulties and are desperately looking for new 'hunting grounds.'

In China and India one can get a subcontract at a better price-quality ratio than in Estonia. Fortunately for Estonia, these countries are far away from the large Western firms. Those who order subcontracts prefer to avoid a large time difference, long air travel; they have problems with an inadequate infrastructure a different culture and food they are not accustomed to. Therefore they have so far preferred Estonia. Estonia's competitive advantage has been its closeness to the market, its ability to produce small quantities, as well as operative and flexible production. Employees of the large firms in Nordic countries and Western Europe, which are up to three hours of travel from Tallinn, prefer Estonia. However, time is not working in favor of Estonia. The price-quality ratio is becoming more and more significant.

Economic competitiveness depends on productivity. The main source of economic growth is the growth of productivity. The productivity of Estonian manufacturing in 2004 was approximately 6 times lower than that of most advanced countries of EU (Eurostat 2009; Arengufond 2008). The gap is growing smaller very slowly and many developments are disturbing. The Estonian Human Development Report (Eesti Koostöö Kogu 2008) shows that the change in the economic structure in Estonia in recent years has gone in the direction of South-European countries rather than towards the desired advanced EU countries. Estonia is 'growing Greek.'

If Estonia were located in the same latitude as Greece, such a development would not be as risky. But Estonia is much farther north and here a lot of energy and money is consumed to compensate for the bad climate. The average annual temperature in Estonia is of course much lower than in Southern Europe. Moreover, the Estonian climate is much more severe - summer and winter, as well as day and night temperatures vary a lot more from each other. Walls are thicker, thermal insulation, storm windows and the roofing that has to resist a lot of snow cost a lot, our constructions are much more expensive than those of southern countries. We need to heat the buildings half a year. Due to the greater difference between internal and external air temperatures, the energy losses are higher. Additionally, employers have to pay higher wages to employees in Estonia than in southern countries - because they have to be able to pay for more expensive northern houses and heating, infrastructure, warmer clothing, more substantial food. Therefore the production costs of Estonian manufacturing enterprises are inevitably higher than those of southern countries, and Estonia is not able to compete with them in many traditional spheres of production in the world market (Kilvits 2004).

A study ordered by the Estonian Development Fund (Arengufond 2008) calculated that if all branches of Estonian manufacturing industry achieved the productivity that is in the respective branch of manufacturing in the most advanced countries in EU while the distribution of Estonian labor between the branches of manufacturing remains the same as now, then productivity in Estonia would attain only 56% of the Irish, 78% of the German, 80% of the Finnish and 90% of the Danish level.

Hence, it is not possible for Estonia to catch up in terms of productivity with the developed industrial countries by simply raising the technological level of enterprises and increasing so-called technical productivity. The structure of Estonian manufacture is out-of-date and requires cardinal and fast changes toward greater value added. For that the target must be set to high-technology production, which, as a rule, guarantees greater value added.

Some positive shifts in that direction have occurred. The structure of Estonian manufacturing improved slightly between 1995 and 2008. For example, the rate of employment with labor-intensive and small value-added textile and clothing industry dropped from 4.5% to 2.9%, whereas in the higher value-added metal, machinery and apparatus industry rose from 5.3% to 5.7% (Statistics Estonia 2009). However, changes have not been as fast as we desire.

Moreover, high-technology branches should not be identified with high-technology production. All branches today contain segments of high-technology production and products, effective marketing channels, well-known brands etc. In the global market a brand owner in a low-technology branch earns as a rule more than most of the subcontractors in high-technology branches. Value added in electronics industry as a whole is definitely higher than in textile industry. However, there are many low-productivity enterprises and entire branches in electronics industry (primitive subcontracting, assembly operations etc.). And, for example, in the textile industry there are old, famous enterprises producing billiard and game table fabric - which own a well-known brand and earn enviably high profits - as well as factories producing various specific products (clothes for firemen and racers; bulletproof fabric etc.) (Kilvits 2004; Labrianidis et al. 2007).

Alternatives and Opportunities for Entrepreneurs

The situation has changed and it is not possible to go on as before. The wages in Estonia will inevitably remain lower than in Western countries for many years yet. But obedient, indulgent and socially submissive workers who are willing to toil selflessly for low wages in bad working conditions in the fear of dismissal in enterprises with uncertain prospects, at the same time earning profit for the employers, are increasingly hard to find in Estonia. The demographic situation in Estonia is bad, manual professions are not popular, but despite the employers' aggressive lobbying, children will not be urged to go to vocational schools or to study engineering and no labor force will be imported in substantial amounts from third countries in the short term. Estonian employers are competing for the work force not only with each other but in the open economic space with all EU, and even with the world private and public sector. The workforce is a limited resource and suffices only for entrepreneurs who have good business plans, who can pay competitive wages.

The success of enterprises depends on what they produce (wooden spoons or cancer medicines), how they produce (primitive manual labor or modern mechanized, automatized, cybernetized production) and how they sell (subcontracting client, in Estonia or an expensive department store in London; directly or through several intermediaries who all want to earn). They need to attempt to develop products, technologies and sales to climb up in the value chain, increase value added and profitability. They need to be innovative in something, do something differently from the competitors.

If, for some reason, an enterprise cannot make production, technology and sales more effective, it has to terminate its activity or move to a region where production costs (labor costs) are lower. It's no use resisting up to the last gasp and then end up with bankruptcy. One must terminate business and quit the market at the right time. The following main options exist: selling the enterprise or part of it; reprofilation; liquidation or bankruptcy; a 'clean-up' strategy. In the last case, the enterprise shall be exploited to depreciation seeking to use as completely as possible all the available production potential. The profit will not be invested in the enterprise but somewhere else. Costs are kept at a minimal level. Fixed assets are not renewed unless it is absolutely necessary; they try to extend the lifespan of the existing ones. The units dealing with the issues of perspectives are liquidated, training of personnel has been stopped (Kilvits 2004).

It is costly to close down an existing enterprise as well as to set up a new one in another country. However, if this investment will pay back within a normal period of time, it will inevitably happen sooner or later and, in a flexible labor market and educational system, it will provide an opportunity for the economy to renew itself. Low-technology and small value-added productions withdraw to give room to high technology and high value-added productions. Low-paid unskilled jobs will be replaced by high-paid skilled jobs.

Alternatives and Opportunities for an Innovation System

The number of people working in the national innovation system in Estonia is not small. Today 220 people are employed with the headquarters of the Enterprise Estonia, and additionally more than 100 with 15 county development centres, 2 regional agencies and 11 in the agency abroad. The Development Fund has 14 employees. There are also Tallinn Entrepreneurship Agency, various techno parks, ministerial units of innovation etc.

The finance of R&D is not small either. In 2006, Estonia spent 1.14% of GDP for this purpose, the EU27 spent 1.84%. Estonia was the 16th among 27 member states. Behind us were two EU old member states – Portugal and Greece (Italy was almost equal with us) and nine new member states. However, there is no unambiguous relationship between the R&D expenditure and economic success. Portugal, Greece and Italy are South-European countries with all the economic logic arising from this fact. However, also the 'lucky dog' of EU and 'our object of envy number one,' Ireland, spent only 1.32% (Eurostat 2009). The Chinese economic success is largely based on just low expenditure on R&D and on efficient industrial espionage and imitation.

As scheduled, the share of Estonian research and development expenditure should rise to 1.9% of GDP by 2010. At the same time, the amount of money would be still diminutive and the situation will stay almost the same. A small, poor and extremely open economy cannot take all the manufacturing industry risks on its shoulders and 'thaw the world.' Innovation policy in a small country cannot be based on the same understandings as in large more closed economies, which use military and space industry spinoffs and possess innovation engines (large enterprises). Only Israel with its population of 7.3 million and in some degree also Sweden (9.2) and Finland (5.3) among the small economies have managed to have relatively similar innovation policies to the great powers of the world. Estonia with its 1.3 million population cannot do it. Estonia's 'small business economy' cannot influence the world economy in a convenient direction. As a small country we can only respond to changes fast and flexibly.

Innovation is nowhere based on the linear model of development today (generation of ideas and fundamental research, applied research and development, production, consumption). R&D activities are increasingly less related to a particular geographical-political space (state). Even worse, benefits from this are largely transmitted to global enterprises.

The technological level of an economy depends not only on research and development activity in that country but also on its ability to adapt technologies worked out elsewhere. Transnational technological transfer is dominating. For example, Finland has only developed 0.5–3.0% of the technologies used in the country on her own; between 97.0 and 99.5% have been taken over from other countries.

The Estonian innovation system has definitely made a lot of useful things, especially by channeling EU resources into our economy. Unfortunately the author cannot name any major Estonian manufacturing enterprises - large employer and taxpayer - that would have been set up or developed due to this. Such enterprises have been established and developed rather thanks to the owners' and executive managers' wisdom or simply good luck in spite of all the difficulties.

It must definitely be taken into consideration in the development and implementation of innovation policies that any state aid inevitably spoils the market. Unprofitable business plans are supported with money coming from the pockets of successful taxpayers. Therefore, an ineffective production might look more effective and an effective one – ineffective. Smart entrepreneurs see a 'milk cow' in the national innovation system. They gladly leave the costs and risks to the state to bear, but keep potential gains to themselves. Entrepreneurs like privatization of income and nationalization of loss. Officials allocating funds are interested in such kind of 'innovation policy.' Administrative units of various small funds spend on themselves one tenth of the funds.

The innovation system in Estonia must promote changes and not the present outdated structure of manufacturing. In order to achieve this, the labor market needs to be as flexible as possible so that the labor force can easily and rapidly move from low-productivity branches to more productive ones. In 2007, Estonia was given the 163rd place in terms of labor market flexibility in the international rating of 181 countries (Eurostat 2009; ILO 2009). The new Employment Contracts Act, which was adopted in December 2008 and will enter into force on 1 July 2009, is expected to improve the situation. The educational system needs to be made more flexible also.

Assistance to development of technologies, purchasing of modern technologies and starting of production in enterprises is a problem. Owners can sell what they have to an international group or relocate into a more suitable country, and the state having spent taxpayers' money will lose both expected jobs and tax revenue.

International corporate enterprises which have financial resources, technologies, market contacts etc. are increasingly more interested in an educated labor force than low wages and taxes. Therefore it is reasonable to stake primarily on human skills and knowledge and make education, including continuous education, accessible to everybody.

University research is financed in the world not only to discover, invent or learn something, but first of all to raise the level of higher education. A parent company wouldn't locate production in a region where it is not possible to hire specialists locally.

The labor force in the EU and in the whole world is much less mobile than capital and production. Language, cultural barriers, social network etc. keep people immobile. The labor force is not leaving en masse, as Estonia is a great place to live in. Therefore, 95 cents of every Kroon spent on education and training serve the purpose.

The state must finance hobby groups much more generously than thus far. The world vision of children develops and expands there, habits grow, talents show up, self-realization opportunities increase. The present success of the Estonian electronics industry is based not only on Tallinn University of Technology and its Institute of Cybernetics, which until 1997 was part of the Estonian Academy of Sciences system. The one-time radio circle at the Tallinn House of Pioneers, which a significant part of the older generation electronics specialists have attended, was also very important.

The state should, more than thus far, cooperate with sectoral unions, which in every way support and promote development in their respective domain – publish professional works; collect, mediate and distribute professional information; develop international contacts between enterprises; organize seminars and public relations events; intermediate subcontracting and other cooperation offers; represent interests of the membership to create a favorable entrepreneurship environment, work out laws, etc. For example, the Federation of Estonian Engineering Industry undoubtedly has a great share in the success story of the branch.

For potential high-technology investors and skilled labor a contemporary living and work environment is also very important. Highly skilled workers (specialists), as a rule, have a well-kept and family that demands modern living conditions. They are willing to live and work only in a region that has a good infrastructure, or they will move to such a place from a place that does not satisfy them. Such families are particularly demanding of the educational facilities (schools) for their children. Therefore it would be reasonable for Estonia to promote immobile, i.e. 'fastened to the ground' infrastructure, as well as creative economy and diverse cultural life.

Delocalization and globalization in general can be a threat or an opportunity, depending on the country's trade mix and its economic and regulatory structure (Rae and Sollie 2007). Economic benefits are evident for the country to which economic activity is relocated, notably through job creation, investment spillovers, and technological transfers. But a relocating country can in principle benefit from relocation too through betterment of economic structure.

Attracting FDI has become a central component of industrial policy in most countries. Investment promotion can be divided into the following areas (Loewendahl 2001; IFC 1997; Christodoulou 1996; Young et al. 1994): 1) strategy and organization (includes setting the national policy context, objectives, structure of investment promotion, competitive positioning, sector targeting strategy); 2) lead activities (marketing; company targeting); 3) facilitation (project handling); 4) investment services (after-care and product improvement; monitoring and evaluation).

The activity of *Enterprise Estonia* in attracting foreign investments includes the following activities:

- Image creation is aimed at the development of the general reputation of Estonia. For that the group advertises in business and sector-specific publications, participate in international investment fairs and seminars, organize seminars to introduce investment possibilities in Estonia, general investment missions and disseminate information materials for investors. For advertising it uses promotional texts about Estonia and ads in newspapers, journals, TV, radio, internet etc.
- Direct marketing. It generates new investment projects and presents Estonia as a host country for foreign investment.
- Investor service is a service for investors in the phase of executing investments and in the post-investment phase.

Enterprise Estonia provides the following complimentary services to potential foreign investors (Enterprise Estonia 2009): 1) general and specific industrial information pertaining to Estonia and its investment opportunities; 2) partner search (subcontractors and joint venture partners); 3) useful contacts in the public and private sector (utilities, law firms, consultants, executive recruitment and more); 4) legal matters (establishing a company, queries regarding visas and residence permits, etc); 5) organization of company visits; 6) assistance in locating industrial property.

Foreign investors may also apply for support through the following programs, upon registration of their company in Estonia (Enterprise Estonia 2009): 1) Start-up program; 2) Business Infrastructure Development Program; 3) Training Program; 4) Consultation Program; 5) R&D Financing Program.

Supporting inflow of high-technology subcontracting is an important tool of Estonian economic policy for using opportunities of delocalization of industries. The state on its part does everything to promote it (importation for inward processing, re-exportation after inward processing, etc.). Branch associations are mainly busy with finding companies that are suitable for ordering high-technology subcontracting. Particularly successful in this respect is the Federation of Estonian Engineering Industry. Largely thanks to the activity of this branch association, more than half of the turnover of the Estonian machine building and metal working industry derives from subcontracting and its technological level and value added is growing well.

Optimism and Intelligent Activity Needed

The state of Estonia has tried – within the limits of its competence and financial resources – to create an innovative economic environment and provide general recommendations for the development of manufacturing (Sikkut, 2008; Kilvits, 2004):

- Make the attempt by developing production, technology and sales to climb up in the value chain, increase value added and profitability. Producers or service providers have in principle three possibilities to raise the value: 1) turn into a product developer; 2) turn into a brand holder; 3) move up to the value chain of higher value added products/services.
- When it is not (yet) possible to be successful with end products, attempts should be made to be competitive at least in the subcontracting market. You should try to shift from single procurement contracts to long-term contracts, become a standing supplier, participate in R&D activity, achieve high technological competence, be aware of the whole production cycle. You should try to orient to such high-technology subcontracting that the customers are not capable of producing themselves. For that you need to own

something that they don't – know-how, specialists, equipment or something else. These are the subcontractors they conclude long-term stable contracts with and assist in introducing standards, management systems etc. For such subcontracts they pay well and such business partners are respected. There is much less sense to orient to such subcontracts that can be produced cheaper than the customer (at better price to quality ratio), for the production of which the contracting entity has no sufficient production capacities or what is ordered from outside to diversify risks (so as not to create production capacities which when the conjuncture grows worse will remain under-utilized).

- Orientation should be taken to main growth domains (sustainable energy and environmental products which enable to prevent or mitigate environmental changes and energy crisis, and/or are environment friendly; health and welfare products which increase human life expectancy and quality).
- Existing capabilities should be utilized better than so far. The area of activity might be updating of traditional activities or movement into new spheres of activity that are related to the traditional ones.
- Also new capabilities should be developed. A target might be bringing new areas of activity from abroad or developing them on the grass-root level. The focus should be on attracting foreign investments to the country, particularly into local entrepreneurship, or on the basis of research and development promoting new knowledge, solutions and setting up of enterprises.
- Attempts should be made to focus on growing markets. Old Europe is suffering from slow growth rates and saturation. Eastern Europe and CIS enjoy fast growth rates. The biggest growth rates are in distant large markets.

Attempts should be made to orient to integration of industry and services, attempting a break-through on the level of business functions, increase the services sector, especially in the direction of export. Management of supply chains and logistics, as well as some spheres of creative economy are worth staking on.

Neither the Enterprise Estonia, the Development Fund, the Government, scientists nor EU say what exactly should be done and can be done to set up a high-value-added manufacturing enterprise. Entrepreneurs themselves have to devise a successful business plan. They have to modernize the structure of manufacturing enterprises fast and successfully. If they cannot do that, the process will pass without their indicative participation through bankruptcies, mergers and takeovers.

The Main Opportunity Is the Forced Development of the Export Sector

Crisis has a purifying and disciplining effect. It enables the elimination of wrong investments and inefficient enterprises from the economy and lowers the proportion of domestic market focused economic sectors as well as the employees' wage growth expectations. Assets are redistributed from passive economic agents to active ones and in the favor of those who have capital for growth financing (RiTo 2008). During boom years the economy is mainly simply expanding; new ideas and more effective ways are searched for just during a decline.

Due to the small domestic market of Estonia the main source of its economic growth is export, i.e. successful sales in the world market. A new economic cycle means that part of the labor force will go from the domestic demand targeted sector to the export sector. Estonia must start consuming less or exporting more. There is no third way.

Compared to the domestic market oriented branches of the manufacturing industry, export oriented branches did quite well in the international economic decline in 2008. The export increased, its structure improved and the share of manufacturing in total exports increased. Estonia was obviously saved by the fact that the structure of exports was differentiated (risks diversified) and largely oriented to so far rather stable European Union member states in the euro zone, especially Finland and Sweden.

And in order to survive the international economic decline as painlessly as possible, to be successful in global competition and develop sustainably, Estonia needs a much faster growth of exports and improvement of its structure. Estonia wants to shift from branches and activities where it is difficult to increase value added to more profitable and promising ones. Unlike the rich industrial countries, Estonia is not in the least interested in keeping its *status quo,* and wants to change it quickly and essentially. The present economic situation provides an exceptionally good chance for this. All sorts of development, international relocation of production and reallocation of economic power in the world are gathering speed. Estonia must quickly find its opportunities in the 'declining' market, a profitable niche. The economic history demonstrates that the best enterprises have been established just in most difficult periods. Estonia might have a splendid opportunity to exit from the global financial and economic crisis not as poor and shabby but rather as a winner, and take up a more dignified position in the international division of labor than now.

Manufacturing entrepreneurs and executives have for several years already complained of shortages in the work force, which, they say, prevents them from implementing new business ideas and expanding production and export. Now cheap loans are no longer available, domestic consumption has diminished and the construction boom is over. This will oust employees from the construction, building materials and wood processing industries as well as from the chemical industry (varnishes and paints, mastics), the manufacture of metal products (metal roofing and wall panels) and from other real estate market related spheres en masse. In the 4th quarter 2007, 84,100 people were employed with construction, a year later 74,600, a reduction of 9,500. And this is only the beginning. Remember that only five years ago – in the 4th quarter 2003 – only 48,000 people were employed in construction (Statistics Estonia 2009). People who have been working in construction are returning also, from Finland and other foreign countries.

In the 4th quarter 2007 there were 28,100 people unemployed in Estonia, and a year later 53,500 already, an increase of 25,400. Although the number of employed people decreased in this period only by 1,200 (Statistics Estonia, 2009), the tendency is obvious – the available workforce is increasing. These people - mostly male blue-collar workers - neither fit into service jobs nor do they want to work there. It would be logical for them to go to manufacturing.

Increased supply of workforce is an opportunity for a forced development of the manufacturing export sector and sharp increase in exports. For that, however, extensive retraining and further education of workforce is required. And money has not vanished from the earth either. Free capital - as much as Estonia has it - is not going into real estate development any more; why not invest it into manufacturing? Maybe the earlier volume of foreign investment will be restored and unlike those days, it will be available primarily for high technology production.

Although the global financial crisis has caused an economic decline in the countries Estonia is exporting to - protectionist tendencies have grown stronger, suppliers demand advance payments, the Estonian Kroon being pegged to the Euro has grown more expensive for some currencies and loan raising is much more difficult than previously - attempts should be made to take the maximum possible advantage of this situation. The more that there are also positive developments for entrepreneurs: raw material prices in the world market have fallen, real estate is cheaper, wage pressure has abated, the failing enterprises disappear from market, leaving gaps, and many enterprises are looking for new cooperation partners, supply chains are changing, international corporations are selling local subsidiaries etc. Our workforce has been much cheaper than in developed industrial countries and so-called technical productivity not very much lower. The problem is rather our position in the value chains and selling skills in general.

Estonia should attempt to take the utmost advantage of international relocation of production - mainly via foreign direct investment and subcontracting. There is a realistic opportunity through production, technology and sales development to enter into more profitable value chains, climb up in the value chain, increase value added and profitability. Those enterprises which can sell in the declining and highly competitive market will survive.

Although in the process of moving towards a post-industrial society, the share of manufacturing in employment, GDP, sales etc. will inevitably fall somewhat in the long-term perspective and the share of services will rise, it is possible that the manufacturing export sector will grow significantly in the short term. 118,900 people were employed in manufacturing in Estonia in the 4th quarter 2008 (Statistics Estonia 2009). Why shouldn't the number of people employed in the manufacturing export sector increase by a few thousand in the short term?

Bibliography

Arengufond (2008), *Eesti majanduse konkurentsivoime hetkeseis ja tulevikuväljavaated.* no. 1.

Armstrong, H. (1995), 'Convergence among Regions of the EU, 1950–1995,' *Papers in Regional Science*, 74(2), pp. 143–152.

Bank of Estonia (2009), (http://eestipank.info/pub/en/dokumendid/statistika/; 1/04/2009).

Brakman, S. and H. Garretsen (2005), *Location and Competition.* Rotledge. London and New York.

CEPII (2004) *European Industry's Place in the International Division of Labour: Situation and Prospects.* Proposed by CEPII-CIREM. European Consortium for Trade-Policy Analysis (ECTA). Report prepared for the Directorate-general for Trade and the European Commission. July 2004.

Christodoulou, P. (1996), *Inward Investment: An Overview and Guide to the Literature,* London, British Library.

Cuny, C. and A. de Crombrugghe (2000), *Guide for the Creation of Industrial Subcontracting Partnership Promotion Centres (of Exchanges).* United Nations Industrial Development Organisation.

Enterprise Estonia (2009), (http://www.eas.ee/?id=1150; 1/04/2009).

Estonian Development Fund (2009), (http://www.arengufond.ee?s= arengufond &lang=en; 1/04/2009).

European Union (2009), (http://europa.eu; 1/04/2009).

Eurostat (2009), (http://epp.eurostat.ec.europe.eu; 1/04/2009).

Gereffi, G. Humphrey, J. Sturgeon, T. (2005), 'The Governance of Global Value Chains,' *Review of International Political Economy.* 12:1, pp. 78–104.

IFC (1997), *Foreign Direct Investment,* Washington, IFC, World Bank.

ILO (2009) – International Labour Organization (http://www.ilo.org/global/ lang-en/index.htm; 1/04/2009).

Johnson, M. (1997), *Outsourcing … in Brief.* Oxford: Butterworth-Heinemann.

Kilvits, K. (2004), 'Some General Tendencies in World Industry,' in *Transatlantic Cooperation. Europe, America & the Baltics: Political & Economic Relations,* A. Charles (ed.), Tallinn, Audentes University, pp. 75–82.

Labrianidis, L., B. Domanski, C. Kalantaridis, K Kilvits and P. Roukova (eds) (2007), *The Moving Frontier: The Changing Geography of Production in Labour Intensive Industries*. PL 001695 MOVE Final Report. Thessaloniki: University of Macedonia of Economics and Social Sciences.

Loewendahl, H. (2001), 'A Framework for FDI Promotion,' *Transnational Corporations*, vol. 10, no. 1, pp. 12–23.

Mack, R. and D. Jacobson (1996), 'The Impact of Peripherality upon Trade Patterns in the European Union,' *European Urban and Regional Studies*, 3(4), pp. 364–369.

Myrdal, G. (1957), *Economic Theory and Under-developed Regions*. London: Duckworth.

Nicoletti, G., Golub, S., Hajkova, D., Mirza, D., Yoo, K.-Y. (2003), 'The Influence of Policies on Trade and Foreign Direct Investment,' *OECD Economic Studies*, 36, 1.

Rae, D. and M. Sollie (2007), *Globalisation and the European Union. Which Countries Are Best Placed to Cope?* OECD Economic Department Working Papers no. 586.

RiTo (2008), *Globaalne kriis tervendab majandust*. Riigikogu Toimetised, 18.

Rodrik, D. (2004), *'Industrial Policy for the Twenty-first Century*. Paper prepared for UNIDO.

Sachs, J. D. (2000), 'Globalisation and Patterns of Economic Development,' *Review of World Economics*, no. 4, pp. 579–600.

Sikkut, S. (2008), 'Eesti tööstus 2018: kus on kasvuvoimalused?' (http://www.arengufond.ee/upload/Editor/industryengines7files/foorum/Siim_Sikkut %20021208.pdf; 4.12.2008).

Statistics Estonia (2009), (http://www.stat.ee; 1/04/2009).

Taynaz, E. and Y. Kilicaslan (2002), *Subcontracting Dynamics and Economic Development: A Study on Textile and Engineering Industries*. Middle East Technical University - Turkey.

Totev, S. and G. Sariiski (2007), 'The Delocalisation of Labour Intensive Industries – Spatial Distribution in the EU,' [in:] *PL 001695 MOVE The Moving Frontier: The Changing Geography of Production in Labour Intensive Industries, Final Report*, L. Labrianidis, B. Domanski, C. Kalantaridis, K. Kilvits, P. Roukova, (eds), Thessaloniki: University of Macedonia of Economics and Social Sciences, pp. 272–302.

UNIDO (2003), *International Subcontracting versus Delocalisation*? Vienna.

Young, S., Hood, N. and Wilson, A. (1994), Targeting Policy as a Competitive Strategy for European Inward Agencies, *European Urban and Regional Studies*, 1 (2), pp. 143–159.

Part II: Migration, Gender, Race, and Identity

Irina Novikova

(In)visibilities of Race, Ethnicity and Gender - Baltic Contexts

> In Vilnius, customers requesting flowers carried by the Somali, 31-year-old Thomas Amaikar, were charged 40 litas (€12) for the service. A white guy in a hussar's uniform only cost 25 litas. In other words, according to a complaint sent to the ombudsman's office, it was a clear case of racial discrimination.
> (Flowers from … 2006)

1. From *Tsyganov* to *Must* - from Gipsy to Black

In 2002, just before the eastern enlargement of the European Union, the Eurovision contest was hosted by Tallinn, Estonia, due to the fact that the winners for the previous Eurovision-2001, Tanel Padar and Dave Benton, had represented Estonia. The duet's victory was instantly converted by Estonian media into the sample case of the racial and ethnic tolerance and multiculturalism flourishing in Estonian society, a particularly important political dividend from the Eurovision victory during the process of access to the European Union. Media emphasized Dave Benton's Afro-Estonianness, even though he was born on the Caribbean island of Aruba and he had lived in Netherlands, moving to Estonia only in 1997 for professional interest such as participation in the Eurovision contest (Picture 1). The song was composed by a Russian, a naturalized citizen of Estonia, who was in the process of Estonianising his name and family-name in the passport, from Igor' Tsyganov to Ivar Must. Let me note here that the family-name *Tsyganov* is a derivative of a Russian word *gipsy (tsygan)* in Russian, whereas his new family-name *Must* means *black* in Estonian.

Picture 1.

At the same time, it is a sort of a commonplace statement among my colleagues, students, friends and acquaintances that Latvia as well as the other two Baltic nations do not have problems with people of other races because – as a student of mine once put it – 'we don't have them.' Baltic societies perceive themselves as monoracial nations, 'despite the invasions from East and West for nearly a thousand years' (Peters 2006: 74). This imagination of national history as 'racially innocent' has secured contemporary Baltic societies with the image of racial homogeneity 'despite invasions.' Also, it is a revealing symptom of persisting hierarchies of racial thinking about identity and national space. Its genealogy should be tracked down to the re-invention of race, central to the universalist vision of the European Enlightenment. As Angus Bankroft argues, 'The development of European modernity and of the concept of race are intertwined, the project of modernity including race as a core innovation in its conceptual framework.' (Bankroft 2007: 35) Reinstated in its Manichean binaries (e.g. 'civilized-savage'), European modernity as a globalizing racial project produced a variety of meanings attached to racial categories and in the constructions of racial whiteness in various national and regional settings and in different historical contexts of Europe[1]. It generated various narratives, discourses and ideas of

1 See, for example, the discussion of the Baltic Cygnet Scheme and being white in Britain in the late forties in *New Geographies of Race and Racism*, Claire Dwyer and Carolyne Bressey, Ashgate, 2008, pp. 56–57.

race, racism and racialization, having inflected national ideologies of cultural nationalism in European societies.

Furthermore, European racial discourses (Eigen 2006; Valls 2005), together with the development of ethnological and anthropological discourses in the 19th century, deserve more attention by those venturing comparative and transnational studies of thinking and practicing race in the Baltic contexts. A populist monoracial image of nation embedded in naturalizing nationality in relation to biological race hides the other side of the moon – how the Baltic nations were conceptualized in racial terms by anthropologists and ethnographers of European modernity. And the Estonian anthropologist Kat Kalling notes, 'Estonians were viewed as "Mongols" by the European scientific community in the 19th century and even later' (Kalling 1999; see also Kalling 2007) in his argument on the racial dualism and eugenics in Estonia. Let me cite a quite lengthy passage from Kalling's article:

Estonians joined the discussions about the anthropological (i.e. biological) aspects of their ethnicity only in the last decades of the 19th century. By that time the theories regarding the Estonians (and other Finnic peoples) as 'Mongols' – and subsequently racially inferior – were already decaying among scientists. The racial theory published by J. Deniker in 1900 described two 'white' races in Europe. These were (as called then) the Nordic and Eastern (Oriental) races. The latter was believed to have some Eastern/Mongoloid influences. According to J. Deniker both could have been represented in Estonia and Finland (Kemiläinen, 1993: 195–198). It could be a turning point in creating attitudes towards Finnic peoples, *incl.* the Estonians, as 'Europeans' and 'whites'. It was also the first time that the racial dualism of Estonians was stressed. Later this theory was 'canonized' by Juhan Aul (Klein) (1897–1994) and others, who admitted the prevalence of two racial types in Estonia, the West-Baltic type in the western and northern parts of the country and the East-Baltic type in the remaining areas. The knowledge about racial dualism was obviously one of the reasons why racial theories could not influence eugenical thinking in Estonia – it was not easy to choose a particular race to represent the national ideal. On the one hand, there was the Eastern race possessing Mongoloid tracks – thus invaluable in the eyes of historical prejudices, but in the light of available archaeological data connecting us with the presumed roots in northern Eurasia. The other and more 'honorable' Nordic (Arian) race was, however, archaeologically not Finnic. [...] One has to admit that educated Estonians of the time, perhaps being well aware of the theories 'suspecting' Estonians and Finns to be 'Mongols,' did not let themselves be influenced and carried away by these ideas and kept Estonian national ideology far from racist issues. Amongst the numerous pre-independence Estonian thinkers, politicians etc. there were no specialists who could concentrate on the biological aspects of the racial issue. The philologist Villem Grünthal-Ridala (1885–1942) was, according to T. Karjahärm, one of the few to preach racial/phrenological theories (Karjahärm, 1993:1351). He was also one of the few to be positive and optimistic about the Estonians' racial background. Other authors remained mainly within the borders of cultural criteria in discussing the word *'toug'* denoting an ethnic/linguistic/cultural issue, and although its biological background was a topic of discussion and in a way a 'self-evident fact,' no racist graduation was considered when evaluating the local ethnic groups. In laying paths for the future national self-consciousness of Estonians, racial and racist aspects could be avoided - morphological markers did not become criteria for a nation.

When returning to the question asked at the beginning of the article, namely whether the racial/ethnic issue was important for Estonian eugenicists, one has to admit that only one (the 25th) sentence of the watch-words contains something to answer this question. It says that too frequent intermarriages between Estonians and aliens are recommendable neither from the point of view of family nor racial aspects (Tulev Eesti, 1925:4). Those suspecting racist attitudes in this should be reminded that 'race' (*'toug'*) in a broad sense meant cultural entity, and the issue was a concern about possible cultural conflicts in an inter-ethnic family, supposedly leading to lower reproduction, poorer education or poverty. Thus the issue was mainly limited to the realm of (cultural) nationalism. The topic is more widely examined in a popular handbook entitled *Pärivus ja Valik* (Heredity and Selection) that also commented on mixed families. The concept, in fact, is positive about blood mixture as such. The issue was a concern about possible cultural domination by Germans and Russians as historical dominants in the particular region of Europe. Thus, intermarriages with the representatives of these two groups should be avoided to stop the denationalization of Estonians. Intermarriages with culturally 'equal' nations, especially with people of other Finnic tribes, would be highly recommendable (Audova et al., 1927:281, Kalling 1999).

Ken Kalling's argument on racial dualism as a panacea against racist issues contains references to the works of Iosif Deniker[2] and reflects a spurring interest to the Russian imperial raciology of the late 19th and early 20th centuries in the post-Soviet anthropological discourses. Deniker's racial classification is used in Kalling's argument on Estonian cultural nationalism and eugenics of the interwar period for disavowing any possible suspicions of racist attitudes in the question on ethnic inter-marriages. Actually, Kalling's argument draws an important political inference of historical analogy between the interwar and post-Soviet periods in the concern with ethnic intermarriages. In this view, cultural nationalism is separated from 'racist attitudes' and advocated, if not justified, as an essential prerequisite of stopping denationalization of Estonians in the light of 'cultural domination' by Germans and Russians. Cultural nationalism defends partialism, exclusionary and discriminating, on behalf of a culture – this is seen as a major difference from racist partialism. However, in my paper I argue that cultural nationalism cannot be divorced from its political and ideological modalities opening ways for the intervention of racial(ized) nationalism, neither in popular views and attitudes nor in practices and doctrines. I will look into some examples of discursive articulations, media representations and populist actions, mainly in the contexts of Latvia and Lithuania, as symptomatic projections of this intimate interconnection between post-Soviet cultural nationalisms towards the issue of Soviet labor migration and racial(ized) thinking that the national *Lebensraum* would be toughly guarded against future 'invasions from East and West' in the age of globalized economy.

2 Iosif Deniker (1852–1918) – a Russian theorist of race typology.

2. Sizes, Flavors, Pleasures/Leisures and Colors of Otherness

'Racial innocence' does not prevent contemporary users of the globalized popular imagescape to feel intrigued with the black male physique and sexuality. In August, 2008, a Latvian news website *apollo.lv* published an article by an anonymous guest author *Are black men ideal partners in bed? (Sizes)*? (Guest author 2008). The article as well as its lively follow-up chat forum reminded me of a huge poster, an advertisement of local liquor production, in downtown Riga of the late 1990s, a fascinating sample of a connection between alcohol advertisement, masculinity and race. The black-and-white poster showed two twin men, nicely smiling and holding identical bottles - in purple and orange colors - in their hands, but with labels informing on two different berry flavors of the same liquor. The word 'different' refers to juicy liquids in the bottles vis-à-vis bottlelike male bodies and was also singled out in a different from black-and-white, purple color. (Picture 2) The picturesque advertisement of the alcoholic beverage was supplied with the text 'Black Balsam: Now two different flavors.' This implicitly sexualized advertisement had an ultimately eye-catching visual element in our 'monoracial' milieu - the black skin color of the male twins. Their background presence embodying 'juicy' differences of alcoholic flavors explicitly demonstrated the racist perception of blackness and masculinity in this 'racially innocent' advertisement. Moreover, unlike other alcoholic advertisements relating masculinity and alcohol to power, this ad delegated the two black men an emasculating 'feminine' position of an object for consumption and pleasure vis-à-vis other ways of representing the relationships between masculinity, power and alcohol.

Another 'juicy' example is drawn from a range of racial images produced by post-Soviet transnational tourist industry. An ad clip of the Russia-based TEZ Tour Agency on Latvian TV shows a quasi-glamorous blonde woman in a dialogue with a male employee of a tourist agency (Picture 3). Their conversation - in Russian - reminds of a visit to a tailor: 'Perhaps, this color would fit?' - 'Are you laughing at me?'(She means that the suggested color - dark beige - does

Picture 2. Black Balsam: Now Two Different Flavors.

not fit the color of her skin). 'Then perhaps, this color – you know, very trendy in this season' – the agent suggests her a sample slip of dark chocolate color.

The woman's reply to the travel agent after a short pause – 'Perhaps I will take it.' The agent, a rather effeminate and smallish white man, demonstrates two pieces of color to his woman client – dark beige (she considers it to be a mismatch with the color of her blue dress) and dark chocolate. The woman chooses the second one, and the next frame shows her in a tropical beach bar at night, dancing with a muscular, handsome black man. More precisely – dark chocolate, and rather humble and silent. While dancing, she is also matching a color sample (dark chocolate) with his skin color, to make sure, probably, that she is having exactly the pleasures for which she has paid. The final episode of the clip shows her, most probably

Picture 3. Tourism - Advertisement of TEZ Tour Agency.

satisfied with her recent trip to the dark-chocolate world, asking for a certain size in centimeters, and the agent looks definitely embarrassed at her (sexual) appetites.

The spectacular celebration of an Afro-Estonian singer, an article about black male sexuality in Latvia, or advertisements about the pleasures of alcohol and tourism circulated in the Baltics from Russia, are rather exemplary products of cultural discourses and practices that treat race on the level of manifest content. Racial categorization is internalized in the case with Igor' Tsyganov changing Ivar Must. On the contrary, the reclamation of the own whiteness was another connotation of existential upgrading added to a popular Russophone vernaculism in Latvia 'let us live like white people do' (*pozhivem kak belye lyudi*).[3]

Seemingly far away from this kind of racialized popular vernaculisms, business can also demonstrate similar racialized thinking and attitudes in the labor market and trade as, for example, in a Latvian ad poster (SIA 'FAMAR – DESI' store 'Buvniecibas ABC'). (Picture 4) It shows a black man who pronounces in a grammatically incorrect way 'Mans gribet remontet Tav's maja!' (Mine want repair Yours house). The *Consumer Rights Protection Centre* fined the company with 5000 Ls for this highly offensive and discriminating poster in terms of race, skin color, national and social background. It was the first time in Latvia that discrimination in public advertisements was punished by an impressively large fine.

Another spectacular advertisement of computers as an example of stereotype activation was published in *'Diena,'* a mainstream daily newspaper in Latvia, and it was also aired on radio. The ad demonstrates two computers (Picture 5). One of them is in black color against white background, and the other one in white against a black background. This black-and-white visual image is coupled with the statement 'While the white rest, the black work.' Pictures of both computers are supplied with a synopsis of their technical characteristics.

The idea behind this advertisement is that, due to their component parts, white-color computers are more suitable for leisure,

3 See also: *The Rise and Fall of the Caucasian Race: A Political History of Racial Identity*. Bruce David Baum. 2006

Picture 4. Mine Want Repair Yours House

Picture 5

and the black ones – for work. In this ad, the technical categorization of computers is visualized by activating an internalized racist sentiment about the socially polarizing 'colors' of existential human activities such as work and leisure. Latvian Ombudsman Romans Apsitis considered this advertisement as discriminating and racist, and demanded that it be removed from media. His argument was that the visual image and text of the ad refer not to the differences in computers, but infer the social categorization of people based on differences in skin color. In his view, the verbs *to rest* and *to work* in combination with the nominalized adjectives *white* and *black*, cannot represent the computers – it is not the technology that relaxes and works, but it is people who do that. However, the state police did not find any trace of racism in this advertisement.

Actually, black and white as colors for giving different meanings of societal polarization have been widely used by Russian speakers in Estonia and Latvia. When both countries introduced the category of non-citizenship for those Russophone people and their offspring who moved to these countries after 1940, this political exclusion was immediately vernaculized into a 'color' label. A massive quantity of non-citizens or 'aliens' in Latvia and Estonia – '*negr*azhdane' (non-citizens) – labeled themselves as *negry* (Negroes)[4], thus, adding the racializing 'color' to their social self-perception of being economically downgraded, politically disenfranchised and ethnically made another. The political inclusion/exclusion divide in the two countries, thus, obtained the connotation of racial binarism, 'belye' and 'negry' (whites and negroes).

The above-discussed Latvian ads with a visual image of a black male body and Baltic Russophone vernaculisms of racial/ized otherness clearly arise from the discourses of race. When race is viewed primarily as access to whiteness (Dyer 1997; Hill 1997; Berger 1999), then the negation to this access defined as 'otherness' is expressed in different ways. Expressions such as color terms and ethnic labels that are not racist in other contexts can be deployed in vernacular and in popular imagery for racializing categorizations of groups or

4 See, for example, http://www.mk-lat.lv/rubrics/society/887, or browse for combination of *негражданин* (status of alien, or non-citizen in Latvia and Estonia) and *негр* (Negro) in Internet.

individuals as, for example, in the case with non-citizens, and race turns into a reflexive attribute, applied to social and ethnic designations of 'otherness.'

3. Our Europe versus Them: Russian Migrants, *Juden raus!*, Asian Dangers, Black Fathers

In the 1990s, the collapse of the socialist statist economy and Soviet political system was accompanied by the reconstruction of political borders in the Baltic region, and this process (re)claimed not only physical borders but also emotional boundaries. The massive labor migration of the Soviet period was treated in the post-Soviet retro-nationalisms as an economic/social/ethnic tool used by Soviet power to destroy ecoethnically balanced economies and the related *Lebensraum* of the nation-state. This nationalist presumption was mainstreamed into the popular feelings about these 'former migrant' communities as essentially alien and hostile to the post-Soviet national(ist) projects.

The 'return to the past,' or 'recovery,' agenda of the early 1990s was proliferated into the political and public discourse of the 'return into Europe,' to get purified from the legacies of communism compared to threats of Asianization.

As the Lithuanian scholar Leonidas Donskis writes:

> ... the new democracies had to catch up with Western European history to qualify for the exclusive and honorable club of Europe. Moreover, 'yet another Europe' had to become even faster than history, transforming itself into a more or less recognizable collective actor in global economy and politics. Capitalism, which was long presented in Soviet high school textbooks as the major menace to the mankind, now seems to be more aggressive and dynamic in post-Soviet societies than in far more moderate, timid, egalitarian, social-democratic, welfare-state-orientated, and post-capitalist Western European countries. (Donskis 2005: 3)

Merje Kuus indicates in her article:

> Taagepera (1999: 24), a prominent academic actively involved in designing the premises of ethnic integration in Estonia, explicitly contrasts Estonia's

> European character with the non-European ways of Russia: Whenever Russia or Serbia consider adopting western ways they must go outside and give up parts of themselves. In contrast, when Estonia or its Baltic neighbors (Latvia and Lithuania) adopt western ways, they only have to reach deeper and actually recover parts of themselves. (Kuus 2002: 97)

In the dominant retro-imagination of that period, recovering a modernist framework of a monocultural nation-state, the major image attached to 'Baltic Russians' (although the category was not used in that period) was one of the 'contaminating' demographic and politically hostile mass, alien and retarding the success of the regional Eurocentrization. For example, the Lithuanian sociologist Gaidys argued:

> The professional composition of Russians in Latvia is similar to that of Lithuanians. The *main problem* there lies not in the Russians' social structure, but *in their greater number.* The same goes for Estonia, especially for its northeastern region [...] Lithuania *was fortunate* in *not having similarly high concentration of Russians;* with *the controversial exception* of Snieckus, which is the site of a nuclear power plant and to which Lithuania can be seen as *a hostage.* For instance, in February 1992 an employee of the nuclear power station, a highly skilled computer specialist who *was suspected of intentionally introducing viruses* into the computers monitoring the operation of the reactors, was arrested' – my italics and underlining (Gaidys 1994: 95)

Family as a problematic political site was already in the foreground of national mass media in the early 1990s. The mid-1990s became the period of active production of *ethno studies*: ethnopolitical, ethnocultural, ethnodemographic, ethnosociological longitudinal surveys and researches of families, with a focus on ethnically mixed families, dynamics of families' ethnic homogeneity/heterogeneity and choices of ethnic belonging among children of ethnically mixed marriages:

By comparing migration waves with resulting changes, ethnic structure of Latvian families has not changed much and it is not changing. Change occurs very slowly, with a generation transforming next generation. We can calm ourselves down that time will cure all wounds – also our nation's scars. The more Russification 'worked on' a generation, the more 'natural' it becomes by revealing itself in the ethnic structure of people born in Latvia, the more it remains in our lives and genes. (Rungule 1995: 21)

The Latvian sociologist Iveta Pavlina insisted:

> A stable family is the basis of the state. [...] The most stable are marriages between a Latvian woman and an ethnic minority man, or a Russian man with an ethnic minority woman [...] The most unstable are marriages between Latvians and Russians: Latvian man – Russian woman, and Russian man – Latvian woman. [...] It seems that in both Russian homogeneous and ethnically mixed families the most frequent divorces are in the families in which one of the partners is Russian. (Pavlina 1995: 59)

The discourse on Russian-speaking migrants of the Soviet period as a quantitative/demographic problem and a hidden political threat has been steadily hegemonized in the Baltic societies since the early 1990s. Furthermore, within the dominant geopolitical pressures in the region, the presence of Russian-speaking populations was approached in the early 1990s as a 'problem' (Clemens 2001) of quantity (!) in terms of European security and the new evolving borders with Russia. From the mid-1990s, the image 'we are the border of Europe,' dominant in the national political rhetoric,[5] was becoming intimately linked with discourses on Russian-speaking communities, proliferating around the meaning and images of 'the fifth column,' 'a hand of Russia,' mafia, corruption, alcoholism. What Vladis Gaidys saw as popular stereotypes of an uneducated Russian in Lithuania, in Latvia, was transplanted into a proliferating image of a degraded, half-wild Russian-speaking migrant, with a touch of 'Asian' threat. (Pictures 6 and 7)

The racialized image of *sovki (*denigrating word for *Soviet people),* with the Orientalized image of threatening and pauperized Russia behind, was activated as an instrument of identity politics in which ethnic, cultural and political differences were framed as incompatible alterities in the Europeanization discourse of the national projects and national visions of joining the EU. This fusion between Russophobia and Orientalism is spectacularly manifested in the interview of Vytautas Landsbergis Junior:

5 'Similarly us hosting the NATO Summit in the month of November is an indication of the area of security and stability that Europe extends now as far as Latvia's eastern borders and on that occasion we will be very pleased to welcome the first ever Prime Minister of Great Britain's visit to the Republic of Latvia,' – from the press-conference transcript of Vaira Vike-freiberga and Tony Blair and a number of speeches of NATO officials (2006. Available at: http://www.number10.gov.uk/Page9812.

Pictures 6 and 7. From the Popular Periodical *Atmoda* of the Early 1990s

> Who would be that traditional Lithuanian, what would be the features of this character? An extinct Lithuanian, first of all, could be characterized by one word – respect. Respect for his place, his woman or her man, his children, his land, his thoughts. A traditional Lithuanian knew, that, idolizing a woman, he himself becomes the god. [...] A mutant, Mongolian variant of a Lithuanian does not have these beautiful features – very often he is unhappy, a drunkard, inclined to blame all and everything, only not himself. Rudeness and egoism are the properties of this mutant. This person does not understand, that the main thing in this world is to understand himself, to be released from complexes, fears and to become a good person caring others [...] Also, he often perceives the woman as a machine for quenching desires, i.e. transforms her into a prostitute, thus, prostituting himself. My friends says, that a popular Mongolian abusive phrase 'f. Mother' is a military command of soldiers-rapers of Ghengis-Khan who ordered the men of enslaved countries ordered to rape their mothers. In this ways occupants instantly broke the outlook of an ordinary person, and he became a slave. [...] Later, often unconsciously using this abusive phrase, a man maintains the century-long slavery already voluntarily. Besides, a raped one often becomes a rapist himself – this psychological law is well remembered by the majority of those who served in the Soviet army. (Landsbergis Jr. 2006)

This discursive framework of living with racialized 'alterity – daily and permanently' (Bauman 1997: 30) in the space of re-claimed nation-state was criticized by the great Lithuanian thinker Tomas Venclova his paper 'Russians and Lithuanians':

> Russians are not Europeans, but Russian-Mongol-Tatar assimilated mixture alien to the phenomena of European culture and even hostile and dangerous in its Soviet scale.' I have an inner protest against these words [...] One can understand hatred. It is particularly simple to understand it in Eastern Europe. But hatred and revenge never contribute to the constructive solution of any social problem. A considerable, if not the majority of Lithuanians look upon Russians without differentiation, led not by reason, but by emotions and even racial instincts.[6] (in Pomeranc 2008)

6 Русские не европейцы, а русско-монголо-татарская ассимиляционная смесь, для которой явления европейской культуры непонятны и чужды, а в советском масштабе даже враждебны и опасны'. Эти слова вызывают во мне внутренний протест. [...] Ненависть можно понять. В Восточной Европе ее понять особенно просто. Но ненависть и чувство мести не способствуют конструктивному решению каких бы то ни было социальных проблем. Большая, а может быть, и большая часть литовцев смотрят на русских недифференцированно, руководствуясь эмоциями и чуть ли не расовыми инстинктами, а не разумом.

In a long-term perspective, the hegemonic sentiment of racialized cultural nationalism has been encouraging for radical nationalist waves manifested, for example, in Lithuania, in the political solidarization of skinheads around the discourse of Russophobia and anti-Semitism:

> Perhaps, the brightest event that stirred up the Lithuanian society in 2008 was The Independence Day of Lithuania on March, 11th. More precisely, its 'celebration' in Vilnius. Along the main street of the country - the central street of Vilnius, the Gediminas Prospect, there was passing a column of some hundred skinheads. 'Russians - out,' 'One-two-three, Lithuania is good without Russians!', 'Juden raus!', 'Kill this Jew!', - such and similar slogans were yelled out by the skinheads. Young men were holding flags and posters with swastika, lifted a hand in a fascist greeting (Foreign students ... 2007)

In Latvia[7], the number of racially-motivated attacks targeting visible minorities has been increasing and the use of racist discourse, by some politicians and in the media, remains a problem (Reports ... 2008). In mid-2006 a man was attacked in central Riga, and the first ever prison sentence for a racially motivated assault was handed down. Later, two teenagers were sentenced for a racially motivated attack against a woman of Brazilian origin in December 2006. As Amnesty International points out: 'The European Union (EU) sent a formal request to Latvia to implement the EU Racial Equality Directive (2000/43/E), which Latvia had to date failed to do.' (Latvia – Amnesty international Report 2008)

Also in Lithuania, in 2008, the prosecutor's office initiated 84 investigations related to discrimination or incitement to racial or ethnic hatred, compared to 37 in 2007 and 17 in 2006. In 2007 there were

> assaults on several foreign students, among them two Africans, of the Lithuanian Christian College in Klaipeda; a fight between Lithuanian and Nigerian youths in May and an attack on a man from Ghana two days later, both in Vilnius; an August attack on an Italian exchange student by assailants who

7 See also National Reports on Responding to Racism http://cms.horus.be/files/99935/MediaArchive/pdf/Lithuania_EN.pdf, http://cms.horus.be/files/99935/MediaArchive/pdf/Latvia_EN.pdf http://cms.horus.be/files/99935/MediaArchive/pdf/Estonia_EN.pdf.

> apparently thought he was a Muslim; and the December death in Vilnius of a former Somali student at Kaunas Medical University after he was beaten in October, allegedly because he spoke on television about racial violence he had experienced in the country. [...] A study by the EU Agency for Fundamental Rights concluded in August 2007 that responses to cases of ethnic discrimination registered in the country were ineffective and that insufficient attention was given to the problem. According to the research, the law provides possibilities to complain about ethnic discrimination; however, the sanctions usually applied in such cases were insufficient, and victims received insufficient or no compensation. The government was revising its National Anti Discrimination Program to address increased levels of discrimination. (Human Rights Report: Lithuania 2008)

The singer Berneen, popular in Lithuania, was attacked in April, 2008. She became famous in Lithuania after her participation in a musical reality-show 'The Way to Stars.' Afterwards, Berneen stayed in Lithuania to continue her musical career on TV. The young woman was attacked by a group of people in downtown Vilnius. Skinheads beat the singer so that she needed medical assistance. During a press conference, Berneen pleaded to pay attention not to her assault, but to a growing number of racist attacks in Lithuania. She also said that she had been attacked by young men in black and with stripes in the colors of the Lithuanian flag and a swastika on their jackets. Black legionaries of the Kaunas basketball club 'Zhalgiris' repeatedly suffered from similar attacks. Later on, Lithuanian court punished Berneen's offender and several participants of the neo-Nazi march for igniting an interethnic conflict.

3. Europe's *Banlieues,* Our Women and *Les Liasons Dangereues*

Race as an (in)visible dimension of post-Soviet national projects in the Baltics has been infiltrating the divide between pressurizing racial and ethnic diversities, on the one hand, and indigenization policies, on the other, and betraying itself in the feeling of racial anxiety in the angry request of a woman voter to a Latvian parliamentary:

> An auntie tells me – my daughter has married a black man and they will have a baby – it will be black! I ask her – how can I help you? She says, but you are a national party! I was a 'fatherlander' at that time. And, if you do nothing in this case, I would not vote for 'fatherlanders' any more! And how she yelled at me by the telephone! It happens, doesn't it? What can I do, right?[8]

An auntie's sentiment fuses her clearly nationalist mindset ('fatherlanders' is the radical nationalist party that demands repatriation of all former Soviet Russian-speaking migrants and their offspring from Latvia) and racist worldview, never shattered in the Soviet period of her life. Her fear of racial miscegenation, in connection with her threat *not* to vote for 'fatherlanders,' indicates something else. The post-Soviet societies, including the Baltic nations, have been witnessing a very slow emergence of new migrant and diasporic groups. By the late 1990s, the nationalist discourses emanating anxiety around former Soviet migrants as hidden enemies 'at the border of Europe' were re-emerging within the public discourses on possible future migrations 'from outside' as an existential threat to the survival of the nation. This discursive connection between past and future threats of migration and Otherness has been solidified and channeled into the public opinion on the historical scale – from Soviet labor migration having 'contaminated' and de-Europeanized the nation, to the future 'colored' migration that would 'contaminate' the nationalist projects of Europeanization.

For example, the clashes in the Paris *banlieues* on October 27, 2005, were actively commented in the Latvian chats as manifestations of black people being an eternal and unchanging disturbance of order and welfare in the European cities. Some comments emphasized the inadequacy of European racialized politics of social exclusion that did not eliminate social and economic discrimination of migrant and colored populations. This rather ambivalent image of 'Europe' loomed, for example, in the Latvian discussions of the Paris unrest in October, 2005:

> After the World War 2, the USA were the richest nation in the world, economically solidified, but internal conflict, protests of black people show that

8 From an interview of a Latvian parliamentary for the project 'FEMCIT Gendered Citizenship in Multicultural Europe: The Impact of the Contemporary Women's Movements'

> welfare is not a wonder wand that would solve many problems. Also, France is a welfare nation, but we see what kind of migrants' unrests happened in the Paris outskirts! (Interview with Oskars Kastens 2007)

Thus, 'Europe' has been looked at, on the one hand, as being in need of finding radical decisions to curb global migration, and on the other, as the modern project that cannot cope with its Others injecting it with millions in migrant transnational flows. 'Europe,' thus, is perceived as a controversial and non-consequential subject in dealing with its postcolonial legacies. Either a generic subject failing in its multicultural ideas and models, or color-'contaminated' urban Europe, never at rest – these views of Europe as a desired space of belonging and identity soak either the skinhead mindset, or the argument of a woman candidate from a marginal political party in Latvia. She openly admitted in a talk show during the 2002 parliamentary elections in Latvia that the party is against repatriating Russians from the country because 'we at least know each other, we have lived many years together; they know our language, our customs. Instead – we don't know who will come instead.'

At the same time, a journalist's question infers the Soviet legacy of labor flows as a reference-point in terms of threatening future migrations in her response to the argument of Oskars Kastens, a former Minister of Integration in Latvia:

> Now about racism. We have the European Union, the community based on the Lisbon strategy, on knowledge. But if we want Latvia to be competitive in long-term perspective, we will need specialists from abroad. I will feel ashamed if somebody who will come to Latvia and bring Latvian business to the world, will be threatened in the streets only because he is from India.
> (Question of a journalist:) Perhaps, wouldn't it be better to invite former Soviet people in order to monitor this process, with their mentality that we know, not people of alien mentality of Islam, the labor force from the countries of East? (Kastens interview 2007)

At the same time, the question actually expresses a journalist's internalized racial privilege voiced in a better option of inviting migrants from post-Soviet Byelorussia and Ukraine to Latvia, thus, acquiring a 'European' component as a nation-recipient. A perceived threat of racial miscegenation and of 'alien mentality of Islam' is referenced in historical terms between socialist and capitalist modernities.

Furthermore, this question as an example of retro/reactive post-Soviet xenophobia[9] reminds us that race figured eminently in the conceptualization and consolidation of a modern nation-state and invites us to explore other discourses in relation to the race/nation bind. As such race has been reclaimed in safeguarding postsocialist nation-states as certain spatial projects (Kuus 2004) and their fundamental social institutions such as family. Family and home are idealized and privatized sanctuaries of a nation-state, and women are expected by nationalists to be the guards of the 'hearth.' Images of space, place and territory link gendered images of home and family with the constructs of race and nation (Penrose, Jackson 1993). To exemplify this link, I will draw on another couple of examples of how blackness and masculinity were used during the 2002 election campaign to the Parliament of Latvia (Saeima). The marginal *Social Democratic Welfare Party* argued against Latvia's joining the European Union and NATO and distributed a leaflet with the image of a NATO soldier with a gun (Picture 8). Next to him stands a lascivious black man, lustfully snatching a woman in Latvian national costume. She is begging for help and protection, under the flag of the European Union but in vain.

Another case of raced and gendered imagery was a TV commercial and a leaflet distributed by *The Party of Freedom* (Picture 9). This scandalous leaflet frames a black man in the uniform of the Army of Latvia. He is pictured at a low angle, next to the Freedom Monument, the symbol of the independent Latvian nation. His heroic low-angle dominates both a viewer's gaze and the text on the monument 'For Fatherland and Freedom' at the background. This visual effect is both magnified and contrasted with an alerting statement: 'Today – a guard of Latvia, tomorrow – perhaps your son-in-law?' The leaflet was printed in both Latvian and Russian languages and distributed via post-boxes in the residential areas of Riga. At the same time, an ad was demonstrated on national TV – the same black soldier embraces an elderly auntie (presumably, his future mother-in-law

9 See the comments on Roma and black people after Ilmars Slapins's article *Melna ada* (Black skin) http://www.delfi.lv/news/comment/comment/article.php?id=22724451.

Picture 8. Advertisement of the *Social Democratic Welfare Party.*

Text under the first picture: 'We refrain from joining the EU and NATO! (We request other parties not to steal our ideas!)' Text under the second picture: 'If you are for NATO and European Union, then already the next Ligo [summer solstice celebration] you will dance obeying foreign reed pipe: 'Pidra-la-la ... Pidra-la-la ..." Text under the third picture: 'Latvia has to stay a free, independent and neutral republic.'

and actually, a figure of a typical voter in election campaigns), and a running line gives the audience the same alerting statement.

Picture 9. Advertisement of *The Party of Freedom*:
'Today – a guard of Latvia, tomorrow – perhaps your son-in-law?'

These particular images, together with the ones that I discussed in the beginning of the article, raise a series of questions: why have these types of images (black men and their bodies) been given such a prominent visual position? What deeper implications emerge from the analysis of images, vernaculars, behaviors in popular discourses vis-à-vis post-Soviet political frameworks and regulatory ideals? A black male body is visualized in the binarism of se(ns)(x)ual desires/threats. It is, thus, turned into a dehumanized spectacle with the familiar 'White Man's' standpoint of racial alterity iconized in its consumed and 'landscaped,' sexualized and seducing/threatening exoticism. However, these images of existential and undifferentiated racial otherness are not simply the local repercussions of the globalized mediascape, political nationalisms and the tourist industry, its pleasures of access to 'all included' leisure. Different images of racial otherness in their various frames (gender or/and sexuality) and colors (from dark beige to dark chocolate) actually articulate white experience (e.g., the discourse of racial innocence or a white woman going for sex tourism). Whiteness secures its dominance by seeming to be nothing in particular because of its perennial nature, either in national knowledge production or through transnational image generation.[10]

On the one hand, the ads of alcoholic beverages and exotic tourism offer racializing views upon the global space as the external continuum of *pleasure and leisure* embodied in a black male figure – beyond national borders. On the other, the ads of a parliamentary campaign center around the images of woman-nation, both domestic and public, to symbolize everything that is *threatened within the borders* – family and nation. The national self-imagination has been discursively operated as being the liberation from the political correctness of Soviet internationalism ('equality irrespective of skin color') and Soviet doctrine of sex equality in the politics of naturalization and essentialization of gender and ethnic identities (Verdery 1996). Actually, the leaflet with a black soldier used the discursive practice of 'externalizing' racial otherness (threat, contamination, miscegenation) by engaging discourses of ethnic nationalism and gender fundamentalism. The visual image and the text directly address women voters of middle age and their 'maternal instincts' – they are one of the major social constituencies among voters in Latvia. Thus, family rhetoric was invoked, deeply implicated in training a feeling of ethnic and racial privilege for safeguarding the national *Lebensraum* in its genealogical purity.

The images of a black male body, either in tourist or political ads, reclaim the racist mythotype of a black male rapist, sexual flesh and barbarian, and re-dress it for the need of motivating a mobilization of the nation against new possible threats – a black perpetrator, a migrant who can become a naturalized citizen, a miscegenator, threatening the national *Lebensraum* with becoming its uninvited 'family member.' Leaflets and a TV ad with a black soldier in Latvian military uniform are a spectacular example of how important the politics of feeling, blood and home is for the process of national

10 The TEZ agency ad is actually a fascinating example of post-Soviet discursive transnationalism in perpetuation of racist attitudes and stereotypes. TEZ Tour is a travel agency based in Russia, having its representative offices in the Baltic countries and purchasing ad time in national and Russian TV-channels available to the Baltic audiences.

re-imagination. These visual materials were circulated in both Latvian and Russian languages to give both communities a shared sentiment of alertness against a racial threat. These visual materials also demonstrate how post-Soviet cultural discourses - in different political contexts like in the Baltics - perpetuate biologization of race whereas the imagery of black/white mutates social, ethnic and gender diversities, differences and legacies into the immobilizing cast of allegedly existential alterities.

5. Genealogies of Innocence?

As a signifier and as a discourse, race possesses a certain .history of ideas of race and ways of thinking in the systems of racial differences in which the 'white' race is the term with the primary meaning in the symbolical racial ordering of the world (Fishkin 1995; Seshadri-Crooks 2000; Bonnett 2000). As Audrey Smedley has argued, 'race [...] [is] a worldview [...] a cosmological ordering system structured out of the political, economic, and social realities of peoples who had emerged as expansionist, conquering, dominating nations on a worldwide quest for wealth and power.' (Smedley 1998: 25). How race was conceptualized in the European North-East, in the societies of Estonia, Lithuania and Latvia, whose experiences in (post)modernity have been marked with varying degrees and modalities of colonization/subordination, not expansion, conquest and domination? How did race evolve as a constituent (in)visible form of identity in these societies to stratify the social system and to reflect social meanings imposed upon these variations?

An important dimension of the studies of a national project as a specific racial(ized) order is a study of how notions of national culture incorporated intellectual views and common beliefs upon race, how different images of race have been (re)produced in media, literature, arts, intellectual production, popular culture, vernaculars in history and today. Further on, the Soviet period was no less important for thinking and imagining 'race' in the Baltic societies. The

Soviet modernist project promoted enthusiastic anti-racist rhetoric in political and media discourses. Soviet ideological and cultural production allegedly maintained the psychogeographic image of the USSR as the country celebrating the ideals of racial equality, but in reality, it perpetuated stereotyping and prejudiced perceptions of race in popular cultural images (Novikova 2004; Novikova 2007; Novikova 2009). Race figured prominently as a stratifying and alienating concept implicated in the delineation of a vast range of Soviet social and cultural practices (Novikova 2004).

Moreover, race as a cultural invention was intimately related to the foundational assumptions of nation-state in European modernity. Racial identification and its derivative - racialization of consciousnesses - are functions of ideology of the ideal subject in a modernist national imaginary. Thus, a broader critique of a post-Soviet racial and racialized imagination should not be isolated from understanding their genealogies in the European ideas of race and in the related anthropological and ethnographic discourses, with their immense influence upon the processes of cultural and political emancipation in the Baltic nations of the early 20th century.

Vytis Ciubrinskas

Lithuanian Transnationalism: Politics of (Trans)migrant Identity

Contemporary global processes of massive flows of population moving through 'locations' and 'territoriality' are usually shaped as multiple human attachments to the place (places) – both to the new places of settlement and to the places of origin (or departure). Actually, much more attention is paid to 'new places,' and the analysis of the processes of integration and acculturation of immigrants is prevailing.

Recent debates on international migration deal with the global flows of human dislocations and translocations and in general with the problems of de-territorialization and re-territorialization, or the new territorialization (Hannerz 1996, Appadurai 1996, Clifford 1997, Eriksen 1999). The growing importance of migration, the influx of immigrants in Old Europe and the increasing amounts of labor migration from New Europe, in particular during and after the recent 2004 and 2007 European Union enlargement periods, fostered a much-increased interchange between roots and routes (Clifford 1997). Not only postcolonial and post-communist immigrants and their offspring are going through the challenges of acculturation in the Western societies, but it increasingly also happens in Eastern Europe, where the same postcolonial and post-communist migrant-producing societies of uncertainty and freedom are now experiencing the repatriation of their former expatriates and transnational migrants.

The Baltic States and Lithuania in particular are a good example of such a situation. Staring in the 1850s, there have been three waves of emigration to the West, mainly to the U.S. Immediately after regaining independence in 1990, they experienced increased attempts of both the post-communist emigration and the Lithuanian diaspora to come 'back home.'

Introduction

Recent employment of the paradigm of transnationalism (Glick-Schiller, Basch, Blanc-Szanton 1995, 1999, Vertovec, Cohen 1999, Glick-Schiller, Levitt 2004) has changed migration research into studying transmigration, i.e. emigration, immigration and return migration. It has also focused particularly on the social relations that migration can produce by questioning the ties and linkages to both places that are touched by migration: the 'old' place, from where the migration came, and the 'new' one, to where migrants have moved. Such analytical framework for understanding of the processes of transnational migration involves 'culture' and 'power' relations as well and implies the symbolic empowerment /disempowerment of culture and politics of identity vis-à-vis the new global flows of human dis- or re-location in relation to places and/or territories and to heritages in particular. It becomes visible when tackling the 'in-rootedness' of ethnic and national cultures and heritages.

The issues of empowerment of culture (as territory, roots and heritage) are widely exemplified by the processes of migration and identity politics of migrants, as it is generally the case for migration from the European continent, which played a role in shaping trans-atlantic identity politics in North America, just to mention transnational Irish (Byron 1999), Jewish (Safran 1991) or Italian (Whyte 1993) identity politics in the US.

In the East European or New European perspective the scale and effect of current transnational migration going from the region drastically challenges the existing patterns of national identities. Nation-state transcending practices of transnationalism are visible in the livelihoods and social strategies of those New European migrants who do construct their own polities of identity and also, according to Gerd Baumann (1997), are affected by the dominant discourses (like for instance 'melting pot' and 'multiculturalism' in the U.S.) and are supposed to adhere to certain homologous (uniform) or hyphenated (multiple) shapes of identity.

In the case of the migratory flows to and from America, the Lithuanian example is conspicuous enough. It has a long and diverse history of waves and generations, with their own politics of identity in the US. Such a complexity could be exemplified by the directions in which the management of the patterns of transatlantic identities went. It is important to stress that Lithuanian migration to the US is transmigration. It challenges the identity not only of those who move, but also of the subsequent generations of those who do adhere to their transatlantic backgrounds. It certainly does identity empowerment work for those who choose to integrate 'with a difference' as well as the opposite for the others and disempower the backgroundness of those who choose to assimilate into mainstream America. It also works differently for those who choose to return back to their or their ancestors' country of emigration.

This chapter provides a case study of the application of identity empowerment of Lithuanian migration to the US and the return back to Lithuania. The aim is, first of all, to point out the issue of migrant identity empowerment vis-à-vis transnationalism. The point of departure in doing this is the conceptualization of cultural identity and politics of identity provided by Jonathan Friedman, Nina Glick-Schiller, Steven Vertovec and James Clifford. It is followed by the application of the identity empowerment perspective for the analysis of the Lithuanian migration to the US and back. In order to show the patterns in which the empowerment of cultural descent or ethnic background is perceived, felt and handled the ways of the transatlantic Lithuanian identity and heritage empowerment are exemplified.

One of the ways is related to the descendants of the Second World War refuges, known as DPs (who came from the Displaced Persons' Camps in Germany), and reluctant to integrate into the 'American dream,' a Lithuanian diaspora. Another case of migration is focused on the local (American) heritage reclaiming. This one comes from the South East Texas communities of descendants of Lithuanians who in 1850s came to the US as pioneers of Texas prairies and through generations and intermarriage eventually almost merged into German-Americans and mainstream Americans. Nevertheless, they did that by being open to the 'difference.' So, the descendants of the latter ones took the heritage reclaiming politics.

The research is based on the anthropological fieldwork conducted in 2002 and 2004 in the US among the Lithuanian background

Americans and on the qualitative social science research done in 2002–2005 in Lithuania among return migrants of the Lithuanian background.

Transnationalism and Empowerment of Migrant Identity: Nation (Ethnicity), Home (Homeland) and Heritage (Roots)

Migrant identity (seen as cultural identity) empowerment, according to Jonathan Friedman, goes through 'objectification, reification and essentialization of culture:

> where culture was an object, whether thing or practice. In this view, culture was contained in its embodiment rather than its generativity; the meaning was in the object, not in the process of its production. This was an identification of peoples in terms of their origins, a project of ethnic mapping analogous to the project of racial mapping that was part of the self-identification of the colonial centers of the world system' (Friedman 1997: 82–85).

The most popular perspective in anthropological studies of migrant identity is transnationalism, which apparently addresses the most important 'building materials' of identity (Castells 1997): nation, home and heritage. According to Glick-Schiller, an internationally acclaimed expert of migration studies, transnationalism is producing 'new social fields' (Glick-Schiller, Levitt 2004) which are different not only from the nation-state pattern but also from diasporic units. Although those are interacting with their homelands they are also creating alternative spaces vis-à-vis dominant society in host countries. She provides the following definition of transnationalism:

> [...] transnationalism [is] a process by which immigrants build social fields that link together their country of origin and their country of settlement. Immigrants who build such social fields are designated 'transmigrants' [...] Transmigrants take actions, make decisions, and feel concerns, and develop identities within social networks that connect them to two or more societies simultaneously (Glick-Schiller, Basch, Blanc-Szanton 1999: 26).

If nation-state nationalism is based on citizenship and participation and is expressed as national identity, transnationalism differs from that. A nation-state usually monopolizes the nation-state narrative of belonging as a forged nationalist narrative (Glick-Schiller, Basch, Blanc-Szanton 1995). Usually both, migrants 'sending' and migrants 'receiving' nation-states, challenge those who move through their national borders as immigrants, but in many cases as emigrants too. For some post-colonial, or for post-socialist 'migrant-sending' nation-states, like Lithuania, emigration can be understood as a loss, and the emigrants themselves, as just temporal settlers abroad, are always ready to answer the question when they will be back. According to Glick-Schiller, this is a nationalist attitude of the 19th and first half of the 20th century because 'national leaders during that period saw their emigrants more as colonists than permanent settlers abroad.'

> [...]...transmigrants were expected to eventually return home, and long-distance nationalism contained a call to come and rebuild the land. To accept permanent settlement elsewhere was generally defined as national betrayal (Glick-Schiller, Fouron 2001: 19).

Thus transnationalism also means a variety of national loyalties and re-located patterns of nationness, and it is extremely important where nationness (as a discourse about and identification with nation) is accommodated, whether it takes place in the homeland, in a neighboring country, or in the diaspora. It is obvious that in our case we have to tackle transnational and thus displaced nationness. Therefore, such 're-located' patterns of identity building appear to be addressed as ethnic patterns rather than belonging to the range of nationness. Clifford (1994) disagrees with that:

> But are diaspora cultures consistently antinationalist? What about their own national aspirations? [...] Indeed some of the most violent articulations of purity and racial exclusivism come from diaspora populations. But such discourses are usually weapons of the (relatively) weak. It is important to distinguish *nationalist critical longing* and *nostalgic* or *eschatological visions* (emphasis mine), from actual nation building-with the help of armies, schools, police and mass media' (Clifford 1994: 220–221).

Diasporic nationalism is thus a conspicuous example of migrant identity empowerment and, according to Vertovec, could be understood as political engagement, as 'politics of homeland' and 'politics of nostalgia' (Vertovec, Cohen 1999). It is related to transnationalism because many migrants 'gain more social power, in terms of leverage over people, property, and locality, with respect to their homeland than they did before migrating' (Glick-Schiller, Levitt 2004).

Furthermore, long distance nationalism (the term coined by Glick-Schiller as the strongest version of diasporic nationalism) is central to understand how

> long-distance nationalist movements have long influenced nation building and national transformation. There are many instances such as the Cuban, Israeli, and Irish communities in which migrants have successfully mobilized host country legislatures to support their homeland projects. Former Iraqi exiles are now playing a critical role in rebuilding the Iraqi state (ibid.).

The diasporic identity, by being built upon homeland nationalism, thus employs the empowerment of 'home' and heritage. From the anthropology of migration perspective, the category of 'home' or 'homeland' is one of the key elements of the nation's repository and is extremely important for understanding transnationalism.

'Home' (homeland) as a category could be defined in two ways: as a socially homogeneous and physically fixed space or as a dynamic, transnational symbolic space. In the traditional connotation, 'home' is a safe, secure, peaceful place linked to 'family,' 'community' and 'homeland' / 'nation' (Al-Ali, Koser 2002). Homeland is the space in which 'the conduct, expectations, attitudes, feelings and reactions of others are predictable and in which one knows the rules of appropriate behavior' (Holy 1996: 186).

From the transnationalist and dynamic perspective, the understanding of 'home' implies a place which undergoes displacement and uprootedness, and becomes crucial for belonging and identity 'work.' It applies mainly to political migrants / refugees to whom the idea of 'home' becomes elevated to a degree of an ideal place and resource for nostalgic feelings. Expatriates settled in diasporas retain a sense of belonging to the 'culture' associated with 'home' as 'homeland' which becomes an important resource of their politics of identity (Ciubrinskas 2004), which becomes elevated into politics of return and missionary identity of 'to be of use for your own country' (Ciubrinskas 2006). But, at the same time, it appears inevitable that the expatriates turned into repatriates find the 'culture,' along with the 'home' or 'homeland' as full of strange, unusual and alien elements: in the Lithuanian case, the lingering Soviet past, even more than a decade after the regime's collapse. If Lithuanian-born repatriates become easily frustrated by facing a 'homeland' so different from what they imagined it to be, this is not a case for second-generation returnees who feel free to shift from one shore of the Atlantic to the other. It is much easier for them to accept the postmodern shaping of 'home' as a place where you develop best and 'home is where you are' (ibid.).

Both the nation-state and diasporic homeland nationalisms heavily employ national heritages. Actually national heritages in the postmodern condition are no longer a codified construction of nationness, like the national flag, anthem or emblem. Instead, the term is used more and more as contested symbolic capital, as a powerful repository of the politics of identity which is extensively manipulated.

As it is pointed elsewhere (Ciubrinskas 2004) the manipulation of any single portion of heritage and especially national heritage, bears its strength from continues circulation and (re)use of it outside, rather than inside of the nation-state. Refuges, deported, émigrés and other displaced individuals and groups share social memories of the country they left, as well as national heritages they transplanted. Even more so, such a virtual adherence to - and charging of value for - common places of origin (home countries) and for the ideas of a common past, becomes a powerful resource of we-ness and acts as a basic foundation of ethnic identity, functioning both for inclusive and exclusive strategies. Thus any single item from the list of the home country's cultural heritage could be treated as shared dignity code and even become an essential cornerstone for the internal identity of one group while at the same time being contested by another group, both being groups of the same ethnic background. Not less substantial, it appears for shaping of the external public and political representations of national prides and moral strengths on foreign soils.

The interest in cultural heritages and in particular in local and family histories is presently strong in the USA. Here it is in vogue and prestigious to be of 'certain particular line and link' and to be able to trace one's own immigrant ancestry line on the world's

map. It is not enough to choose or to prove adherence to one of five American categories that could be described as: Afro-American, Asian-American, Euro-American, Latino-American or 'Native American.' One needs to be aware of his/her own background and ancestral line in order to be proud of being American with 'certain cultural and historical' but not necessary ethnic background. So the 'historification' and 'genealogization' of such ancestries, in Jonathan Friedman's words. '[...] is a question of the practice of a particular kind of identity, an identity of rootedness, of genealogy as it relates to territory' (Friedman 2004:69).
It brings a need for documentation and publicity, and it is easy to turn that need into claims for and/or reclamations of the recognition of certain history and heritage.

David Hollinger (1995: 2–3) once described the identity processes in contemporary America in regard to 'today's greater sensitivity to roots' and as existing 'beyond multiculturalism,' saying they need to be understood in a 'post-ethnic' perspective. Beyond multiculturalism, the America situation implies a dynamic and changing character of many groups and promotes multiple identities, and it gives room for the revisiting of identities and for discovering, emerging, or building a new one. One can add to already multiple identities – for example, American, Texan, German-American, – one more: perhaps an 'of Lithuanian background' identity. Hollinger terms this multiplicity of identities as a form of 'rooted cosmopolitanism.' Thus, following contemporary trends in America, sensitivity to roots (in particular the European) invokes a delineation of background which could be ambivalent, civic rather than ethnic.

Lithuanian Migration to the United States

After having done an overview of the analytical perspectives of identity empowerment in relation to migration through such resources as nation, home and heritage, we will try to apply them by scrutinizing examples of transatlantic Lithuanianness. It is the way to understand how migrant identities and/or cultures are constructed in the everyday lives of migrants and how identity empowerment can occur through certain manipulations of culture and locality. In this case, we will focus on one-culture and one-territory transcending migratory avenues of social interaction which shapes adherence to homeland nationalism, missionary identity and local ethnic heritage reclaiming.

First we start with an overview of Lithuanian migration to the US. As was mentioned, Lithuania is one of those European countries from which large numbers of people immigrated to the United States. Due to an especially large-scale emigration, and its long duration from the 1850s onward until World War I, approximately one quarter of the total Lithuanian population emigrated and came to be concentrated mainly in the United States. In the early 1920's there were more ethnic Lithuanians in Chicago than in the Lithuanian capital itself and the largest city in the country of the time, Kaunas. One of the last censuses of the United States in 1990 shows that 811,865 persons claim Lithuanian ancestry (Kavoliunas 1994).

From the very outset, at the end of the nineteenth century the role of immigrant communities in the U.S. was one of 'Lithuanian nation building' so that America became a second birthplace of modern Lithuanian nationalism. It was actually in America that a Lithuanian national consciousness or 'nationalist Lithuanianness,' had developed at the end of the nineteen century, often at a faster pace than in Lithuania itself (Fainhauz 1991: 9) and, significantly, influenced the emergence of the independent nation state, the Lithuanian Republic, in 1918. Similar nationalistic zeal occurred in the second half of the twentieth century, during the Soviet occupation of Lithuania. This time the phrase of 'retaining nationness,' was crucial for the most Lithuanian-Americans and even popular after the reestablishment of the independent Lithuanian State in 1990. It actually significantly fostered the return migration.

The period, the wave of immigration, the way it happened and in particular the rootedness in the American soil are basic markers for a distinct pattern of Lithuanianness to be recognized. Any one of these patterns falls into the ascription of a certain social strategy, ideology and politics of identity and is motivated and reinforced by 'symbolic capital' taken from 'repository' of national or ethnic heritage. The key point of reference to the ethnic identity construction and reconstruction processes, which seems to be basic for shaping categories of Lithuanian-Americans, is the role of the homeland.

Generally speaking, Lithuanian-Americans fall into one of the following waves or categories of immigration. The first of these relates to economic immigration from the 1850s to the 1930s. The predominant feature of these Lithuanian-Americans is their rootedness and in-born relationship to their 'new' home country. Today this category has already been applied to at least four generations. Their ethnic identity, as Lithuanian-American anthropologist Liucija Baskauskas (1981) argues, relies on a flexible set of standards (of culture and heritage) for ethnic behavior and they feel proud to be 'sort of' Lithuanians. They share a distinct identity even without proof of inborn ethnicity based on strong attachments to core issues of identity such as language, endogamy or references to the homeland, which for the most of the American born was left behind before it became nation-state in 1918.

The second ways of emigration related to political refugee immigration of the late 1940s. The forced migrants of Lithuania included those political refuges and exiles who, at the end of the Second World War, fled from the Soviet-sponsored communist regime to the West, and became concentrated in the Displaced Persons camps in Germany. At the end of the 1940s they received the opportunity to move to the U.S., Canada, Britain, Australia and other countries. At least 30,000 of these Lithuanians from the Displaced Persons camps (DPs) settled in the U.S.; of those between 12,000 and 15,000 settled in Chicago (Kucas 1975). *Dipukai* (Dee Pees) is a term derived from the Displaced Persons Camps located in the Western part of Germany of World War II and afterwards. It is used by and for the individuals who immigrated to the U.S. after they had lived or were born in the DP Camps. The relationship to the country of refuge eventually made most of this category of middle class Lithuanians in exile feel as strongly attached to it as to their 'second birthplace' and most of them (especially the second and the third, American born generations) have built self-identification as Lithuanian-Americans. Despite that, and at the same time, their adherence towards ethnic belonging and nationness were fixed entities directly tied to Lithuania as homeland and even more as a nation state. Their experience in the

DP Camps, became a resource of social memory for the later generations, was an exercise in living in a society without really being a part of it, and served as a model after they settled in the U.S.

In terms of social capital the political wave of migrants is different from earlier labor migrants. The former belong to the lower middle class and middle class, and most of them are professionals with a university education (Ciubrinskas 2005). Most, if not all, of them underwent ethnic 'Lithuanian' enculturation in their families and Saturday schools, and through the efforts of the Lithuanian American Community. The Lithuanian American Community was and still is the major Lithuanian organization in the U.S., with its sections in each large city, and it also acts as an umbrella organization for almost all activities focused on retaining Lithuanian ethnicity and nationness.

Return migrants are mainly springing from this wave of immigration. Generally they are not the offspring of the labor migrants, hundreds of thousands of whom immigrated to the U.S. since 1850s, but the political émigrés and their offspring who constitute the major part of the returnees. These expatriates and their offspring, in the second and third generation, are the largest group of returnees and/or settlers in Lithuania, the majority coming from the U.S. and Canada and in much smaller numbers from Australia.

The final wave of immigration relates to recent (from the late 1980s onwards) labor immigration from Lithuania during the period of Perestroika and especially after reestablishment of independence in 1990. *Tarybukai* (little Soviets) is a term invented by DPs or Lithuanian-Americans to define incoming immigrants as being marked by the Soviet regime. Lithuanians of this category are challenged the most because of their non-rootedness in the America, even if they are rapidly undergoing the process of naturalization and acculturation and becoming hyphened Lithuanian-Americans.

Transnational Lithuanianness. A Quest for a Model

The transatlantic, or transnational Lithuanianness as a model of identity has been coined and recoined in different periods and in diverse settings of North America and elsewhere and thus has to be understood in a variety of migrant identity politics of which we will concentrate on three. First and the most conspicuous one is transnational identity or diasporic Lithuanianness, the second one is the identity of return migrants to Lithuania, and the third one is identity of descendants of early immigrants to Texas. The first and second will be approached from the diaspora nationalism framework and the third one from the roots identity perspective.

Diasporic Identity: Politics of Retention

The Lithuanian pattern of diasporic community in the US refers to the political immigration. It includes those political refugees and exiles who belong to the DP wave of immigration. Inevitably most of the diaspora Lithuanians and their offspring undergo ethnic enculturation in their families, ethnic schools, and in the Lithuanian Community. The Lithuanian Community was, and still is, the major Lithuanian organization in the US. With its sections in each large city, it is also like an umbrella organization or an overwhelming network of almost all *lietuviskoji veikla* (Lithuanian activities and agency) focused on retaining the Lithuanianness.

The homeland nationalism ideology which penetrates *lietuviskoji veikla* in the trans-Atlantic diaspora worked as a kind of prescribed identity enshrined first of all, as mentioned above, in the enculturation of refugees and their offspring. Lithuania to them has become a mythical reference, an idea and not a country and a place. *Lietuviskoji veikla* as the Lithuanian activity and agency in the diaspora was, and is, extremely pro-'retaining Lithuanianness' and oriented to the independent Lithuania nation state of the 1920s–1940. It is a kind of idealized version of nationalism:

> Our parents were young when they left Lithuania. They were nurtured in the interwar spirit. In those times in Europe, it was a nationalist and national-socialist spirit. It influenced the organizations of emigrants. It helped to keep Lithuanian culture, nurture the young generation which more ore less could speak Lithuanian. This implies that nationalism helped to keep the Lithuanian spirit. Under this influence, an idealized portrait of the interwar period was created (Lithuanian-Canadian, 35, male).

> We were escaping from [Soviet] occupation, and it was such a sacred thing to retain the Lithuanianness [*lietuvybe*]. Strictly to speak only Lithuanian in families and avoid integration [...] it was like a protest against occupation (Lithuanian-Canadian, 75, female).

A diasporic image of the home country was constructed from the typical political refuge's experience, especially the image of a homeland under siege (Kelly 2000). The occupied and suffering country left behind at the end of World War II encouraged them to stay identified with 'their own nation' and to retain its culture. Basically, it was a very strong feeling of duty and mission, both moral and civic, to do what was possible to retain the culture as well as to liberate the country.

It was clearly assumed that the Lithuanian cultural heritage was challenged by the Soviet regime. One of my informants, who belongs to the second generation of DPs, by acknowledging the importance of 'finding roots,' emphasized:

> I feel we are a generation that has been robbed of our heritage. I play the national anthem and cry, as we were born here [in the US] and have lost a touch (or were forced to lose the touch) with our roots (Rita, 36).

Such an idealistic nationalism was functional in the diaspora and in the 1950s–1980s turned into charity and political campaigns to help by the soviets occupied Lithuania.

Every Lithuanian expatriate was expected to be ready to turn into a repatriate one day and the 'obligation to return' was a central imperative to the Lithuanian activities throughout the Lithuanian diasporas after World War II. It was inscribed, as it was mentioned, in the enculturation model used in the families of DPs.

> In my family, parents didn't allow us to watch TV. While at home we had to speak Lithuanian only. Each word pronounced in English was fined with a 10-cent fine. There were always some talks about Lithuania, as it needs to be

> helped to be liberated and that we will obviously return to it right after it will be free (American-born, 51, male).

So the Lithuanian diaspora's identity was based on the strategy of cherishing, perpetuating and retaining nationness in terms of culture, language, traditions and heritage. Such an identity became empowered by being juxtaposed to the communist regime which 'denied' Lithuanian culture in the homeland. Thus, it was altered by the obligation to retain culture in order to return it back after communism would be defeated.

Missionary Identity: Politics of Return

For political immigrants, the home country appears as a destiny where they belong as the nationals of the nation and where they are obliged to return. As it was argued elsewhere (Ciubrinskas 2006, Ciubrinskas 2009) a sort of missionary identity with the formula 'to be of use to your own country' was implied to, if not imposed upon, second and even third generation Lithuanian-Americans. So even the American-born generations have been supposed to treat Lithuania, but not the United States, the country they were born in, as their 'own' country.

Nevertheless, sociological research conducted in the 1950s, 1970s and in 2002 among American-born Lithuanian-Americans has shown that the 'obligation to return' is far from a constant imperative. It changes depending on age groups and generations, and even certainty about the return, not to talk about the practice of returning, has decreased sharply in the last years (Cernius 2005: 149).

However, as it was mentioned, the imperative of the 'obligation to return' was materialized by the dominance of DP émigrés among the Lithuanian background Americans, hundreds of whom came to settle in Lithuania over the past twenty years. This implies that the Lithuanian patriotism of the diaspora played an outstanding role among the commitments of expatriates and their American born offspring for repatriation. It also becomes a core for the politics of missionary identity which actually act as long-distance politics of retention.

Returnees (the majority of whom are former political émigrés and their offspring, second and third generation foreign-born Lithuanians) upon returning to Lithuania used to feel that they were 'experts on the retention of Lithuanianess.' Such an 'expert' position is based on the experience of acculturation in the countries that gave them refuge after 1945 and on knowledge of the 'free world' and the codes of conduct elaborated in the diaspora community life as a ready-made formula of 'how to be Lithuanian in the free democratic world.' This formula in the end of 1980s and beginning of 1990s, for example, was used in the U.S. to confront the newly arrived Lithuanian immigrants of the third wave from the former communist bloc. They were said to be marked by a 'lack of culture' and 'contaminated' by being exposed to the communist way. Post-communist immigrants were met by 'culture experts' - diaspora Lithuanians, who acted as 'gatekeepers' (cf. Corra and Willer 2002) or advisers, both in approaching general American society as well as getting into the ethnic Lithuanian community (Kuzmickaite 2003; Ciubrinskas 2004).

Lithuanian transmigrants living in diasporas, particularly in the U.S., put a great deal of effort into ensuring that their ethnicity was, in Reginald Byron's words, furnished with a culture and a history (Byron 1999). Lithuanian ethnicity was not only shared as an ancestry myth, as a common heritage and a social memory, it was seen as Lithuanian 'national' culture. The DP generation, in particular, assumed a nationalist mission to contribute to Lithuanian culture by devoting their private lives to a range of Lithuanian cultural projects and practices, such as the completion and publication of a thirty-six volume universal encyclopedia in the Lithuanian language in Boston, in the 1970s (Kucas 1975). The Lithuanian-American intelligentsia took on the responsibility to instruct the younger generation and to reproduce their culture in ethnic schools, organizations, and churches.

Large charitable donations, including IT equipment, books, consumer goods and financial assets, were arranged and brought to Lithuania by the returnees, and these were extremely significant in the late 1980s and the beginning of 1990s, just before, during and immediately after the Singing Revolution. Another good example of 'missionary' work for Lithuania was the reestablishment of the

University in Kaunas, the second largest city in the country, in 1989. With the support of the Lithuanian diaspora in the U.S. and Canada, the Vytautas Magnus University was reopened as a modern Western university, becoming a prime example of the postcolonialist-style export of Western standards. The first two university presidents were Lithuanian-Americans. They established a system along the North American model with a strong 'Anglo-Saxon' bias, an emphasis on English, a friendly attitude to foreign faculties, and a flexible system designed to accommodate visiting faculty staff. Some faculty from the diaspora came to stay and devote themselves to the implementation of Western academic standards (Vastokas 2005).

Sympathy for the needs of post-soviet Lithuanians among the diaspora is particularly rooted in the U.S. Lithuanian diaspora intellectual group 'Santara-Sviesa.' With the broad-minded attitude inscribed in its logo: 'open face to Lithuania,' Santara-Sviesa was opposed by the radical wing of the diaspora who refused any possibility of public cooperation with Soviet Lithuania, despite their proclaimed 'enlightened campaigns for spreading information about democracy and the free world' (Dapkute 2001). It was, and still is, the case for Santara-Sviesa members like the current President of Lithuania and his wife, Valdas and Alma Adamkus, to be strongly motivated and devoted to helping the country and its people.

> For the first time I came to Lithuania as a tourist, in 1988. I stayed longer in 1992. Just came here to work in the parliament [Auksciausioji Taryba]. I was working in the Secretariat of Landsbergis, later in the Department of Information. I stayed here by accident. I didn't have plans to come here, and to stay. I just wanted to do some work and then go back to continue my studies in the U.S. […] I came here because of my overwhelming idealism; I wanted to help [Lithuania] somehow. Soon I understood that my help is not needed. I understood I just have to work. That's it. […] I have started to work here and invested my time. So, as it is going well, it pays to work here, if it doesn't, than, maybe, I would live somewhere else. (Lithuanian-American male, 30)

Despite the returnees' most common self-image of being faithful to their patriotic mission, they are contested in the public sphere. The local image of the returnee is different and controversial (Vastokas 1993; Sidrys 1996). In the returnees' personal encounters with 'locals' in the public sphere, particularly in their competition for social statuses and positions, differences arise in terms of their right and authority to represent Lithuanianness. This compares with the data from Latvia collected by M.A. Herloff-Mortensen:

> [Returnees] occupy important positions in different ministries, newspapers and so on, where they have a lot of contact with foreigners. They explain Latvia, they do translations, and they are advisors. Basically they are the transmission belt in the middle between Latvia and the West. Most local Latvians don't understand how to do that, they don't understand the West. (Herloff-Mortensen 1999)

In such cases, returnees, especially professionals, are accepted as experts, but at the same time they are constantly challenged, both publicly, by local preconceptions about foreigners coming from the West, and privately, in James Scott's terminology, by exercising the weapons of the weak, 'hidden transcripts' (Scott 1985, 1990). Labels and stereotypes of 'Westerners moved to the East' are based on the schema of them – as 'prosperous and successful enough to do what they want' – and of us – as 'having unique local experience.'

So in delineating the identity of returnees as transmigrants or 'migrants of nostalgia' in post-communist Lithuania we notice that their identity consists of the strategies of retention of nationness in terms of culture, heritage and ethnic belonging. Coined in diaspora, and encultured in the ethnic institutions there, it was transplanted back to the country of departure as missionary identity politics. It included both the 'obligation to retain the culture' and 'to be of use for Lithuania.' So returnees, by becoming 'missionaries,' were keen to implement their own Lithuanian culture-codifying standards in a country 'devastated by communism.' Actually such, by ethnic nationalism enshrined 'cultural fundamentalism,' fitted well into early 1990s mainstream Lithuanian cultural politics promoting Lithuanian ethnic culture (traditional folk culture) and heritage.

Roots Identity: Politics of Reclaiming Ethnic and Local Heritage

The Lithuanian connection in Texas is the oldest in the whole of the US. It opens the history of the Lithuanian migration to North America. It started in early 1850s and despite the fact that it lasted only for about twenty years, was quite small and consisted of no more than two hundred immigrants who eventually assimilated, the contemporary descendents 'discovered' the fact of being 'sort of Lithuanians' themselves. Generation after generation, stories, records, letters and pictures about that were passed on and survived.

In East Texas, since the early 1990s, a group of descendants of early Lithuanian immigrants made a network of 'searching for the genealogical roots and ancestry' and heritage, and in 1994 a historical marker 'Lithuanians in Texas,' with an inscription on it about the Lithuanian immigration, was erected on the road crossing the main area of the former Lithuanian colony. It says:

> Among the many European immigrants arriving to Texas in the mid-19th century was a small group of Lithuanians who settled in the Yorktown vicinity of De Witt County. Due to their eventual assimilation with the numerous German immigrants in the area, the Lithuanians and their contributions to the history of this region were overlooked for generations. [...] They arrived in about 1852, making them among the earliest documented Lithuanian immigrants to America. [...] Leaving their homeland for a variety of religious and political reasons, the Lithuanians arrived in Texas primarily through the ports of Galveston and Indianola. Establishing farms in the area, the Lithuanians became American citizens and contributed to the history and culture of this area. Men from the community fought on both sides of the American Civil War. [...]
> [Location: FM 119 and Alvis Road about 4 miles south (near Royal Oaks), Yorktown]

Most of Lithuanians coming from Lithuania Minor to Texas were native Lithuanian speakers with some command of German. No doubt some Lithuanians came without knowledge of German, but it was also the case that some of them, even those born in the US, still spoke preferably only Lithuanian. This was the case with George Lundschen. His great-granddaughter Patricia Hand recalls:

> Back in the 1968 when I started my quest for my roots, my grandmother Agnes Lundschen Rabenaldt said that her parents, Robert and Emma Schuenmann Lundschen, could not speak the same language. She said her father spoke Lithuanian though he was born American (Wolff 2002).

It is an example of intermarriage in a family history, which in our case led to awareness of a particular heritage which was approached as 'overlooked' and thus in a need to reclaim. It could be added that Lithuanian language skills, along with the 'transplanted' European values of diligence as well as pietism of the Lutheran faith and a few other things perhaps comprised that 'culture' and heritage of early immigrants. At least it was fixed and also later evoked in the social memory of my informants and thus became a platform for their identity search.

Even if we totally follow the Daniel Hollinger's concept of contemporary America being 'post-ethnic' (Hollinger 1995), ethnicity still matters a lot. It could be evoked, empowered, even 'invented' by the ethnic heritage alone. In our case, material heritage (graveyards, churches, historical sites, also historical objects and artifacts) and collective memory (inscribed in family stories, letters, documents and visual materials) came into the focus of those 'searching for the genealogical roots and ancestry.' It resulted in the reclaim of Lithuanian heritage through genealogy.

Genealogical Reclaims of Heritage and Re-Writing of Local History

Genealogical and Historical Societies as well as Commissions in Texas are the most important institutions in documenting Lithuanian ancestry in the area. They are central in exploring the Lithuanian pioneer history in the area. Local historians and members of those societies are most instrumental in compiling Lithuanian family histories-genealogies. From time to time they initiate new topic-oriented databases, and in the early 1980s Lithuanian family genealogies & directories were created.

The Lithuanian descendants undertake genealogical activities of making ancestry lists and genealogical studies by writing family histories themselves as well. Especially active are members of the mentioned network of those 'searching for the genealogical roots' who are eager to regain the loss of the local history of Texas 'overlooked by generations,' with the claim of the Lithuanian fragment to be present among other 'early pioneers.' It is also a group with interest to regain 'the past' by making a documentary proof of it. This is mainly managed by the individual persons who used to become aware of their family ethnic background not in the regular way of enculturation, but 'by discovering' it and building their family history and genealogical research interests out of curiosity. Their own family histories are of particular interest to them, especially after they 'discover' themselves having, besides German, also Lithuanian background.

They are instrumental by taking the initiatives in retaining material heritage, for example, in designation of Lithuanian heritage sites to be given the status of a memorial site protected by the state of Texas.

Thus do the genealogical and historical societies and genealogists as well as local historian networks (mainly of the Lithuanian ancestry) as well as interest groups (networks) of descendants enact heritage reclaim in Texas. Those societies and networks are central for all public activities (including, for example, commemoration activities or assistance in maintaining ethnic graveyards) to take place. The networks of 'regainists' that act to reclaim and 'rewrite' the local Texas multicultural past also play a role.

Most of the activity and also most of interest in the whole endeavor of Lithuanianness in Texas are related to family histories and family reunions. Family reunions started in the area of the former Lithuanian colony in late 1970s, and annual meetings are extremely popular among the families of Lithuanian descendants. For example, family reunions of the Lithuanian Kirlicks' family near Yorktown are held every summer and in 1994 numbered over 1000 members.

Such activities are used for creating new networks of genealogy as well as ethnic and local heritage interest groups.

Conclusions

Contemporary focus on the notions of transnationalism and transmigration signals a concern with attachment to a place of origin, which is quite new within migration research. The overview of analytical perspectives of identity empowerment vis-à-vis transnationalism that we have made provides the understanding that culture and territory are bound as homeland or/and as heritage. They can be used as analytical categories to explain the complexity of the identity empowerment in particular for transnational Lithuanianness, which attempts to retain the culture and identity of migrants and their descendants. The category of heritage is a good framework to explain how family heritages could be tightly bound with ethnic and local cultural heritages, how those could be reclaimed as 'roots,' and also how it could work as an analytical category to address the roots of identity politics.

To sum up the resources for mobilization of the identity politics of the Lithuanian background Americans, it is worth noting that the issue of heritage transplanted from Europe and retained in the US and even eventually brought back to the homeland is of focal importance to shape the Lithuanian transnationalism. Different Lithuanian background groups are competing for 'their own heritages' among themselves and with the mainstream societies in Chicago, Texas and in Vilnius. Homeland nationalism embraces a heritage where culture stands for nation and mobilizes into a politics of Lithuanianness. This movement is the best-represented and institutionalized in ethnic institutions and the most visible in the whole heritage display of the Lithuanian-background groups in the U.S. But the picture becomes more complex if other Lithuanian-background groups are approached as also sharing and empowering their own (ethnic) heritages. Namely, the heritage of 'local ethnic survivors' in Texas is seen as history (ethnic and local) and as 'roots' (patrimonial and cultural), and it is claimed as 'overlooked for generations' in the traces of the deeds of pioneer ancestors.

Transatlantic Lithuanianness is manipulated and articulated in diasporic communities and among other groups and individuals of Lithuanian background in many ways with many meanings. It is retained, evoked, reclaimed and in particular ways enacted in the politics of (trans)migrant identity. We have explored three patterns of it.

The first pattern consists of diasporic communities that retain culture and nationness. The generations related to this category of Lithuanian-Americans are accustomed to approach their heritage as Lithuanianness in terms of nationness. Their ethnic enculturation has been predominantly focused on cherishing the independent Lithuanian nation-state culture and history transplanted from pre-communist Eastern Europe. It became empowered not only by the retention but also by the standardization of 'Lithuanian culture.' For example, a codified overview of Lithuanian culture and heritage was used in the textbooks produced by the diaspora for the ethnic schools. A moral formula of global Lithuanianness 'a Lithuanian is always a Lithuanian' was used in the U.S. to confront the newly arrived third wave Lithuanian immigrants from the former communist bloc. They were said to be marked by a 'lack of culture' and 'contaminated' by being exposed to the communist way. So in this respect diaspora identity politics acted as 'the Lithuanian culture expert' and the 'gatekeeper' for post-communist immigrants both in approaching main stream American society as well as getting into the ethnic community.

The second pattern – returnees with a mission – consists of small fraction of the total global Lithuanian diaspora, the majority of whom are former political émigrés and their offspring, second and third generation foreign-born Lithuanians. This pattern of identity is very close to the diasporic one. Its strategies of retention of nationness in terms of culture, heritage and ethnic belonging (encultured and coined in the ethnic institutions) were transplanted back to the country of departure. In the terms of Glick-Schiller, it was the same 'long distance nationalism' nationalists' politics of identity. The retainers of homeland culture as well as the adherents to a missionary imperative of returning it back home after the fall of communism. Besides that, at the core of missionary identity politics' there was an imperative 'to be of use for Lithuania devastated by communism' which actually was welcomed by the mainstream society especially during the period of Perestroika and just after regaining Lithuanian independence in early 1990s.

The third pattern is that of a community searching for its roots and striving for the recognition and regaining of 'its own,' Lithuanian-Texan, heritage. It consists of Texans with Lithuanian background and their identity politics are built upon the strategy of regaining recognition for the 'overlooked for generations' ethnic Lithuanian heritage of multiethnic Texas. By documenting and marking (by erecting historical markers signifying Lithuanian heritage on the roads) 'Lithuanians – Texas pioneer' ancestors' pasts, such politics reclaim the ethnic heritage. It serves for the representation of that reclaimed heritage of the Lithuanian pioneers ('heroes of the past') to be seen back on the local (Texas) parade of immigrant cultures dominated by German-American Texans' culture. Actually, it is also the reclaiming of certain (Lithuanian) roots, culture and history and also an ambition of re-writing the already 'invented' and standardized history of Texas by adding the Lithuanian dimension to it.

Those who feel their heritage 'overlooked by generations' are actually crafting a politics of identity by striving to achieve recognition of 'their culture,' based on traces of it in the area. This is mainly because the dominant identity politics and dominant discourse of the state of Texas, emphasizing its pioneer past, and the multicultural present of the state provokes certain activities by descendants. These descendants are themselves encouraged to attain recognition of 'their social status' as bearers of a certain social memory. They are winning social prestige by being involved in continuous discourses and practices of 'Lithuanian ancestry/heritage' and by becoming experts of the history of local culture and/or of particular genealogical line of ancestry.

Bibliography

Al-Ali, N.; Koser, K. (eds) (2002), New Approaches to Migration? Transnational Communities and the Transformation of Home. London and New York: Routledge.

Appadurai, A. (1996), Modernity at Large. Cultural Dimensions of Globalization. Minnesota University Press.

Baskauskas, L.(1981), 'The Lithuanian Refugee Experience and Grief,' *Immigration and Migration Review*, 15(1), pp. 276–291.

Baumann, G. (1997), 'Dominant and Demotic Discourses of Culture: Their Relevance to Multi-Ethnic Alliances' In: P. Werbner and T. Modood (eds), *Debating Cultural Hybridity. Multi-Cultural Identities and the Politics of Anti-Racism*, London & New Jersey: Zed Books), pp. 209–225.

Byron, R. (1999), *Irish America*, Oxford: Oxford University Press.

Castells, M. (1997), *The Power of Identity*. Oxford: Blackwell.

Cernius, V. (2005), 'Acculturation of Lithuanian Immigrants Who Arrived in the United States after World War II.' In: D. Kuiziniene (ed.), *Beginnings and Ends of Emigration*, The Lithuanian Emigration Institute, Vilnius: Versus Aureus, pp. 123–156.

Ciubrinskas, V. (2004), 'Transnational Identity and Heritage: Lithuania Imagined, Constructed and Contested.' In: U. Kockel and M. Nick Craith (eds), *Communicating Cultures*, Munster: LIT Verlag, pp. 42–66.

Ciubrinskas, V. (2006), 'To Be of Use to Your Own Country': Missionary Identity of the Lithuanian Transmigrants, *Socialiniai Mokslai. Social Sciences* 3(53), pp. 25–32.

Ciubrinskas, V. (2009), 'Diasporas Coming Home. Identity and Uncertainty of Transnational Returnees in Postcommunist Lithuania.' In: L. Kurti and P. Skalnik (eds), *Postsocialist Europe. Perspective from Home*, London: Berhahn, pp. 95–117.

Ciubrinskas , V. (2005), 'Lithuanian Transnationalism: Constructed, Imagined and Contested Identity of Lithuanian Americans.' In: D. Kuiziniene (ed.), *Beginnings and Ends of Emigration.* The Lithuanian Emigration Institute, Vilnius: Versus Aureus, pp. 33–50.

Clifford, J. (1994), 'Diasporas,' *Cultural Anthropology* 9(3), pp. 302–338.

Clifford, J. (1997), *Routes, Travel and Translation in the Late Twentieth Century*, Cambridge, MA, London: Harvard University Press.

Corra, M. and D. Willer. (2002), 'The Gatekeeper,' *Sociological Theory*, 20(2), pp. 180–207.

Dapkute, D. (2001), 'Lietuviu iseivijos santykiu su okupuota Lietuva dinamika 20 a. 6-9 desimtmeciais,' *Istorija*, vol. 47, pp. 34–47.

Eriksen, T. H. (1999), 'Globalization and Politics of Identity,' *UN Chronicle*, vol. 36 (Autumn).

Fainhauz, D. (1991), *Lithuanians in the USA. Aspects of Ethnic Identity.* Chicago: Lithuanian Library Press, Inc.

Friedman, J. (1996), *Cultural Identity and Global Process.* London: Sage.

Friedman, J. (1997), 'Global Crises, the Struggle for Cultural Identity and Intellectual Porkbarrelling: Cosmopolitans versus Locals, Ethnics and Nationals in an Era of De-hegemonisation.' In: P. Werbner and T. Modood (eds), *Debating Cultural Hybridity. Multi-Cultural Identities and the Politics of Anti-Racism*, London &New Jersey: ZED Books, pp. 70–89.

Glick-Schiller, N.; Basch, L.; Blanc-Szanton, C. (1995), 'From Immigrant to Transmigrant: Theorizing Transnational Migration,' *Anthropological Quarterly*, 68(1), pp. 48–63.

Glick-Schiller, N.; Fouron, G. E. (2001), *Georges Woke up Laughing. Long Distance Nationalism and the Search for Home.* Durham / London: Duke University Press.

Glick-Schiller, N., Levitt (2004), 'Transnational Perspectives on Migration: Conceptualizing Simularity,' *International Migration Review*, vol. 37 (Fall).

Glick-Schiller, N.; Basch, L.; Blanc-Szanton, C. (1999), 'Transnationalism: A New Analytical Framework for Understanding Migration.' In: S. Vertovec and R. Cohen (eds), Migration, Diaspora and Transnationalism Cheltenham and Northamton: Edward Elgar Pub., pp. 26–49.

Hannerz, U. (1996), *Transnational Connections. Culture, People, Places*, New York: Routledge.

Herloff Mortensen, M.-A. (1999), 'The Latvian Thing: Narratives of Place and Identity among Local and Diasporic Latvians,' M.A. dissertation. Copenhagen: Institute of Anthropology, University of Copenhagen.

Hollinger, D. A. (1995), *Postethnic America: Beyond Multiculturalism*, Basic Books, A Division of Harper Collins Publishers.

Holy, V. (1996), *The Little Czech and the Great Czech Nation: National Identity and the Post-Communist Social Transformation*, Cambridge: Cambridge University Press.

Kavoliunas, J. (1994), 'Lithuanian-American Population Growing, Becoming more Geographically Dispersed,' *Lituanus*, vol. 40(2).

Kelly, M. E. (2000), 'Ethnic Pilgrimages: People of Lithuanian Descent in Lithuania,' *Sociological Spectrum* vol. 20, pp. 65–91.

Kucas, A. (1975), *Lithuanians in America*, Boston: Encyclopedia Lituanica Press.

Kuzmickaite, D. (2003), *Between Two Worlds: Recent Lithuanian Immigrants in Chicago (1988–2000)*,Vilnius: Versus Aureus.

Safran, W. (1991), 'Diasporas in Modern Societies. Myths of Homeland and Return,' *Diaspora*, vol. 1(1), pp. 83–99.

Scott, J. (1985), *Weapons of the Weak: Everyday Forms of Peasant Resistance*, New Haven, CT: Yale University Press.

Scott, J.(1990), *Domination and the Arts of Resistance: Hidden Transcripts*, New Haven, CT: Yale University Press.

Sidrys, R. (1996), 'Lithuanians on Lithuanian Americans,' *Observer* 1(2): pp. 4–9.

Vastokas, R. (1993), 'Lietuvos ir iseivijos sankryza,' *Europos Lietuvis*, vol. 32(47), pp. 1–4.

Vastokas R. (2005), 'From Glasnost to NATO: Retired and Restless in a Post-Soviet State,' *Trent University Newsletters*, vol. 2, pp. 14–16.

Vertovec, S.; Cohen, R. (1999), 'Introduction.' In: S. Vertovec; R. Cohen (eds), *Migration, Diaspora and Transnationalism*, Cheltenham and Northamton: Edward Elgar Pub, pp. xiii–xxviii.

White, W.F. (1993), *Street Corner Society. The Social Structure of an Italian Slum*, Chicago: University of Chicago Press.

Wolff, H. (2002), 'Many in DeWitt have Lithuanian roots,' *Victoria Advocate*, May 29.

Part III:
Language, Media, and the Public Domain

Gabrielle Hogan-Brun

Crossing Boundaries? Negotiating Diversity from East to West

This contribution focuses on means of using language and culture to stake boundaries in the (re-) consolidation of national identity and on challenges that can arise in this process. In considering language ideological debates on this topic we explore implications for questions of difference and tolerance. Throughout the cultural history of Europe, language and culture have been a site for constructing and contesting different versions of collective identity, or of delineation and assertion (Busch 2009: 46). Functioning as an arbitrary divide between national entities, they have over time increasingly become part of hegemonic discourse and political practice. As epistemological constructs, their role is sustained and promoted by a number of institutional and discursive means. During processes of transition, this social practice tends to be reactivated through a narrative (re-) consolidation of a sense of national (id)entity. This social habitus, to use a term coined by Bourdieu, can serve as a means to strengthen outward boundaries.

In order to qualify for European Union (EU) membership, the boundaries of this paradigm needed to be (re-) negotiated in Central and Eastern Europe (CEE). EU accession and identity negotiations went hand in hand and were influenced by social perceptions implying a reciprocal view of 'Self 'and 'Others,' and reciprocal representations of 'core' and 'periphery' (Giordano & Zvinkliene 2003: 9f). In this process, EU conditionalities that had to be complied with presented a not inconsiderable hurdle for the (relatively late) newcomers from CEE, whose societies were expected to cross established boundaries in becoming more closely aligned with Western democratic principles (Hogan-Brun *et al.* 2007). Social reforms that were carried out as part of this process needed to ensure minority protection provisions in accordance with standards set by international frameworks (for more information see ECRML and FCPNM weblinks in references). Language policy developments, on the other hand, which have mainly remained the prerogative of member states, have undergone less decisive molding in accommodating diversity. Moreover, the region's embeddedness with the West is also dependent on broader global developments, which will require additional re-adjustments, both in terms of language and identity politics.

Boundary-Staking through Language and Identity: Traditions and Challenges

Collective conceptions that are based on language and culture are the outcome of accelerating, nationalizing activities seeking to intensify the power of the state over the population from the 17th century onwards. In this process, language began to play a central role in identity marking and, as a corollary, boundary setting. The consequences of this idea have been widely documented in commentaries on language, culture and nationalism (Barbour and Carmichael 2000; Wright 2000; May 2003). An ideology evolved that is reflected in the dominant discourse found in most European nation-states, which, although nowadays *de facto* multicultural and multilingual, nonetheless still see themselves as essentially monolingual. This dogma of linguistic homogeneity (whether or not inscribed in constitutional and other legal apparatus) has been mainly maintained in implicitly embedding the idea of a 'national language' in state institutions such as (above all) education and public employment. Indigenous or long-standing ethnolinguistic/national minorities have been absorbed into this homogeneous political culture to a large extent uncontroversially by granting limited linguistic rights on the one hand and promoting what Kymlicka (2001a: 25) calls a 'societal culture' on the other: 'all liberal democracies,' he argues, 'have encouraged citizens to view their life-chances as tied up with participation in common societal institutions that operate in [the 'national' language].'

Nowadays it is particularly in times of socio-political turnover as in the post-communist settings of CEE that language and culture tend to be deployed for the (re-) consolidation of national identity. In the Baltic settings, the restitution of independence was paralleled by the reinstatement of the official status of the titular languages, whose position was further strengthened by various language laws and regulations. This led to an education policy that made the national language a compulsory subject for all students and it also involved the introduction of occupational language certification measures for speakers of other languages, and national naturalization procedures based on an examination of language competence and cultural knowledge.

In this context of transition ethno-cultural diversity risks to be perceived as an existential threat to states, which can engender discourses on sameness and difference that are embedded in a 'security/loyalty' framework (cf. Kymlicka 2001b: 22; Hogan-Brun 2005). Hence, throughout CEE identity politics have increasingly become part of hegemonic discourses and political practice (O'Reilly 2001: 2). But whilst language and culture continue to play a principal role in these nationalist ideologies, this is taking place against a largely heterogeneous reality that is mainly a legacy of past conditions.

Whilst amply critiqued in the scholarly literature, language and culture have also been redeployed in Western Europe to firm up porous national boundaries in curbing the growing rate of immigration. This has involved the conceptualization of gate keeping procedures that serve along new lines in an attempt to deal with (real and/or perceived) challenges which have arisen through the social impact of continuing cross-border flows of people in the wake of recent eastward EU enlargements. Perceived threats to national sovereignty (in economic, political and cultural terms), and in particular in relation to the idea of national integrity, have increasingly led governments to pursue policy agendas that have accentuated a 'politics of difference.' This has particularly manifested itself through the proliferation of national naturalization procedures for applicants that involve examining their language competence and cultural knowledge[1]. These are

1 More information on naturalization procedures is available in G. Extra *et al.* (2009), and a cross-Baltic overview is offered in Hogan-Brun *et al.* (2007).

means that are based on what Blommaert and Verschueren (1998: 194–195) call the 'dogma of homogeneism: a view of society in which differences are seen as dangerous and centrifugal and in which the 'best' society is suggested to be one without inter-group differences.' Along these lines it can be argued that national migration policies were developed not merely as instruments of political 'management' but also as part of a larger ideological process.

In an era then when nation-states have reasserted their role as protectors of national culture, the dynamics of contemporary political debates about language, identity and citizenship have gained a powerful momentum, across Europe (Hogan-Brun *et al.* 2009). Particularly in the West, discourses on hybridity and multiple belongings circulate freely within intellectual settings. It is argued that the denial of societal multilingualism fuels discourses that ignore, or reject, the very real situations created by migration. Stevenson (2006: 148) goes further in stating that political activities inspired by ideological intentions seeking to salvage the integrity of the nation are based on the myth of a stable monolingual norm and increasingly at odds with, and under assault from, multilingual realities. Whilst this is evidently the case, the promotion and management of cultural and linguistic diversity are naturally also conditional upon their acceptance in nation-states. As we shall see below, this has meant that in re-consolidating their westward orientation for EU membership, set social boundaries needed to be somewhat softened in CEE to dislodge entrenched perceptions of 'self' and 'others,' or 'core' and 'periphery.'

Changing Orientations and the Politics of Recognition in an Enlarging EU

Based on the principles of liberal democracy that foster a sense of commonality upon which modern societies can be built, EU accession has introduced the notion of a 'politics of recognition.' Initially based on equality and a heightened emphasis on the individual, it has increasingly taken on a group-based nature, and includes demands for recognition by social and ethnic groups, and not least by nations. One particularly interesting and potentially controversial claim is that each culture is unique and of equal value. The nature of these demands that have been increasingly oriented to recognition of uniqueness relates to what is also termed the 'politics of difference.' An important discernible effect of these developments within Central and Eastern European contexts is that there has been heightened tension between various claims for protection of difference or uniqueness and the perceived equal validity of each culture.

As part of recent developments connected with EU accession, the predominant focus on titular differences was challenged in CEE when local groups and nationalisms began to question the nation-state from below as a representative and accountable power system. Their claims for recognition, often manifested through assertions of difference, show that the politics of recognition holds potential for political conflicts. Since recognition revolves around matters of identity, in particular how identities are shaped, who contributes to the shaping, and how a person's and a group's sense of identity can be violated or harmed, the politics of difference also highlights the role and salience of groups in the shaping of political identities (cf. Fossum 2001).

The recognition of difference and negotiation of identity has presented challenges in the politically reconsolidating settings of CEE. As Schöpflin (2003: 277f) argues, with external influences repeatedly having impacted on existing collectives in this region, the task of inward processes over time became that of securing cohesion on an ongoing basis through discursive activities of identity re-construction. A corollary was the erection of boundaries, where language was, and continues to be, used as the principal mechanism in the process of differentiation through identity marking. Hence locally adopted discursive constructs of nation and national identity have tended to foreground national uniformity over intra-national differences. Shaped through collective memory, the political and cultural thought styles in this region have been found to often involve a 'historicizing' approach that is somewhat out of alignment with those of the West where emphasis is more on procedure and pragmatics (ibid.: 488). In our context, this is most markedly noticeable in terms of different ways of embracing diversity. As became evident during the course of EU membership negotiations, the largely technocratic accession conditions imposed by the West at times demonstrated a lack of engagement with the symbolic and historic dimension of European enlargement so vital to Central and Eastern Europe's sense of self-esteem. Belonging, and eventual EU and NATO membership, could only be achieved by conforming to Western norms in the absence of domestic models of modernity. Whilst the notion of collective identity is likely to continue to be instrumentally deployed in the (re-) shaping of modern consciousness and the social reality of CEE, this will in time need to evolve further to become more inclusive and fluid, and to reconcile locally democratizing ideals with those of an increasingly multicultural Europe. In what follows we now focus on means of boundary staking through language from either 'above,' by elites, and of negotiations and possible adjustments through social practice 'from below.' In doing so we adopt a comparative perspective starting with a diachronic focus on Lithuania.

Negotiating Language Boundaries

Historically, multilingual language groups have evolved in a number of ways. This has happened either through conquest, migration, colonization or linguistic imperialism (Spolsky 1998: 52f). The unique blend of multilingualism in the Baltic region echoes such a variegated past, and it determines to a large extent approaches adopted to the local management of language diversity. Stepping back a few centuries, an example can be drawn from Lithuania. Several different languages were already used as written and spoken ones in the old, multiethnic Lithuanian state of King Mindaugas. The range of languages used increased significantly, and this was no issue as Lithuania's territory was subsequently extended from the Baltic Sea to the Black Sea under the Grand Dukes Algirdas and Kestutis. Tolerance of language diversity was customary in those days, and practiced in previous eras as well, e.g. during the time of the Roman and

Persian empires. It was much later that the principle *cujus regio, ejus lingua* or 'the ruler determines the language' started to be applied, with limited tolerance for languages other than that of the ruler (see Spolsky 2005; May 2001; Wright 2004). This kind of approach has proliferated after the watershed of political ideas and ideologies stemming from the French Revolution and German Romanticism. Laying the foundations of what came to be termed 'national habitus,' this mode has since functioned as a template for the formulation and implementation of language management procedures in many emergent nations, from West to East. It was following the post WW border changes that the realization emerged of the need to provide group (language) rights to the many minorities who had survived population movements and territorial adjustments.

There are, on the other hand, countries that recognize the fact that they are highly multilingual. On independence, India adopted a constitution that recognized a dozen official languages, allowed for initial education in other vernaculars, and planned the replacement of English by Hindi as a working national official language within a few years. Releasing a flurry of language management activity, this was not without conflicts, as was also the case in newly independent South Africa when seven selected local languages were given constitutional status besides English and Afrikaans. Other multilingual states such as Switzerland and Belgium came into existence through a federation of different, territorially settled, language communities, which elicited different language management practices. In both countries, the major languages were made official according to their demographic distribution, and language policy follows the territoriality principle. Belgium makes allowances for sub-groups from the other major communities and has Dutch-speaking regions in some of which French has a special status; there are also French-speaking regions in some of which Dutch has a special status; and in some regions German is recognized for certain functions; the capital Brussels is legally bilingual. In quadrilingual Switzerland, the twenty-six administrative divisions (*Cantons*) are allowed linguistic autonomy according to the Swiss constitution (which was adopted in 1848), and they designate their own official language(s). Three Cantons are bilingual and one is trilingual. This localized system, however, also entails challenges, particularly in terms of infrastructural differences between the four language regions. Concerns over this have resulted in calls for a more active language policy at the national level (Watts 1997; Grin 1999). It is a fact which is somewhat echoed at the EU level as well, as we shall see below.

Managing Multilingualism from Above

In our days, growing movements of people across and into Europe further increase existing levels of language contact and diversity. The consequences of globalization, which manifest themselves in the latent spread of languages through commerce, high technology, advanced research, higher education, sports & entertainment, and formal education, add to existing challenges of maintaining language diversity. Given their impact on our changing sociolinguistic ecologies the whole pattern is becoming ever more complex. In the absence of an overarching language policy at EU level, the approaches chosen in dealing with challenges that have arisen as a consequence of this increasing mix are context-dependent and vary from East to West. In the East, the trend is to preserve and strengthen the national languages and cultures whilst also meeting the present day challenges of globalization. Many states in the West on the other hand see themselves confronted with (how) to address issues of increasing linguistic and cultural pluralism at the macro-political level. At the micro level too, services and organizations are seeking ways to accommodate existing language, and hence social, needs.

From its beginning, the EU has adopted a paradoxical and far from consistent position towards linguistic pluralism. On the one hand, it backs national sovereignty over language and the theoretical equality of the official languages of all its members. At the same time, it has re-asserted the rights of indigenous minority languages, checking the risks inherent in this by permitting its existing members to define which minority languages to recognize and what rights to give them. But as new members of the expanded EU are expected to grant language rights to all minorities, those of migrants are often considered a problem. With other parts of the world (e.g. the US, Africa and China) also experiencing similar complexities and uncertainties, the consequences of globalization add to existing challenges of maintaining language diversity.

With respect to these developments a model of language policy has been proposed (Spolsky 2005) that distinguishes between language practices (what people do), language beliefs and ideology (what people think should be done), and language management (the efforts of putative language managers to effectuate changes). Language management focuses at the macro level on status planning, language cultivation as well as on adding speakers. It can however also risk changing the language practices and sometimes beliefs of others. The model therefore suggests that successful language management needs to adequately take into account existing language beliefs and practices.

Language management then, whilst potentially effective *per se*, is not without issues. What can make this activity difficult is the fact that the complexity of the task is seldom realized. There are those who argue that managing is controlling. Others are questioning whether language management can be justified at all, and whether anyone, whatever their claim to authority, has a right to try to change existing language settings. Some are wondering whether language management can in fact be achieved at all (Jernudd, 1991). Whatever the positions, it is crucial to point out that all language planning activities always take place in particular sociolinguistic settings, and that the nature and scope of the planning can only be fully understood in relation to these contexts. As became evident during the last EU accession negotiations, moral and legal standards provided in international charters should therefore aim to allow for choices to be adopted in various political constellations (Hogan-Brun 2005). In other words, it should always be borne in mind that legal frameworks and norms ought to permit a flexible implementation in particular settings, at the macro as well and also micro levels, which we now focus on.

Managing Multilingualism from Below

No central language policy can reach out into the complexity of language practices throughout society, be this at the smaller organizational or at the private realms. It is a fact and needs to be acknowledged that languages are being used and managed in various ways at all levels of society. Walking down the streets of any major city, increasingly in the Baltic as well, will attest to an at times *ad hoc* management of languages in contact from below, both acoustically and visually. In stores, places of worship or of entertainment, local languages have started to mix in many creative ways with those of tourists. Streetscapes (Shohamy & Gorter, 2008) can also boast innovative solutions in multilingually catering for passers-by.

At the family level, languages can also co-exist and be used in myriads of complementary and hybrid ways. Studies of language management at this micro unit and of interactions between community members in different localities serve to establish tendencies from below to resist simple national language planning priorities. For instance, interviews in South-Eastern Lithuanian family settings have produced evidence that whilst there is a strong trend to use Lithuanian across the generations this is not necessarily a linear move (Hogan-Brun et al. 2007: 580). Amongst a wider circle of minority groups, languages can also function as a dynamic source for in-group solidarity or for exercising power over the out-group as has been observed in this region too. Furthermore, many religious institutions and groups such as the Karaims have their own language policies, and these too may be different from that of the nation.

Business, commerce and the needs of multilingual workplace settings may also encourage different language practices and provide various motivations for acquiring these. Mastery of a specific language often enables job seekers to gain access to desired positions within the labor market. Increased levels of bilingualism with the titular language across the Baltic States generally, and a continuing demand for certification for occupational language use, attest to the phenomenon of instrumental motivation governing language choice in this domain. Such language preferences act as symbolic capital with inherent value in the linguistic marketplace.

But there is an important second side to the management of multilingualism from below. With greater heterogeneity of cultures and languages in mixed social groups significant challenges can arise in linguistically diverse organizations such as the workplace or schools. Concerns over levels of productivity on the one hand and achievement rates on the other have resulted in a greater focus on the management of communicative practices whose aim it is ultimately to foster integration at the micro level.

Concluding Remarks and Outlook

It is a fact that the sociolinguistic ecology of our modern societies is changing rapidly. As countries from East to West are increasingly becoming hosts to diverse speech communities new challenges arise with growing trans-border movements of people across the EU. Many governments struggle to find ways (how) to host these newcomers and (how) to address newly arising issues in connection with linguistic and cultural pluralism. The varying approaches adopted at the national level to deal with rising levels of diversity are naturally contextually determined. In the East re-evolving multilingualisms which are taking place against a national project that is intent on strengthening the status and increase use of the titular languages are symbolic of changing orientations that are socially, politically and economically motivated. In the more stable settings of Western Europe, a discourse of language management design and planning is now intensifying to control increasing levels of diversity caused by more complex migration flows.

Given some of the deep divisions which less constructive language policies of the previous centuries have created among different language groups, implementation of language management activities and initiatives to promote plurilingualism can admittedly be challenging. Issues of power and status often remain to be resolved, both among different community language groups and between them and those who speak only the dominant language of their society. In considering the various gate-keeping means employed by states to deal with the supposed 'crisis of multiculturalism' in an age of migration the existence and nature of different, contextually determined national perceptions on this subject need to be taken into account. Whilst some countries have adopted a multicultural discourse, others, particularly new or newly independent nation-states, are more intent on fostering cultural (and linguistic) unity.

In order to address existing challenges, international framework conventions (as elaborated on by Hogan-Brun & Wolff 2003; see also Grin 2004) in support of regional and minority languages will need to be extended to also grant language rights to immigrant groups (cf. Extra & Yağmur 2004). The EU too has to address this issue at the supra-national level. Overall, it can be stated that policies which promote multiculturalism are a relatively recent Western phenomenon and still have a long way to go until they produce a 'model of integration that permits recognition of sameness as well as of difference' (Nic Craith 2004: 16), both in the East and in the West.

Tolerance is a key orientation political communities require in accommodating diversity. The recognition of (cultural, linguistic and religious) difference, however, varies from one setting to another. Hence, since culture and context tend to play a significant role in shaping approaches to the management of diversity, proposals on the management of multilingualism at the EU level need to consider language-related issues that arise in different regional settings in a context-sensitive manner. It follows that questions of transferability of diversity management models must always involve situated, critical and diachronic analyses to take account of human agency, political intervention, power and authority in the formation of particular (national) language ideologies (Blommaert 1999). Such an approach will serve to counteract a tendency to simplify and 'sanitize' language histories (May, 2003: 128f) in debates on the relationships between language and power/social structure and encourage locally sensitive approaches to language policy and management.

With the increasingly multicultural nature of virtually every European state an emerging challenge is whether codes of solidarity and reciprocal loyalty will be developed that allow for centrifugal and centripetal forces to co-exist fruitfully, particularly at the national level. As has been argued (see Hall, in Wodak 1999: 17) globalization may increasingly create conditions that are favorable to cultural hybridization. This is for the time being likely to be reflected more in Western than in Central and Eastern European discourse that (still) needs to embrace negotiation of diversity more fully for the constructive crossing of societal boundaries.

Note

This contribution is an elaborated version of a keynote talk entitled 'Multilingualism - Micro and Macro Connections from East to West,' presented at an international conference on '*National Language Policy: School, Society, State,*' held at the *Seimas* (Lithuanian Parliament) in Vilnius, 19–20 September 2008.

References

Barbour, S. & C. Carmichael (2000), *Language and Nationalism in Europe.* Oxford: Oxford University Press.

Blommaert, J. (ed.) (1999), *Language Ideological Debates.* Berlin: Mouton de Gruyter.

Blommaert, J. & J. Verschueren (1998), 'The Role of Language in European Nationalist Ideologies,' in B., Schieffelin, K. Woolard & P. Kroskrity (eds), *Language Ideologies: Practice and Theory.* New York: Oxford University Press, pp. 189–210.

Bourdieu, P. (1973), 'Cultural Reproduction and Social Reproduction,' in R. Brown (ed.), *Knowledge, Education and Cultural Change: Papers in the Sociology of Education.* London: Tavistock, pp. 71–112.

Busch, B. (2009), 'Reflecting Social Heteroglossia and Accommodating Diverse Audiences - A Challenge to the Media,' in A. Galasińska & M. Krzyżanowski (eds), *Discourse and Social Change – Post-Communism and Beyond.* Houndsmills: Palgrave/Macmillan, pp. 43–58.

Extra, G. and K. Yağmur (2004), *Urban Multilingualism in Europe. Immigrant Minority Languages at Home and School.* Clevedon: Multilingual Matters.

Fossum, J. E. (2001), Identity-politics in the European Union, ARENA Working Papers WP 01/17. University of Oslo: Centre for European Studies. Retrieved 30 March 2008 from: <http://www.arena.uio.no/publications/wp01_17.htm>.

Framework Convention for the Protection of National Minorities (FCPNM). Retrieved 15 March 2009 from: <http://conventions.coe.int/Treaty/EN/WhatYouWant.asp?NT=157 and CM=1 and DF=10/02/03>.

European Charter for Regional or Minority Languages (ECRML). Retrieved 15 March 2009 from: <http://conventions.coe.int/Treaty/EN/WhatYouWant.asp?NT=148 and CM=1 and DF=10/02/03>.

European Convention on Human Rights (ECHR). Retrieved 15 March 2009 from: <http://www.un.org/aboutun/charter/index.html>.

Extra, G., M. Spotti and P. Van Avermaet (eds) (2009), *Testing Regimes: Cross- National Perspectives on Language, Migration & Citizenship.* Advances in Sociolinguistics. London/New York: Continuum.

Giordano, C. & Zvinkliene, A (2003), 'Introduction: Europeans from *Remote* Regions,' in C. Giordano, A. Zvinkliene, and D. Hensler (eds), *Baltic States. Looking at Small Societies on Europe's Margins.* Fribourg: Fribourg University Press, pp. 9–27.

Grin, F. (1999), *Language Policy in Multilingual Switzerland: Overview and Recent Developments.* Flensburg: Germany. European Centre for Minority Issues.

Grin, F. (2004), *Language Policy Evaluation and the European Charter for Regional or Minority Languages.* Houndsmills/New York: Palgrave/Macmillan.

Hogan-Brun, G., U. Ozolins, M. Ramoniene and M. Rannut (2007), *Language Policies and Practices in the Baltic States.* Polity series of 'Current Issues in Language Planning,' 8: 4. Clevedon: Multilingual Matters.

Hogan-Brun, G., C. Mar-Molinero and P. Stevenson. (eds) (2009), *Discourses on Language and Integration: Critical Perspectives on Language Testing Regimes in Europe.* Amsterdam: J. Benjamins.

Hogan-Brun, G. (2005), 'The Baltic Republics and Language Ideological Debates Surrounding their EU Accession,' in G. Hogan-Brun (guest ed.), *Language and Social Processes in the Baltic Republics Surrounding EU Accession, Journal of Multilingual and Multicultural Development* 26/5. Special Issue, pp. 367–377.

Hogan-Brun, G. & S. Wolff (2003), 'Language Minorities in Europe: An Introduction to the Current Debate,' in G. Hogan-Brun & S. Wolff (eds), *Minority Languages in Europe: Frameworks – Status – Prospects.* Pagrave/Macmillan, Houndsmills/New York, pp. 3–15.

Jernudd, B.H. (1991), *Lectures on Language Problems.* Dehli: Bahri.

Kymlicka, W. (2001a), *Politics in the Vernacular: Nationalism, Multiculturalism and Citizenship.* Oxford: Oxford University Press.

Kymlicka, W. (2001b), 'Universal Minority Rights?' Editorial, *Ethnicities* 1(1), pp. 21–24.

May, S. (2001), *Language and Minority Rights. Ethnicity, Nationalism and the Politics of Language,* London: Longman.

May, S. (2003), 'Misconceiving Minority Language Rights: Implications for Liberal Political Theory,' in W. Kymlicka and A. Patten (eds), *Language Rights and Political Theory.* Oxford: Oxford University Press, pp. 123–152.

Nic Craith, M. (2004), 'Why I believe that Academics should take Lead in the Debate on Multiculturalism,' *Times Higher Educational Supplement,* 22 April, p. 16.

O'Reilly, C. (2001), *Language, Ethnicity and the State*, vol II, Minority Languages in Eastern Europe post-1998. Basingstoke/New York: Palgrave Macmillan.
Schöpflin, G. (2003), 'Identities, Politics and post-Communism in Central Europe,' *Nations and Nationalism*, 9(4), pp. 477–490.
Shohamy, E. & D. Gorter (2008), *Linguistic Landscape.* London/New York: Routledge.
Spolsky, B. (1998), *Sociolinguistics.* Oxford: Oxford University Press.
Spolsky, B. (2005), 'Language in its Social Context, Baltic Sociolinguistic Review, *Journal of Baltic Studies* (guest ed. G. Hogan-Brun), pp. 254–272.
Stevenson, P. (2006), 'National Languages in Transnational Contexts: Language, Migration and Citizenship in Europe,' in C. Mar-Molinero & P. Stevenson (eds), *Language Ideologies, Policies and Practices: Language and the Future of Europe.* Basingstoke/New York: Palgrave Macmillan, 147–162.
Watts, R. (1997), 'Language Policies and Education in Switzerland', in R. Watts and J. Smodicezc (eds), *Cultural Democracy and Ethnic Pluralism: Multicultural and Multilingual Policies in Education.* Frankfurt: Peter Lang, pp. 271–302.
Wodak, R., R. de Cilla, M. Reisigl & K. Liebhart (1999), *The Discursive Construction of National Identity.* Edinburgh: Edinburgh University Press.
Wright, S. (2000), *Community and Communication. The Role of Language in Nation-State Building and European Integration.* Clevedon: Multilingual Matters.
Wright, S. (2004), *Language Policy and Language Planning. From Nationalism to Globalisation.* Houndsmills/New York: Palgrave MacMillan.

Aukse Balcytiene

The Baltic Media and Journalism in Context: Sketching the Regional Picture

Introduction: Changing Politics, Changing Media

In the early 1990s different analysts made predictions about social developments in the transition countries of Central and Eastern Europe. According to them, the former socialist societies would need to solve at least four major problems related to the processes of stabilization and development of parliamentary democracy, the development of a market economy, technological improvement and the resurgence and evolution of a civil society (see, for example, Splichal, 1994; Gross, 2002). Consequently, following the prescribed idea of 'Westernization,' new democratic countries have extensively applied market liberalization and de-regulation policies as their normative ideals in the fields of politics and economy as well as the social sphere (including media institutions) (Jakubowicz and Sükösd, 2008).

A decade or so later, according to different measures, the attempts of market liberalization and gradual nationalization (i.e. national system building) of media have succeeded. Democracy, economy and the media system in the Baltic States constitute stability[1]. The use of new technologies is steadily growing and in some small East European countries (e.g., Estonia) Internet usage numbers outreached those in more economically advanced and older member states of the European Union.

1 Stabilization is indicated by the following indicators: 1) different types of dailies (mid-market and tabloid) exist in print media market, 2) broadcasting comprises both public service and commercial TV stations, and 3) an entirely new online news space has emerged.

Briefly, there is a structural diversity of media reported in Central and Eastern Europe. At the same time, however, contemporary developments in media of those countries have also disclosed certain drawbacks. Market oriented journalism dominates, the public service media is weak and other requirements of media democratic performance are not adequately met in the countries of young democracy. Also, despite different attempts to analyze media transitions and transformations in this region of Europe, fundamental questions - why media is as it is and why media fail to meet democratic performance expectations - are not answered (Voltmer, 2008).

This lack of answers is perhaps a natural outcome of the fact that the democratic revolutions in Central and Eastern Europe originated in different social circumstances and differed in their acceleration (or delay); therefore they had different results. Indeed, these countries represent highly complex systems which differ across a range of historical, political, economic and sociocultural dimensions. Some of these countries are large (Poland), others are medium size (Czech Republic, Hungary, Bulgaria and Romania) and others are small or very small (Slovakia, the three Baltic States and Slovenia) markets. In some of these countries civil society structures and journalism traditions were not completely destroyed by the socialist regime. This makes drafting of single theoretical model of media and social transformations a complicated matter indeed.

Limited scholarship, limited comparative analyses, limited publications in other than national languages, but most importantly lack of analytical studies contribute that these countries are still 'terra incognita' for many scholars outside this geographic and cultural region. Therefore, this paper aims to fill this gap. It seeks to disclose a few of the most important contemporary characteristics of mainstream Baltic journalism. To state this more precisely, it aims to disclose the historical roots of Baltic journalism and to incorporate this knowledge into the analysis of more recent developments such as the commercialization and marketization of journalism and politics manifested in small Baltic nations.

This discussion applies an approach that is focused on 'what is the case.' Instead of describing major structural changes (such as giving the names of main media owners and media concentration as well as technological diffusion parameters) emerging in the Baltic countries media, it argues that despite similarities of the Baltic journalism to media developments in many countries around the world, the concrete occurrence of certain phenomena such as the ongoing restructuring of the media market and commercialization of journalism remarkably differ from those developments in the West due to historical legacies and (national) specifics in the development of journalism culture.

Indeed, one cannot understand the media (its content and media functions, also media usage characteristics by the audience) without comprehending the nature and diversity of society, namely the system of political parties and relations between different interests, the development of a civil society and so forth. A historical perspective in the assessment of changes in contemporary media and its context is very important, too. Media institutions (their structures, professionalism ideals) evolve over time. At each step of their evolution past events and institutional patterns inherited from earlier periods have an influence on the direction they take at present. Disclosing these historical legacies will be one of the core aims of this paper.

In spite of major changes and advancements in societal development, one of the critical indications in the Baltic societies is the observation that civil structures are weak there. Obviously, the media contribute to the evolution of a civil society. Their role in transmitting and cultivating political culture rests on several factors. Firstly, contemporary societies cannot exist without widespread and rapid communications and due to that they rely on the media. Secondly, the notion of political culture itself is bound to participation and civic engagement based on information supplied by the media. As will be discussed in this paper, 'stabilization' achieved in the Baltic States is not the final state of the media system within democratization. A broader understanding would imply Baltic media's 'openness,' which means that, in addition to being commercial, journalism has also a function to be societal in scope (Balcytiene, 2006).

Contextualizing the Baltic Media: A Retrospective Look at Media Functions in Small Nations

From the Western point of view, the Baltic countries have always represented the East. While looking from the East, these countries always seemed to belong to the West. Such a duality and oppositions in various interpretations mixed with geo-political and cultural marginality of the Baltic States has contributed to the development in media policies of a certain rhetoric of intellectual and cultural preservation and self-realization. For example, the recognition and protection of national languages and national identities has been an instrumental part in the national awakenings through several centuries in the countries of the Baltic Sea region (see, for example, Hoyer et al., 1993; Vihalemm et al., 1997; Lieven, 1994; Salovaara-Moring, 2008).

The three Baltic countries are similar in their geo-political situation, thus their political histories have certain similarities. The three Baltic countries (as well as parts of Poland and Finland) were incorporated into the territories of Tsarist Russia and became distant and marginal provinces of the great empire (since the end of the 18th century). In the first half of the 20th century the Baltic countries established independent statehoods (1918–1940), and then again disappeared from the world map by becoming incorporated into the Soviet Union (1944–1990). Yet, according to their cultural (ethnic, linguistic, religious and educational) peculiarities, the developments of media in those countries resulted in slightly different systems[2].

Indeed, it is not possible to modify or change some of the variables defining the dominating cultural and political narratives in contemporary media regulation policies of these nations. As will be demonstrated here, for example, the country's geo-political situation

2 These differences are noticed in media (print, TV or online) consumption patterns. Also, social organizational factors, such as dominating social and cultural values of discipline and self-education, come into play here (this is especially true for Finland, also to some extent to Estonia) (see Castels and Himanen, 2002; Salovaara-Moring, 2008).

(its geographic location as well as country's neighbors) and the size of the country are among those variables which have contributed to certain historical and political experiences.

The Smallness of the Market as an Analytical Dimension and its Impact on Dominating Media Policies

Small countries have many peculiar characteristics which directly or indirectly affect their media structures and media regulation (Puppis, 2009). The issue of size is among the crucial ones affecting policies of regulation. A media policy dilemma arises in the instance what to support – diversity amongst media actors by liberalizing market entrance conditions for new owners (as in the Baltic countries), or diversity of media content by, for example, providing subsidies to the media and promoting media education and media literacy programs in schools (as in the Nordic countries).

A shortage of resources and the small audience and advertising markets directly affect the journalistic production. It is a truism that larger and wealthier markets with greater resources available for the provision of media can afford a greater diversity of content output than smaller markets. Obviously, the resources available for media provision in a small market are less than the resources available for even a minority group in a larger market (Doyle, 2002).

Another observation is that small countries are also less influential in global terms. To say it more precisely, small countries are more severely affected by global influences of cultural infusion and commercialization because they have fewer resources (human as well as financial) to produce high quality domestic products to compete with foreign production. A particular concern, therefore, for smaller markets is the availability of resources (money and ideas) to support domestic content, as opposed to less expensive but imported content.

In their regulation policies, traditionally, small countries tend to an interventionist approach. As these countries face difficulties in fulfilling their cultural and social obligations, different kinds of regulation (for example, through state interventions such as subsidizing domestic production) become crucial. At the same time, small countries with exclusive languages are less vulnerable and less exposed to competition from abroad. This is exactly the case in the Baltic States where media regulation is very liberal, meaning that all kinds of concentration (cross-media ownership, diagonal concentration) are possible and there are no restrictions on media ownership by foreign investors. On the other hand, in Lithuania, Latvia and Estonia development of culturally sensitive policies (to protect the language, the country's cultural heritage, its folklore and national traditions) are perceived as a fundamental role of the state alongside the policies to act in the name of a public interest.

To sum up, media and journalism development in small markets is indeed a very interesting research case. As observed, European Union policies towards media concentrate too much on large markets. Small countries are very different. The resources they have are very different, too. The markets of such countries are different as well as their scales. For example, large countries have the volume of resources (money, companies as well as critical mass of talent) to produce a lot of original content in the native language while small countries very often must import a lot. The languages are also very different. In many small countries public service broadcasting continues to have a key role as a guardian of national culture while in large countries that is not so common today. All these indicators contribute to the fact that media structures in small and large countries and their performance are not the same.

The next section of this paper will concentrate on the geo-political and cultural marginality of the Baltic nations and its impact on development of media institutions and journalism.

The Literary Tradition of Baltic Journalism and Its Historical and Cultural Roots

In order to better understand the characteristics of the present-day media and journalism in the Baltic States, it is crucially important to take into account several factors such as the social and cultural history of written languages and book publishing traditions, as well as the history of national resistance and liberation movements. As will be argued here, these factors have strongly contributed to the development of both – national self-consciousness in the Baltic nations and also the media.

This section will focus on the emergence of Lithuanian journalism in more detail, but relevant examples will also be provided from the other two Baltic countries Estonia and Latvia.

Generally, the development of Baltic journalism was always closely related to the history and the social role of language in the intellectual life of these countries. For example, the Lithuanian language for many centuries had especially close contacts to two living languages, German and Polish, as well as Latin and East Slavic as written languages. In the early modern times (16–17th centuries), Lithuanian culture was strongly influenced by German culture from East Prussia[3]. After the formation of the Polish–Lithuanian Commonwealth in the 16th century, and then later, when both Poland and Lithuania were incorporated into the Russian Empire (from 1795), the Lithuanian language was strongly influenced by Polish which gradually became the language of culture. Latvia and Estonia in those times remained in the intellectual and cultural sphere of Baltic Germans.

For more than one hundred years, throughout the 19th century, the small nations were subdued by the Tsarist regime and went through strident Russification which was especially severe in Lithuania, where press prohibition was installed following the national uprisings in 1861 and 1863. Despite the fact that using the Lithuanian language in schools and churches was prohibited, the intellectual life continued[4]. By the end of the 19th century the nation consolidated

3 In the East Prussia region a large number of books such as translations of the Bible, psalm books, grammars, dictionaries and primers were published. The first periodical publication in the national language, *Nusidavimai Dievo karalysteje*, was printed in Lithuania Minor in 1823. The first newspapers in Lithuanian were published significantly later than in many other European languages. It appeared later than the Estonian *Luhhike Oppetus* (1766), the Latvian *Latviesu Arste* (1768), the Polish *Merkuriusz Polski* (1661) or the first Finnish newspaper founded in 1771 by the Aurora Society in Turku.

4 As Lithuanian schools were banned, children were secretly taught the Lithuanian language in unofficial, underground schools from books that were

in protests against the press ban. The resistance was chiefly spurred by religious motives[5], but it was massive. Different groups of people took part in the protests and deeply influenced the national consciousness. The Tsar was thus forced to recognize them. According to historians, when the Russians imposed the press ban in the mid-19th century, the authorities did not consider the Lithuanians to be a distinctive nationality. But by lifting the ban, the Tsarist government essentially recognized the existence of the Lithuanians as a nationality[6].

Certain similarities to the events described above can also be noticed in the developments of protest movements in the second half of the 20th century, namely in the times of the Soviet Lithuania.

With the secret protocols of Molotov–Ribbentrop pact in 1939, Nazi Germany and the Soviet Union divided the countries of Central and Eastern Europe between themselves and the three Baltic States were incorporated into the Soviet Union[7]. The Baltic States underwent a radical social and political transformation. In the public sphere, the Soviet state was keen on having control over the content and distribution of public information. The media was strictly supervised, regulated and controlled by the Communist Party and its apparatus. Control included not only censorship of the press and electronic media. All information – books, film, theatre and

forbidden to print and distribute. The books were published in East Prussia (which is also often called Lithuania Minor) and the book smugglers brought the forbidden literature to Lithuania Major.

5 Significant numbers of protest letters were written to the Tsar claiming that due to the ban on the Lithuanian language press the nation lacked publications for the education of its children and therefore public morality suffered. Initiatives like these became a catalyst for organized actions. It was necessary to show initiative and to organize public events in order to sign protest letters. About a hundred protest letters were written and signed by entire villages. The organizers included the priests, government servants, and members of the intelligentsia.

6 Unpublished manuscript 'How Russia has Acknowledged the Lithuanian Nation' by Alfred Erich Senn.

7 By this agreement, Lithuania fell into the German 'sphere of interest': Nazi Germany subsequently traded Lithuania to the Soviet Union in exchange for a part of Poland that had first been designated for Soviet occupation. Moscow had forced the Lithuanians to accept the presence of Soviet troops within their borders.

cinema performances, exhibitions, and advertising – was subject to censorship.

At the same time, despite the system of total control, many underground publications[8] of persistent value were published and a kind of 'semi participatory' channel was born in the subdued Baltic countries, namely the cultural sphere. According to Aleksandras Stromas[9], when free communications is suppressed or otherwise impossible, a cultural sphere acquires a certain consolidative function. Indeed, in Soviet times, the Baltic nations were maintained through certain cultural functions (cultural traditions, folk songs and distinctive poetry) – such a common heritage allowed all ethnic community members to communicate[10] on a free and understandable basis which also required a specific literacy to comprehend hidden meanings in Aesopian language.

In all Baltic countries, by paying the lip service to the official ideology, the media developed and maintained a tradition of participation in the national opposition to the regime. Creativity (in all its forms: theatre, literary press, song and dance festivals, etc.) became a substitute for other functions such as political participation, which under democratic conditions may be performed without any help from the arts. Despite the careful ideological control, topics such as the preservation of the cultural heritage, the protection of language from Russification, problems with education, and the pollution of the environment were always present.

In brief, it seems that Lithuanian journalism (and Latvian and Estonian as well) grew from literary tradition and was cultivated as a part of the cultural sphere. In different periods (especially in the Soviet times) it was the cultural sphere (literary and cultural

8 Among the samizdat publications *Kataliku Baznycios kronika* (The Chronicle of the Catholic Church) was the biggest (self-published) publication in the Soviet Union, continuously published from 1972–1989. Other samizdat publications were the publications of partisan poems, songs, and diaries (many of these authors remained unknown).

9 Lithuanian émigré political scientist.

10 Such kind of culture had to be complex, elitist and tricky because otherwise it would not be able to cross the barriers of censorship. This type of culture also had to have common denominators, otherwise people would not be able to understand and use it.

press, theatre performances, national song and folk dance festivals, etc.) that accommodated the most diverse functions (of education, of development of national consciousness and, later - in times of Gorbachiov's perestroika - of political mobilization).

Even in the times of their First Republics (1918–1940), in the print media of Lithuania, Latvia and Estonia the cultural topics and the literary genre were among the most developed. The press at that time acted as a public catalyst in all three countries - dailies published translations, opinions and reviews. The press also motivated young writers to produce and publish their works and thus intellectually enlightened the public. Through such activities the publications enabled the Lithuanians to identify themselves as Lithuanian. 'Lietuvos sulietuvinimas' (making Lithuania Lithuanian) was a key phrase of that time. In search for a national identity, the Lithuanians rejected elements of culture that seemed not appropriate to them. At the same time, appropriate approaches to the development of a national culture were searched for, particularly in Scandinavia and France (Gudaitis, 2001). Similar practices also occurred in the development of print media in Estonia and Latvia. Differently from Lithuania, the tradition of publishing political dailies in these countries lasted a bit longer. Over the years, the literary perspective has changed into a political one - it gradually changed from erudite and literary journalism to journalism that incorporated the myth-making power of fiction and political advocacy. The writing dealt with the actuality of observed life, but due to its literary character the press was opinionated. It attempted to convey impressions and fuel emotions, rather than to provide facts. Close linkage between journalism and literature is also apparent when examiniong how professional organizations of journalists and publishers as well as journalism training and education evolved[11].

11 The Union of Lithuanian Writers and Journalists held its first meeting in Kaunas in 1922, with 22 founding members. The organization was reorganized in 1929 into Lithuanian Journalists' Union (LJU) with about 70 members. At that time, the most popular form of journalism training included courses organized by the Lithuanian News Agency ELTA (founded in 1920), newspapers (e.g., *Trimitas*, 1926), as well as extramural studies called Journalism Courses at Home (1933) for which over 500 participants registered. Academic institutionalization of the profession began with the establishment of the

To conclude, in its emergence, Baltic journalism was closely associated with culture and politics, but not so strongly with the profit-making business. Baltic countries had periods of democratic development in the first half of the 20th century, but even then, in times of their First Republics, newspapers were strongly financed and subsidized by the parties (for short periods) or by the state. The press, therefore, had very limited possibilities to become profitable through market mechanisms. Indeed, paid advertising expanded in newspapers and brought profit to the publishers, but the market structures were weak. Furthermore, at the beginning of the 20th century, the reading of newspapers in the Baltic countries (especially in Lithuania) was an activity associated with the educated strata of society (writers, lawyers, politicians, doctors and teachers) and, of course, with the clergy.

Although this historical retrospection is quite brief it nevertheless gives an account on the importance of language, the emerging book publishing tradition as well as religion as means of national consolidation in these countries. In the interwar period, media and journalism in the Baltic countries was elite-oriented, aiming at the educated class. This also had a strong influence in determining the character of the press at that time. Later, in Soviet times, the literary publications, in particular, and the cultural sphere, in general, have continued its consolidative mission. The cultural sphere developed as an alternative sphere where semi-free public discourse was cultivated through Aesopian language and other symbols, as well as underground publications.

Department of Sociology and Journalism at Vytautas Magnus University in Kaunas in 1941.

The Breakthrough of the 1990s and After: New Functions of the Baltic Media for the New Times

In the past two decades in the Baltic countries, the democratic consolidation developed alongside the creation of a complex media market and mixed media system comprising both commercial and public service media as well as not-for-profit publications. In the early 1990s, in these countries, the construction of a new media landscape had to start almost from scratch and the laws were generally liberal in character. In the new democracies there was little sympathy for economic regulation which led to the formation of a variety of systems that today reflect the most deregulated systems in the Western world. In the Baltic States, in a similar way to other post communist countries of Central and Eastern Europe (Poland, Hungary, Czech Republic), the primary goal was to remove the media's governmental subordination and to nationalize the media system (through such steps as abolishment of censorship, change of media ownership patterns and so forth) (Lauk and Harro, 2003; Balcytiene, 2009; Jakubowicz and Sükösd, 2008).

Commercialism hits Baltic Countries

Journalism in the Baltic States has faced serious changes in recent years. The number of media channels has increased and overall circulation of tabloids and specialized magazines has multiplied in all countries. Scholars have started discussing the homogenization of journalism, the emergence of more sensational and more entertainment oriented reporting, as well as blurring boundaries between news, public relations and advertising (Harro-Loit and Saks, 2006; Balcytiene, 2006). Briefly, a very liberal business environment with liberal state policies, absence of party press and direct political parallelism, weak professionalism of media institutions and the absence of adequate public control as well as other country specific factors have contributed to the emergence of a commercial media with a very active role in the Baltic States. In other words, in the Baltic countries, where political organizations and interest groups are weak and fragmented, the definition of political issues and decisions and also their public interpretation is left to the mainstream media.

In the media system which has such a peculiar function the profit motive becomes crucial. As research studies disclose, in the Baltic States, media organizations obey profit oriented motives of highest audience reach and highest advertising revenues (Balcytiene and Lauk, 2005; Harro-Loit and Saks, 2007; Lauk, 2008; Balcytiene, 2009). The media uses formats which promise high public attention. Moreover, the media generic diversity is decreasing and issues are covered with personalized and human touch aspects and so forth.

Indeed, the trend towards media commercialization is reported in many countries around the world (Hallin and Mancini, 2004). In the Baltic States, however, this process has its country specific character. To say it more precisely, the institutional and constitutional design in the Baltic States produce a mediatized public sphere. Although such arrangements are noticed in many countries, an aggressive media commercialization is more dangerous in small nations. In small markets where media regulation is very liberal (where marketizaton of journalism as well as media concentration is increasing) and civil society structures are very weak, media commercialization could lead to situations in which material politics no longer plays a role in the public discourse. Although transferring political messages, such media gradually depoliticize public discourse on politics. In the long run a situation could arise in which the public can no longer recognize the connection between issues and political performance and decision making. Consequently, the democracy will suffer.

Although it may look like a simplistic explanation, it seems that the new democracies have jumped into the period of secularization surpassing the period of media dependence on political leanings. As this vision may have truism in it and capture the essential global developments in media systems in different countries around the world with emerging discussions about modernization, secularization and fragmentation, at the same time a relevant account of historical reasons for the absence of ideologically diverse party press tradition in the Baltic countries must be given as well.

Historically speaking, throughout the centuries freedom of the press has been a problematic issue in Lithuania as well as in the other two Baltic countries and also Finland (Hoyer et al, 1993; Salovaara-Moring, 2008). The historical conditions for the development of press freedom in these countries were closely intertwined with the countries' geographical position between East and West and their borders with Russia. All these countries have gone through harsh periods of press censorship (up to the prohibition of publications in the Lithuanian language) and strident Russification in the second half of the 19th century. The bans on national publications were lifted in 1904 but the censorship endured and freedom of the press was achieved only when independent states were established on the Eastern side of the Baltic Sea in 1918 (Hoyer et al, 1993; Vaisnys, 1998).

Even during the time of the independent statehoods, as early as in the third decade of the 20th century, democratic regimes in newly established national states were overthrown and media censorship became a norm in the three countries (Vaisnys, 1998). In Lithuania this happened in 1926, in Latvia and Estonia 7 years later, in 1934. In Lithuania, the military coup d'etat that brought the Nationalist Union to power in December 1926 reinstated press censorship. The state imposed a ban on ideologically and politically-varied publications, especially those produced by the Christian-Democrats and the Peasants' Party. The ruling Nationalist Union presented information through political lenses, and propaganda was almost equated with journalism. The new law on media in 1936 installed even more severe restrictions on the party press.

In the Soviet period, the partisanship of the press in those countries (socialist republics) meant that it accommodated ideological views, but just those that included certain Marxist ideology were present. As discussed in the previous section of this paper, in such a highly complex situation, a specific substitute for the political public sphere gradually emerged in the subdued nations of the Baltic States – the cultural sphere. It may be hypothesized that because of different factors – a relative cultural negligence and linguistic distinctiveness – the literature and the literary genres in journalism helped to develop a style of allegoric tales, metaphors, and symbols that told another story among the initiated. Thus, a national morale could be bolstered (Stromas, 2001; Vihalemm et al., 1997; Balcytiene, 2006).

Around the breakthrough years (the period between the late 1980s and the early 1990s), in the Baltic countries, the party-press parallelism (or political parallelism) was very strong for quite some years. The media started to reflect major political divisions in society with the political breakthrough events (in 1987), a varied party press emerged and culminated some years later, but then gradually decreased and disappeared by the mid 1990s. At present, absence of political parallelism is reported in the Baltic States.

Briefly, the absence of partisanship traditions in media has contributed to the situation where clear political leanings were not able to develop, and, consequently, partisan press where these leanings could be discussed, explained and defended is absent in the Baltic States. In such context commercialism rules – media discourse is filled with sensations which give a very fragmented view of society. For most journalists, the production of news which meets audience needs is a major guiding professional principle. Although regarding themselves as mediators, journalists often see themselves as facilitators of rational (consumer) choice. This kind of journalism can be called 'secular' journalism as it takes great interest in public opinion. In other words, media is structuring its news agenda by carefully observing what audience groups read and watch. Such journalism is also clearly market driven, therefore it is flexible to pressures of audience demand.

As a regulator, the state in Lithuania, Latvia and Estonia has not engaged in interventions to modify the market, for example by regulating cross-media ownership and concentration, imposing stricter regulation on advertising in media and so forth. Indeed, the state in its media related policies rhetorically stresses the importance of service to public interest, consensus finding and transparency. In practice, however, little application of these principles by the media can be noticed. The Baltic media themselves seldom observe the principles of public accountability. In addition, they are suspicious of outside interventions into their field (such as public discussions and academic criticism of media performance) so they rather sympathize with aggressive commercialization and the function of a 'attack dog' (Lauk and Harro, 2003). The situation is indeed complicated and journalistic professionalism suffers because of that.

One more observation can be mentioned here. In addition to what has been indicated as dominating secular discourse as proliferating in media in the Baltic countries, in Lithuania, another observation is noticed, namely the literary tradition in news presentation. In publications, information (facts) is often mixed with opinions and assessments. On the one hand, as has been discussed earlier, there are country specific (historical) constraints which have brought these developments to the present day. On the other hand, the dominating genres in the media such as extended news reports (to a lesser extent), features and publicistics accommodate an evaluative aspect themselves. Briefly, having a long history of active resistance against the attempts to destroy the national language as well as national traditions, Lithuanians have developed a certain conscious relationship to the Lithuanian language seeking to preserve it from outside influences. Thus figurative expressions and literary elements have also endured in modern commercial journalism.

To conclude, the media oriented communication culture which is registered in the mainstream media in the Baltic countries has some similarities to what is found in other Western countries with liberal media traditions. But small nations with linguistically restricted audiences and (politically) active mainstream media focused on commercialization have contributed to their country specific communication nuances, thus leaving these countries on the periphery of global developments.

A Way Forward: Contemporary Challenges to Media Professionalization

Generally speaking, media liberalization policies which were applied in these countries in the early 1990s opened the media field for the emergence of different actors in the small Baltic markets. Content diversity was promoted and gradually achieved through moderate state interventions, such as subsidies to culture and minority media. With the exception of Latvia, these countries also have institutionalized media self-regulation systems. However, establishment of institutions is important but not a sufficient factor for the consolidation of democracy. As practice reveals, in many post communist countries the institutions are there, but there is no (or very little) public support and compliance with behavioral norms of these institutions because adequate values are not there.

The absence of political parallelism, dominating secular discourses in the mainstream media as well as other features of (politically) active commercial media contribute to the peculiar social structures in the Baltic societies. Briefly, there is some kind of social 'shapelessness' reported in Lithuania, Latvia and Estonia. As discussed earlier, lacking traditions, well defined and clear values as well as ideological strength on the scale of 'left-right' leanings, the political parties delegate their institutionalization functions to the media, especially to commercial press and television. Consequently, instead of being a channel or mediator of political issues the media becomes an active player in this field and the news which gives the maximum profit is in the core interest of such media. A one-sided (commercial) approach towards politics fragments the public agenda – those issues which have highest relevance to the national political agenda are those that lie at the core interest of media professionals; thus they have the highest probability to be reflected in the public sphere. Therefore, it seems that the aggressive commercialization reported in the media of the Baltic countries is a direct result of country specific conditions (so called historical legacies such as a long tradition of media censorship and lack of party-press parallelism in these countries) rather than external pressures and developments on a global scale such as the marketization of politics and media.

What can be done in this situation, by whom and (if possible) how?

Different analysts of post communist transformations mention at least two phases which are crucial in the institutional development and democratization of societies, namely the phase of transition and the phase of consolidation (Gross, 2002; Jakubowicz and Sükösd, 2008). The phase of transition (or revolution) deals with the emergence of institutions while the phase of consolidation (or evolution) deals with the further development of institutions and adequate culture, the latter comprising both attitudinal and behavioral patterns. From the point of view of transformations in the media field, the concept of media freedom appears to be very useful in the analysis of the emergence of attitudinal and behavioral foundations of certain professional culture, as Bajomi-Lazar (2008) proposes. According to this author, the concept of media freedom is disclosed through three dimensions such as the institutional (legal establishment of media institutions such as laws, regulatory authorities, funds to support media), the behavioral (development of consensus among political elites and media that democracy and media freedom is the only 'game in town') and the attitudinal (commitment of citizens and their understanding that media freedom is a value which is inseparable from democracy). This line of reasoning stresses that public support and commitment enhances the consolidation of media freedom while public alienation hinders it. In short, democratic consolidation evolves through civil society, political society and the rule of law. Therefore, the fundamental question to be asked here is whether civil society believes in democratic values.

It seems that in many post communist countries there is a certain delay in transformations in the fields of politics and society. To say it more precisely, there is a delay between democratic consolidation (development of institutions) and media freedom consolidation (development of adequate culture supporting professional values and norms). What emerges from this discussion is that these two processes are not parallel. When culture emerges, the institutions will function.

Conclusions and Outlook

Being small corresponds with a number of operating constraints and problems. It is indeed more difficult to be small. As has been demonstrated with media development examples and traditions in the Baltic nations, small countries do many things to meet their various needs and sometimes these strategies are rather contradictory. For example, the role of the state in small Baltic nations is quite mixed. On the one hand, liberal media regulation promotes the ideals of market liberalization while, on the other hand, protectionism policies are implemented to financially support cultural publications through subsidies.

Indeed, the countries on the North Eastern side of Europe and the Eastern side of the Baltic Sea (the three Baltic States and also Finland) have remained on the periphery of global developments for a long time[12]. As was disclosed in previous sections of this paper, Christianity came to these countries later than in the neighboring countries. Publications in their native languages also appeared much later than in other languages in the same region. As demonstrated in this paper, the media in these countries have acquired different functions in different periods of time. At the same time, cultural protection, survival and self-preservation have been dominating narratives (either consciously or subconsciously) and primary collective aims in media related policies of those countries.

In spite of certain drawbacks, with democratic reforms and emerging professional cultures, the contemporary evidence gives signs of the evolution of professional media. Although, as discussed here, the mainstream commercial media remain subordinated to the market goals and political establishment functions, alternative media outlets (diverse online-only news portals, social and critical media, literary and cultural magazines) are developing social responsibility and public service orientation. On the other hand, mainstream journalism in the Baltic States, has not yet developed as an autonomous institution. There is a lack of consensus on professional journalistic standards as well as clarity among journalists on professional ideals (for example, the watchdog function lacks adequate definition; also, evaluative and advocacy journalism tradition persists in the media which shows its historical literary roots), professional organizations are weak and clear career paths for journalists do not exist (D'Haenens et al., 2009). In addition, although institutionalized in legal regulation, the practice of professional self-regulation process also has its ups and downs in the countries of young democracy.

12 Surprisingly enough, in international contexts, very often, these countries are represented in a rather mystified, sometimes also romantic way (from Prosper Merimee and his novel 'Lokis' to contemporary novels as 'The Corrections' by Jonathan Franzen or the thriller 'Hannibal Rising').

In spite of the above mentioned characteristics, media systems in the the Baltic States are all affected by the same processes of change as the countries in the West. At the same time, there are certain differences in media commercialization patterns, for example, between small Baltic and small Nordic countries.

Small Nordic countries, for example, have cherished the ideal of social responsibility as part of their national media systems, thus professional values of freedom of expression, diversity of opinions and controlling those in power are realized as professional norms even in competition-oriented and media marketization situations (Nord, 2008). In contrast, the new democracies across the Baltic Sea have jumped into a market-oriented news production model without a period of such an adjustment to a public service and media accountability tradition. Thus their media performance manifests a completely different practice. Indeed, we have to stress that quality journalism exists in the Baltic countries - public service ideals are being re-discovered and stressed by some media organizations, but these are clearly non-mainstream media which represent, for example, business dailies, social and critical media as well as online-only news portals.

To conclude, the journalistic culture of the Baltic States is affected by the professional media model which stresses liberalism and competition. However, as discussed earlier, certain objective parameters (such as geo-political situation and the size of these countries) combined with historical legacies (such as histories of press censorship and development of book publishing and reading traditions) have caused distortions in the present-day media performance in these countries from the directions that, for example, the Nordic media is moving towards. Therefore media secularization and consumerism are typical keywords describing journalistic culture in the Baltic countries today.

Indeed, there is no need to stop media commercialization in the Baltic States. Rather, finding adequate means to open-up the media field for other actors (public intellectuals as well as the general public) to critically assess social and cultural changes in these countries seems to be of crucial importance. Concrete steps in this direction are being taken through the expansion of new alternative media such as social and critical media (political weeklies, business dailies, cultural and literary magazines) as well as citizen journalism (blogs) and interactive social networks of citizens.

Bibliography

Bajomi-Lazar, Peter (2008), 'The Consolidation of Media Freedom in Post Communist Countries.' In: Jakubowicz, Karol, and Sükösd, Miklos (eds), *Finding the Right Place on the Map: Central and Eastern European Media Change in a Global Perspective*, Bristol: Intellect, pp. 73–85.

Balcytiene, Aukse (2009), 'Market-Led Reforms as Incentives for Media Change, Development and Diversification in the Baltic States,' *International Communication Gazette*, vol. 71, no. 1-2, pp. 39–49.

Balcytiene, Aukse (2006), *Mass Media in Lithuania: Changes, Development, and Journalism Culture*. Berlin: Vistas.

Balcytiene, Aukse and Lauk, Epp (2005), 'Media Transformations: The Post Transition Lessons in Lithuania and Estonia,' *Informacijos mokslai*, vol. 33, pp. 96–109.

Castels, Manuel, and Himanen, Pekka (2002), *The Information Society and the Welfare State*. Oxford: Oxford University Press.

D'Haenens, Leen, Marcinkowski, Frank, Donk, Andre, Maniglio, Tanja, Trappel, Josef, Fidalgo, Joachim, Balcytiene, Aukse and Napryte, Egle (2009), 'The Media and Democracy Monitor Applied to Five Countries: A Selection of Indicators and Their Measurement,' *Communications: The European Journal of Communication Research*, vol. 34, pp. 203–220.

Doyle, Gillian (2002), *Media Ownership*. London: Sage.

Gross, Peter (2002), *Entangled Evolutions: Media and Democratization in Eastern Europe*. Baltimore: The Johns Hopkins University Press.

Gudaitis, Leonas (2001), *Zurnalistikos mokslas ir mokymas Lietuvoje 1922–1943*. Kaunas: Vytauto Didziojo universiteto leidykla.

Hallin, C. Daniel, and Mancini, Paolo (2004), *Comparing Media Systems: Three Models of Media and Politics*. Cambridge: Cambridge University Press.

Harro-Loit, Halliki, and Saks, Kertu (2007), 'The Diminishing Border Between Advertising and Journalism in Estonia,' *Journalism Studies*, vol. 7, no. 2, pp. 312–322.

Hoyer, Svennik, Lauk, Epp and Vihalemm, Peeter (1993), *Towards a Civic Society: The Baltic Media's Long Road to Freedom*. Tartu: Nota Baltica.

Jakubowicz, Karol and Sükösd, Miklos (2008), 'Twelwe Concepts Regarding Media System Evolution and Democratization in Post Communist Societies.' In: Jakubowicz, Karol and Sükösd, Miklos (eds), *Finding the Right Place on the Map: Central and Eastern European Media Change in a Global Perspective*, Bristol: Intellect, pp. 9–41.

Lauk, Epp (2008), 'How will it all Unfold? Media Systems and Journalism Cultures in Post Communist Countries.' In: Jakubowicz, Karol and Sükösd, Miklos (eds), *Finding the Right Place on the Map. Central and Eastern European Media Change in a Global Perspective*, Bristol: Intellect, pp. 193–212.

Lauk, Epp, and Harro, Halliki (2003), 'A Landscape after the Storm: Development of the Estonian Media in the 1990s.' In: Paletz, David and Jakubowicz, Karol (eds), *Business as Usual: Continuity and Change in Central and Eastern Europe*, New Jersey: Hampton Press.

Lieven, Anatol (1994), *The Baltic Revolution. Estonia, Latvia, Lithuania and the Path to Independence*. Yale University Press.

Nord, Lars (2008), 'Swedish Media between Politics and Market,' *Informacijos mokslai*, vol. 47, pp. 9–22.

Puppis, Manuel (2009), 'Media Regulation in Small States,' *International Communication Gazette*, vol. 71, pp. 7–17.

Salovaara-Moring, Inka (2009), 'Mind the Gap? Press Freedom and Pluralism in Finland.' In: Czepek, Andrea, Hellwig, Melanie and Nowak, Eva (eds), *Press Freedom and Pluralism in Europe: Concepts and Conditions*, Bristol: Intellect, pp. 213–229.

Splichal, Slavko (1994), *Media Beyond Socialism: Theory and Practice in East-Central Europe*. San Francisco: Westview Press.

Stromas, Aleksandras (2001), *Laisves horizontai*. Vilnius: Baltos lankos.

Vaisnys, Andrius (1998), *Spauda ir valstybe 1918–1940*. Vilnius: Biznio masinu kompanija.

Vihalemm, Peter, Lauk, Epp, and Lauristin, Marju (1997), 'Estonian Media in the Process of Change.' In: Lauristin, Marju and Vihalemm, Peter (eds), *Return to the Western World: Cultural and Political Perspectives on the Estonian Post Communist Transition*, Tartu: Tartu University Press, pp. 227–241.

Voltmer, Katrin (2008), 'Comparing Media Systems in New Democracies: East Meets South Meets East,' *Central European Journal of Communication*, vol. 1., no. 1, pp. 23–41.

Kristina Juraite, Epp Lauk and Vita Zelce

The Professionalization of Journalism in the Baltic States: The Origins of Practices, Structures and Cultures (until 1940) [1]

This article attempts at first to compare the early stage of the development of journalism as a profession and cultural phenomenon in the Baltic countries – Estonia, Latvia and Lithuania. Therefore, the historical dimension of the paper is complemented with social, economic and political contexts. The second focus of this paper is the international co-operation of the Baltic journalists' organizations in the early 1900s. These organizations had a significant role in developing a common Baltic public sphere and supporting political and cultural interaction between the three countries. The Baltic Press Association was founded in 1933, in Tallinn, with National Committee representation in each country. The Soviet occupation in the summer of 1940 dealt a fatal blow to journalism in the Baltic States, and in destroying the community of journalists of the independence period ruined the profession. Finally, a retrospective insight into the cultures of Baltic journalism is necessary for a better understanding of the contemporary journalism of the three countries, as 'a large part of the explanation of the present lies in the past. We are what we are because we were what we were.' (Schudson 2003: 65)

1 Research for this paper was enabled by the Estonian Science Foundation research grant no. 7547 'Changing Journalism Cultures: A Comparative Perspective.' An early version of the paper was presented at the International Association for Media and Communication Research (IAMCR) Conference 'Media and Global Divides,' Stockholm, July 20–25, 2008.

Comparative Perspective in the Baltic Journalism History Research

When attempting comparative research one needs to ask at least four questions: what exactly does comparative research mean; and what, how and why do we compare? Historians have answered this question in the following way:

> Comparative history is the systematic comparing and contrasting of two or more historical cases in order to identify and explain their important similarities and differences. Such comparison has two primary goals. First, by examining more than one instance of historical change, comparative history tries to identify significant aspects or features of each instance, which might have escaped the notice of historians focused on a single case. Second, in the process of identifying those features and comparing their presence or absence across cases, comparative historians hypothesise and test generalisable theories or principles of historical change (Andrews 1994: 162).

This kind of comparative approach was used quite frequently in the 20th century by researchers in the field of history, and particularly social history. Comparisons are inevitable when evaluating big structures and large processes (Tilly 1984: 81). Comparisons between countries, media industries, periods of time, the past and the present can also help to explain the present-day media industry and to better understand the history of national media systems (Chapmann 2005: 1). Historians, however, often criticize the comparison of historical processes on the basis that this reduces the importance of individuals, social groups, and the individual and unique nature of events and processes; all of which are very important if history is to be understood (Tosh 2006: 223).

The first and until now last attempt to use a comparative approach in dealing with the history of the Baltic media systems was made in 1993. Under the leadership of Professor Svennik Høyer from the University of Oslo, Norway, a group of Estonian, Latvian and Lithuanian media scholars developed the volume *Towards a Civic Society: the Baltic Media's Long Road to Freedom*, which provides a panoramic view on the development of the media in each of the Baltic countries from the beginning of their journalism tradition in the 17th century until 1993.

Since then, research in journalism history has continued along separate paths in each Baltic country (Lauk 2000; Gudaitis 2001; Urbonas 2002; Balcytiene 2006). More has been achieved on the comparative analysis of media and journalism changes in the Baltic countries in the recent past and present time (Vihalemm 2002, Baerug 2005).

Our paper is the second attempt at comparing the early stages of journalism development in the three Baltic countries. How can one analyze national media systems from a comparative perspective? How can a comparative approach aid journalism history research? The aforementioned questions are not yet sufficiently discussed and there is no consensus as to how to do comparative research in journalism. Furthermore, there is no significant theoretical groundwork. Cross-cultural study of journalism is poorly conceptualized and comparative methodology is still rarely discussed. This concerns journalism research from both historical and contemporary perspectives and definitely deserves wider scholarly attention and discussion.

Most probably, the lack of a theoretically grounded conceptual framework is also a reason why the cross-cultural and cross-national comparative studies mostly follow the conventional pattern of national studies – describing the development of various aspects of journalism throughout certain periods.

These *comparative descriptions* as Lennart Weibull (1997: 61) calls them or *descriptive comparisons*, as others have called them (see for example Hanitzsch 2005), allow some general parallels to be drawn in the development of journalism in different countries. They also enable the uniqueness and universality in the development of a particular national journalistic system to be defined. Hallin and Mancini (2004: 3) emphasize the importance of comparisons which improve our comprehension and conceptualization of the complexities of the national media systems: 'Comparative analysis makes it possible to notice things we did not notice and therefore had not conceptualized, and it also forces us to clarify the scope and applicability of the concepts we do employ.' Thus, comparative perspective with the focus on the patterns of similarities and differences across national cases is a key for investigating the development of professional journalism cultures in the three Baltic countries.

Comparative analysis of the Baltic journalism development will be structured around the following dimensions: emergence of the national press, establishment of professional associations, journalism training and education, and transnational cooperation of journalists in the Baltics up until 1940.

The Emergence of Journalism as a Profession

We use the concept of professionalization as the theoretical framework in comparing the historical development of journalistic associations in the Baltic countries. When viewed through the narrow frame of a classical sociology of professions, journalism is not regarded as a 'true' profession equal to law, medicine or education. On the other hand, there are various characteristics that allow viewing journalism at least as a professionalizing occupation. The perspective here is that journalism is professional by its abstract nature, its demand for specialized competences and skills provided in the process of education, and its ambitions to correspond to high professional standards. Journalism is professional also by its sense of group identity based on occupation-related communication and boundary formation in relation to other groups when seeking occupational power.

Professionalization may be seen as a way of the social legitimization of a developing occupation. In the process of formation and self-definition, an occupational group needs to construct and maintain occupational boundaries, 'which are social or cultural divisions that help signify a group's work, societal roles and legitimacy' (Dooley 1997: 7). In fact, the process of boundary building contains most of the aspects of professionalization. The boundary building activities include the definition of certain work tasks and normative occupational values, establishing professional standards (a code of Conduct), seeking control over education and recruitment of newcomers. The process of establishing and maintaining boundaries is central to an occupational group in acquiring social legitimacy. A professional association supports the attempts at seeking legal rights to control their field as well as resist external efforts to control the activities of the occupation's members. In return for autonomy and a certain measure of authority that journalism and journalists enjoy in a democratic society, the professional association takes the responsibility of guaranteeing a certain quality of professional performance including penalizing those who violate the group's standards.

The Formation of a Journalistic Occupational Identity

The development of journalism and every media system largely depends on a historically set cultural and political environment. It would be erroneous to assume that the histories and cultures of the Baltic countries took the same path. There are certain similarities and parallels between Estonia and Latvia, especially in their political histories. All the three Baltic nations had been subdued by Tsarist Russia by the end of the 18th century. However, Lithuania remained under the cultural influence of the Polonized nobility and gentry, while Baltic Germans ruled Estonia and Latvia. Therefore, the first printers and publishers were either Polish or German, rather than Lithuanian, Latvian and Estonian. For instance, the first newspapers ever published in the Baltic area – *Ordinary Freytags* (later *Donnerstags*) *Post-Zeitung* (1675–1678 in Tallinn) and *Rigische Montags (Donnerstags) Ordinari Post-Zeitung* (1680–1710 in Riga) – appeared in German. The first periodical publication that emerged in Lithuanian territory was a Polish-language newspaper *Kurier Litewski* (1760–1763).

From the economic perspective, Estonians and Latvians were peasants with rare exceptions until the 1870s, when intelligentsia of Estonian and Latvian origin started to appear. Several educated Baltic Germans from the ruling elite considered it their mission to enlighten and educate the Estonian and Latvian people. They published the first local language magazines in 1766 and 1768, respectively. At the same time, numerous German language newspapers were issued in Riga, Tallinn and Tartu. The target audience for these newspapers was the German-speaking elite, which was relatively small in number. This meant that newspaper publishing could not be a profitable business, and editors and publishers had to accept the absence of commercial advantage in the process. This limited any expansion in staff numbers. Even in the mid-19th century, all but a few newspapers were written and edited by just one or two individuals. The editors of the first Estonian language (1806–1807) and Latvian language (1822–1915) newspapers were also German Lutheran clergymen. They partly produced the content of the newspapers and partly translated the remainder from German newspapers. Paradoxically, in this way, Estonian and Latvian peasants read the same news that their masters had in their German language newspapers.

A relatively late start of national publishing in Lithuania was due to a variety of political, social and economic reasons. After the third partition of the Lithuanian-Polish Commonwealth in 1795, Lithuanian territory was subjected to the Russian Tsarist's authority and its Russification policy. In 1832, the University of Vilnius was closed down; it reopened only in 1919. After national uprisings against Russian Empire in 1830–1831 and 1863–1864, the Lithuanian language was banned from schools and offices, and no Lithuanians were accepted for the civil service. The prohibition of publishing, distributing, and reading of Lithuanian books and press continued for 40 years until 1904. Consequently, Lithuanian journalism could only develop outside the borders of the Russian Empire, mainly in Lithuania Minor and the USA as well as Latvia, Russia and Poland.

From the end of the 18th century to the latter decades of the 19th century Lithuania Minor (also known as East Prussia) became a cradle of Lithuanian publishing till the start of the 20th century. The first periodical publication in Lithuanian language, *Nusidavimai Dievo Karalysteje* (Legends about the Kingdom of God), appeared as late as 1823–1824 in Tilsit, Lithuania Minor. In 1849, the first regular weeklies were launched, including *Keleivis* (The Traveller), published in Lithuania Minor, and *Lietuviskas Prietelis* (The Friend of Lithuanians), published in Lithuania proper (Høyer, Lauk, Vihalemm 1993). Vast smuggling operations of the publications regularly involved locals who took the risk of secretly transporting and distributing books and newspapers from Lithuania Minor to the mainland (Balcytiene 2006).[2]

After the national revolt in 1863–1864, the first wave of emigration started; it resulted in over fifty thousand people settling in the USA by the end of 19th century. In 1879–1882, the first Lithuanian newspaper *Gazieta Lietuviszka* (The Lithuanian Newspaper) was published weekly in the USA (Bulota 1992). Clearly, the Lithuanian press and publishing era had begun outside the mainland in the 19th century, laying strong foundations for the future development of the Lithuanian journalism culture, as well as serving as a voice of the national movement. One of the most influential publications for the Lithuanian national rebirth movement was the literary magazine *Ausra* (Dawn), published in Tilsit, Lithuania Minor by Jonas Basanavicius (1851–1927), one of the leaders and main ideologists of the movement. With more than 70 contributors, and a circulation of about 1,000 copies, the magazine had a particular mission to awaken public historical memory and promote Lithuanian language and culture. Another periodical of particular importance to the national movement was the magazine *Varpas* (Bell), also published in Tilsit in 1889–1905 by Vincas Kudirka (1858–1899), a talented writer, translator and publicist (Høyer, Lauk, Vihalemm 1993). *Varpas* proclaimed the ideals of national solidarity, democracy, tolerance and pragmatism.

Estonia and Latvia had shared a relatively similar historical path, as well as emerging journalistic practices. The development of Estonia's and Latvia's intelligentsia and their increasing engagement from the 1870s onwards in professions (priesthood, medicine, education and law) led to the forming of the occupational group of journalists. In many European countries editors were recruited from these social layers when the professions modernized in the 19th century. For instance, during the first five decades of the 19th century half of the 114 newspaper editors in Finland were university teach-

2 In the period of 1864–1904, when Tsarist Russia banned all publications in Lithuanian, more than 3320 books and 130 periodicals were issued outside Lithuania proper, mainly in Lithuania Minor and USA. Because of massive smugglings of Lithuanian books and press, over 3000 people were arrested and 2000 sentenced (Bulota 1992; Urbonas 2002).

ers or schoolmasters and had academic degrees (Tommila 1988). The situation was the same in Germany at that time (Koszyk 1966).

The first Latvian and Estonian full-time editors appeared in the late 1850s, early 1860s. Almost simultaneously, in 1856, two weekly newspapers were established that quickly gained popularity among their readers and became leading newspapers of the time: *Majas Viesis (Guest of the Home)* in Latvia and *Perno Postimees (Postman of Perno)* in Estonia. The editors of these newspapers (Ansis Leitans and Johann Voldemar Jannsen) became leading figures during the national awakening of Estonians and Latvians in the second half of the 19th century. Jannsen was a schoolmaster and author who also initiated the first Estonian song festival and theatre. When he started his second Estonian newspaper in Tartu in 1864 (*Eesti Postimees/Estonian Postman*), he became the first full-time Estonian newspaper editor.

Leitans was a popular author, and his works were among the most widely read of the day. The job of editor only enhanced his social prestige (Zelce 2000: 147–149).[3] Leitans was paid for his work as editor of *Majas Viesis*. Contemporaries recall that the payment was small, especially in comparison to the work which the man did (Leitans et al. 1875). From the perspective of media development, the paid job of an editor signified the development towards an independent occupation of journalism.

The same was true of the editors of other newspapers which emerged over subsequent decades. During the first decades of what is known as the Latvian national renaissance (from the 1850s to the 1870s), newspapers and their editors performed important functions in society. Newspapers organized events, served as consultation centres, collected and helped to prepare complaints from peasants, and offered assistance to readers who wanted to find a job, to choose an educational institution, purchase land or a building, etc. The

3 Numerous Latvian authors would later recall from their childhood and adolescence that Leitans was a hero, a spiritual giant. Anyone who actually met the great man was surprised, because in fact he was tiny, and his body was wracked by disease. This did not reduce respect for him, and it encouraged the idea that an individual's achievements and personality are more important than his physical properties.

history of the newspaper *Peterburgas Avizes* (*St Petersburg Newspapers*) (1862–1865) offers excellent evidence of this. The newspaper had an editor, an assistant editor, and an employee who was responsible for sending the paper to its subscribers. The editor received an annual salary (700 roubles at first), as well as bonuses for subscription numbers and honoraria for published articles. The editor was responsible for the content of the newspaper, including the news columns. He maintained links with correspondents and readers, and he also dealt with aspects of censorship (Zelce 2009: 375–386).

In 1880, the first Latvian publishing company was established in Riga –*Bernhards Dirikis & Co.* The company took over the weekly newspaper *Baltijas Vestnesis* (*Baltic Herold*), which had been published since 1868 and was quite popular. The first Latvian daily, *Rigas Lapa* (*The News-Sheet of Riga*), appeared in 1877, followed one year later by the newspaper *Balss* (*Voice*), which was published twice a week and was aimed at rural residents. The publishing company transformed *Baltijas Vestnesis* into a daily, while *Balss* became a weekly. In the first half of the 1880s, the company's share of the Latvian newspaper reading market was nearly 50% (Zelce 1994: 34–36).

The actual history of Estonian and Latvian journalists starts in the late 1880s, when, despite the continuing censorship and other restrictions, the Estonian and Latvian press markets began to expand and the number of jobs gradually increased. There were only 6 newspapers and 2 magazines in Latvian in 1860, but by 1890 their number had increased to 10 and 8, and by 1900, altogether 28 titles in Latvian appeared. There are no data about the number of Latvian journalists in the late 19th and early 20th century. The largest newspapers employed between 5 and 15 people, and thematic specialization began to emerge. Most newspapers had a domestic editor, a foreign affairs editor, a literature editor, an editorial page editor, and a judicial and economic affairs editor. Newspapers also employed people to translate telegrams from abroad, as well as a variety of technical employees.

While there were only 6 titles of periodical publications in Estonian in 1857, in 1887 their number was 27. In 1891 the first daily newspaper started to appear. The potential audience for the Estonian press already existed in the 18th century (according to the censuses, the rate of literacy among the adult population was 60% at the end of the 18th century and increased to 95% in 1897). A sufficient technological potential for printing and publishing had also emerged. In 1890, 30 printing shops were in operation, and in 1900 their number was 44 (Lauk & Pallas 2008).

The first signs of the occupational awareness of Estonian, Latvian and Lithuanian journalists appeared simultaneously by the end of the 1890s. According to our data, 23 Estonian journalists were permanently employed in 1896 and 27 in 1897. The first meetings of Estonian editors in these years give evidence of the emergence of a new occupational group that clearly identified itself with the field of journalism. The editors were in similar social and occupational positions; they had common problems to discuss (e.g., emerging competition among their publications and ethical matters), and common professional rhetoric. Similar problems were raised among Lithuanian journalists in the United States, in their first attempt to establish a professional organization. *The Writing Society* was founded in 1892 with the aim at supporting contributors to the Lithuanian newspapers in the U.S.A.

In the Latvian press, the discussions about the specifics of journalists' work and role started at the same time. In 1892, the newspaper *Dienas Lapa* (*The Daily News-sheet*) declared that a journalist must be very talented and must work very hard in order to fill the columns of a newspaper, to satisfy the needs and interests of all kinds of readers, to observe all the details of everyday life, and to report and discuss them. A reporter must be aware of what is going on, and have a thorough understanding of the processes and people to be able to present in brief the main ideas about complicated issues to the readers. Finally, the work of a journalist is hard, 'his strength (nerves) will probably be damaged more than in any other job,' admitted the paper. Usually, the paper concluded, a person is not strong enough to work as a journalist for 20 or 30 years 'without breaking his neck.'[4]

As all Estonian, Latvian and Lithuanian journalists had learned their craft only from experience, the issue of professional training was raised for the first time. Several newspaper articles proposed

4 'Jaunlaiku rakstnieciba' ('Writing Today'), *Dienas Lapa*, 15 and 17 April 1892.

starting special training courses for journalists and to send them on study trips to abroad. But neither conditions nor possibilities enabled these ideas to be realized at that time. In 1902, however, a textbook for Lithuanian journalists (*Spauda ir Kultura /The Press and Culture*) was published in the United States. This book was a translation from German and dealt with the professional standards and interests of journalists (Bulota 1992). The question of journalistic ethics was also touched upon for the first time. In 1906, *Postimees (The Postman*) in Estonia presented an idea to establish a court of honor for journalists. The editors, thus, were beginning to realize that journalism was not simply one trade among many. 'It is a distinct way of experiencing the world. It is a separate consciousness' as Schudson (1995:31) argues.

The beginning of the 20th century was a period of rapid modernization covering all spheres of social life in the Baltic countries, in which the press had a crucial role. This was the period of both ideological and structural diversification and of a rapid expansion of the Estonian press despite continuing censorship. During the first five years of the century, the number of fully employed journalists doubled: 29 journalists were employed in 1900 and 57 in 1905, whereas in 1906 the number was already 77. Alongside the growth of the number of publications, the editorial staffs of the newspapers also grew and the division of labor developed further. For example, the staff of the only daily, *Postimees* consisted of 5 journalists in 1900, and in 1909 the number was 12 (Lauk & Pallas 2008). These numbers are comparable, for example, with Finnish data. In Finland, there were 3.2 journalists per newspaper in 1900 and 3.9 in 1910. The total number of Finnish journalists was 283 (Nygård 1987). At different times in 1905–1918, 210 journalists were employed in the Estonian press (24 women among them), in 1919–1940 their number was 632 (including 73 women) (Pallas 2000).

In Lithuania, no statistical data is available on the number of practicing journalists until the early 20th century. The Press Society of Lithuania Minor, established in 1915, had 30 members (Urbonas 2002). The Lithuanian Journalists' Union had over 100 members in 1932, 135 members in 1934, and 208 in 1940 (Raguotis 1992). However, a fuller picture of the number of people involved in journalism activities could be reconstructed on the basis of the numbers involved in journalism training initiatives. In 1933, over 500 people subscribed for *Journalism Courses at Home* which could be equated with extramural studies for those interested in journalism (Urbonas 2002).

First Congresses of Journalists of the Baltic Area

By the early 20th century, with the growth of the number of fully employed journalists, and thoroughly altered working environments, the need for determining commonly shared professional standards, responsibility, methods of training, and employment and recruitment conditions became inevitable. 'Who should be considered a journalist?' clearly became a question of establishing the occupational boundaries and the legitimacy of the occupation.

In early April 1905, an all-Russian Congress of journalists and literati took place in St. Petersburg. The Congress was the first large forum of literary intelligentsia that invited Baltic representatives to participate. Soon after that, in late April 1905, a meeting of Estonian and Latvian journalists took place in St. Petersburg, in which about 20 editors from Tallinn, Tartu, Riga and Jelgava participated. This group agreed upon convening a Congress of Baltic Journalists in Riga. The Congress, however, was only held on 21–22 April 1909. The official organizer was the Riga Association of Writers and Artists. For organizational reasons, the invitation to Estonian journalists was delayed, and so the Congress was attended by Baltic German, Latvian and Russian press people. Estonians were represented by one journalist, who worked for the Estonian newspaper *Postimees (Postman)*. On the second day, delegates learned of a telegram from the editors of four Estonian newspapers: 'Because of the delay, our arrival is not possible. We wish success to the Congress. We shall discuss the resolutions of the Congress amongst ourselves and with our colleagues in Tartu, and we will approve them if that is possible.'[5]

5 'Pirmais Baltijas zurnalistu kongress Riga 21. un 22. marta' (First Congress of Baltic Journalists in Riga on March 21 and 22), *Dzimtenes Vestnesis*, 26 March 1909.

The Congress declared its major aim to bring Baltic journalists (Estonians, Latvians, Germans) closer together. There were proposals to establish an Association of Baltic Journalists and Writers, with chapters in Jelgava, Liepaja (Libau), Tallinn and Tartu. Another suggestion was to establish a special newspaper for journalists, one that would be published in Latvian, Estonian, German and Russian. There was also much discussion about the overall situation of journalism and literature in the Baltic provinces, with delegates calling for a system in which they could help one another. There were also debates about the status of reporters. One newspaper reported that delegates felt that a reporter had a difficult time: 'He supposedly has to be everywhere and know everything, he is said to be responsible for his editors, for the law and for each private individual, he has a great burden of obligations and responsibilities, but he has no rights at all. Delegates said that his work is not properly compensated, and often he has to cover expenses from his own pocket when gathering the news.'[6] Other speakers said that the qualifications of many reporters were poor and that the results of their work were not worthy of a high level of compensation. There were proposals for contractual relations with journalists and on the establishment of a bureau for their work. The Congress agreed to establish a central system for collecting the news. In another resolution, they agreed to observe confidentiality in terms of not disclosing the names of the authors of press articles to private individuals. Future plans included trips for Baltic journalists so that they could learn more about the Baltic region.

The most difficult issue for the Congress of Baltic Journalists concerned inter-ethnic relations in the region. The Baltic German press was accused of disruption in society because of its activities in 1905 and later. All in all, the Congress did not attract much attention, because the larger Latvian newspapers felt that it had been organized in the interests of Baltic Germans and thus had a reserved attitude toward the event.

6 'Pirmais Baltijas zurnalistu kongress Riga 21. un 22. marta' (First Congress of Baltic Journalists in Riga on March 21 and 22), *Dzimtenes Vestnesis*, 23 March 1909.

The Congress of Estonian journalists was held soon after the Riga Congress, in May 1909 in Tallinn. The Congress brought together two thirds of all Estonian journalists (40 of 65 employed in 1909) from most of the newspapers and magazines. There were also four female journalists among the participants and three guests from Finland (Lauk 1995). The agenda concentrated around the core questions that determine the framework of the occupation: the journalists' professional role and status, ethical problems, education and employment conditions. The Congress also discussed and approved the resolutions of the Congress of Baltic Journalists. A resolution was passed to establish an organization of journalists and authors.

The Second Congress of Baltic Journalists was held on May 26 and 27, 1910, again in Riga. There were 45 journalists representing 20 newspapers participating – 19 Latvians, 9 Estonians, 9 Russians and 8 Germans,. The most important issue on the agenda was how to establish closer links among the nations of the Baltic region, and debates focused mostly on this issue. The resolutions of the Congress also contain an idea to establish an Association of Baltic Journalists that should promote the inter-ethnic co-operation among journalists. In the subsequent years, attempts by Baltic journalists to work together subsided.

The question of a professional organization of journalists in Lithuania could only arise after the ban on the Lithuanian press was abolished in 1904. In 1907, for the first time an idea was presented to arrange a meeting of Lithuanian journalists from Lithuania proper, Lithuania Minor and the United States. Unfortunately, the idea did not work out due to the lack of any common ground. The first conference of the Lithuanian press, however, was arranged in the United States by American-Lithuanians in 1910. The first association of Lithuanian journalists, the *Press Society of American-Lithuanians*, grew out of this conference. Its primary objectives were targeted at journalists, editors and publishers, their relationships, professional ethics, language and editing. This organization did not last because of political dissent among the members, and gradually fell apart within a few years (Lauk et al. 1993:113).

These meetings demonstrate that an important qualitative development had occurred in Baltic journalism: professional activity in the newspaper field had finally been clearly separated from other fields and journalism had become a full-time occupation. The need for determining commonly shared professional standards, responsibility, methods of training, and employment and recruitment conditions became inevitable. 'Who should be considered a journalist?' clearly became a question of establishing the occupational boundaries and the legitimacy of the occupation. At that time, however, unlike the situation in some other countries, the role and status differences inside the occupation were not yet distinct enough. It was still difficult to draw a clear dividing line between a publisher and editor as well as a journalist and external contributor. Thus, the staff members, the permanent contributors and the publishers were all considered journalists. In Germany, for instance, publishing had already become an independent occupation by the 1840s (Koszyk 1966) and in Sweden, Norway and Finland the publishers had established their associations before the journalists did.

Establishing Professional Associations

The period before and during WWI was not favorable for the development of the press in the Baltic nations. After the 1905–1907 Revolution the Tsarist authorities tightened censorship and it was difficult to establish new publications. In 1907, over 600 publications were closed throughout the Russian Empire (Lauk 2000:26). The press was also hindered by economic hardships caused by the outbreak of WWI, and also by the enforcement of military censorship all over the Russian Empire in 1914. After the February Revolution 1917, press freedom was declared for a short while. By July 1917 new restricting regulations were enforced and the military censorship restored.

Lithuania was occupied by German troops by September 1915, Riga by the end of August 1917, and the rest of Latvia and also Estonia in February 1918. The conditions for the functioning of national presses depended entirely on the occupying authorities. Most of the national newspapers were closed down and only a few publications loyal to the occupying power were issued under strict censorship.

The same situation was repeated during the Communist rule from the end of 1918 to May 1919. Free development of the press was not possible before 1920, when the peace treaties with the Soviets were signed and the Baltic States were consolidated into parliamentary democracies.

During these periods of political turmoil, however, the associations of Latvian and Estonian journalists were founded. In 1917, the *Latvian Association of Writers and Journalists* was established, initially with 27 members. The organization was initially very active, but its activities were suppressed during the consequent German occupation and by the Bolshevik regime. The Association re-established itself in 1920. Its main focus was on professional issues and protection of the profession's interests. In 1922, the Association organized a celebration of the 100th anniversary of the first press publication in the Latvian language, which attracted a great deal of attention. The central event was attended by all of the country's top political officials, along with diplomats and representatives of many foreign press publications and news agencies. Greetings were presented by the *Estonian Journalists' Association*, the *Lithuanian Union of Writers and Journalists*, as well as representatives from several publications in the two neighboring countries. Also in honor of the anniversary, a first comprehensive review of the history of the Latvian press was published. The centennial celebration also launched a new tradition – the Press Ball, which would subsequently become one of the most important and prestigious events of the year. In a way, the high social status of the Press Ball helped to ensure the prestige of Latvian journalists and the mass media. Similar Press Balls became a tradition of the Estonian Journalists' Association as well.

The Latvian Association of Writers and Journalists was very much a trade organization in that it worked to defend the interests of its members – particularly their material interests (pensions, working conditions, sickness insurances etc.). In 1924, the Association had more than 200 members. In 1925, the association achieved a collective agreement with publishers on norms related to honoraria and the amount of working hours. In 1931, the Association resolved the issue of pensions and sickness insurance for journalists, and it also took over the handling of copyright issues. The Association organized congresses and helped journalists to establish international contacts. In 1927, the *Latvian Association of Writers and Journalists* was admitted to the International Federation of Journalists (Treijs 1996: 88–94). In Latvia, two minority journalists' associations were also established in these years. The *Association of German Journalists* was founded in 1927 and the *Association of Jewish Journalists* in 1930. *The Latvian Association of Writers and Journalists* experienced a schism in 1931, with rightist members decamping and establishing the *Latvian Press Association*.

A coup on May 15, 1934, was the end of democracy in Latvia. The authoritarian regime of Karlis Ulmanis banned nearly all organizations, but the *Latvian Association of Writers and Journalists* and the *Latvian Press Association* were not closed. At the same time, however, 54 newspapers and 14 magazines were banned by the Government. The leading commercial publications that remained began to support the authoritarian regime very actively. In 1934, the *Latvian Association of Writers and Journalists* merged with the *Latvian Press Association,* taking on the latter's name. In 1938, it had 342 members. It also supported and praised the regime of Ulmanis (Treijs 1994: 355–361).

The *Estonian Journalists' Association* was established in 1919 with 30 founding members. This was the time of the Estonia's War for Independence and many journalists also served as soldiers. Until the end of the war the most essential activity of the *Association* involved communication with the journalists-combatants in the battlefields and the dispatch of the newspapers to the front. When the war was over, the *Association* stopped working. In April 1921 the Congress of Estonian journalists in Tallinn revived the *Association*. In 1925, new statutes of the organization were adopted and the association was renamed the *Estonian Journalists' Union* (EJU). In the new statutes the membership was more distinctively defined than before. The membership was determined in two ways: 1) active members (who had been regular staff members for at least two years) and 2) associate members (who actively contributed to the newspapers and magazines). The activities that the Union declared as its main tasks, included: 1) the improvement of journalists' educational and professional qualities and publication of the Union's yearbook, 2) protecting journalists' interests in relations with employers and improving journalists' social and economic conditions, 3) developing international co-operation (Lauk 1993: 134–135). In 1930, the EJU became a member of the International Federation of Journalists. In the 1920s, the Union had approcimately 100 members, in the 1930s about 120. It is estimated that one fifth of all journalists belonged to the Union. Although the EJU admitted journalists from all over the country, the members came mainly from the larger newspapers and magazines that were published in Tallinn and Tartu.

In Lithuania, journalists began to organize only in 1920, when journalists and authors established their separate section within the *Lithuanian Artists' Association*. The emphasis, however, was more on the creative work in literature, promotion of translations and literary publishing, than on journalism. Immediately after the first Baltic Journalists Conference arranged in Kaunas in 1921, Lithuanian journalists decided to separate from the Artists' Association and establish an independent organization for journalists and writers. The *Union of Lithuanian Writers and Journalists* held its first meeting in Kaunas in 1922, with 22 founding members on board. The organization was reorganized in 1929 into the *Lithuanian Journalists' Union* (LJU) with about 70 members. The membership increased up to 208 by 1940. The statutes of LJU adopted in 1930 emphasized professional solidarity, cooperation and ethics among all. LJU took care of the members' moral and material interests, legal status, as well as the quality of press which was supposed to serve the honor, culture and welfare of the public. The membership could be granted to those who were practicing journalism as their major activity at least for two years (full members), as well as those who were contributing to different media outlets, but this was not their major occupation (correspondents) (Urbonas 2002).

Except for Estonia, the Baltic journalists' associations were first established as joint organizations for journalists and authors. The initial idea in Estonia was also a common organization. This reflects the fact that historically, the authors were the most productive and regular contributors for the press, and at times also the staff members. In Norway, for instance, the share of authors-editors in the press was 58 per cent by the middle of the 19th century (Høyer 1995: 326–327). The distinction between a journalist and an author or freelance contributor in the Baltic journalism remained turbid until the early 20th century. The role of authors-editors had been especially significant in Baltic nation building. They frequently published their novels first in the newspapers; they wrote literary criticism that became a particular journalistic format. The best feuilleton and political satire writers also came from among the authors. The prominence of authors diminished along the growth of journalism into a news industry and business. Growing competition in the newspaper market brought along changes in news presentation and journalistic methods (Harro 2001). Newspaper content gradually diversified and also required more specific skills of newsgathering and presentation. The work tasks and skills of journalists as well as the division of labor within the editorial offices was specified. Journalism became a distinct career of itself by the end of the 1920s. This is also the time when the professional organizations were actively involved in 'profession-building.' They used various strategies including the dissemination of professionalizing rhetoric in a variety of forms to legitimize the occupation (Dooley 1997). They began to make efforts for having a say in the press-related legislation. For instance, in the 1930s, the Estonian Journalists' Union took steps toward adoption of a Press Law that would regulate work and pay terms, lay down rules for signing contracts, fix the minimum rates of wages and salaries, etc. (Lauk 1993:137). In Latvia, a collective contract had been used for the press since the 1920s that determined wages, working conditions and terms of employment.

Attempts at Legitimating Journalism in the Baltics

The associations aspired to raise the prestige of the occupation and status of journalists by trying to define professional standards and educational requirements. Clear-cut professional standards also serve as a means for controlling the entry to the field. In 1924, the *Latvian Association of Writers and Journalists* suggested the Government establish a Press Chamber, but the idea was rejected. In connection with the preparation of new regulations on publishing in 1933 and 1938, the *Estonian Journalists' Union* (EJU) suggested that an article be included concerning a journalist's professional requirements and standards. This was not, however, followed up on. Nevertheless, leading journalists, editors and authors discussed the issue of occupational standards in the newspapers and public meetings. The EJU took several initiatives to improve journalists' education (e.g., scholarships for study trips abroad, reporters' courses, publishing a reporter's handbook etc.). Proposals were also made to establish a state-funded training system or to open a faculty of journalism at Tartu University. These ideas, however, were never realized.

Early efforts to professionalize journalism and include it into the academic curriculum took place at Vytautas Magnus University in Kaunas, Lithuania, which at that time was the only place in the Baltic countries where journalism was taught. Since the early 20th century those Lithuanian activists involved in journalism activities emphasized the need for professional competence for editors and press leaders. The most popular form of journalism training included courses organized by the Lithuanian News Agency ELTA (1922), newspapers (eg., Trimitas, 1926), as well as extramural studies called *Journalism Courses at Home* (1933) for which over 500 participants registered (Raguotis 1992). In 1925, the first journalism courses were provided at the University of Lithuania (renamed Vytautas Magnus University in 1930). Later in 1941, the Department of Sociology and Journalism was established to provide students with professional journalism education and training. Unfortunately, a few years later the department was closed down by the Nazi authorities (Gudaitis 2001).

One of the *Latvian Press Association's* leading figures, Arturs Kroders, designed a three-year training programme for Latvian journalists. Steps were taken to set up a school for journalists. A curriculum was designed on the basis of those of similar schools in Germany, France, Belgium and the United States. Regulations for the school's operations were drafted, and instructors were chosen. The Latvian Chamber of Writing and Art, which administered and supervised the mass media in Latvia prepared to open a three-year Institute of Journalism in the autumn of 1940. These plans were cancelled when the Soviet Union occupied Latvia in June of that year.

The issue of moral values and ethical standards of journalistic work was also raised. A code of professional conduct is regarded as an important attribute that distinguishes a profession. Although several discussions were held in the press and in the meetings and congresses of the EJU, a formal code of ethics was not adopted. In 1930, a court of honor was established for handling ethical issues. The statutes of the court contained some general ethical principles for journalists that were compulsory only for the members of the EJU. There is no evidence of the actual activities of this court. As late as in 1939, the EJU adopted the ethical code of the International Federation of Journalists (IFJ). Estonian journalists adopted an ethical code of their own only in 1997.

The *Lithuanian Journalists' Union* emphasized the importance of professional ethics and quality of press in its statutes adopted in 1930. However, no particular code of professional conduct was accepted till 1996, when the code of ethics of the Lithuanian Journalists and Publishers was adopted.

Transnational Cooperation of the Baltic Journalists' Associations

An important indicator of a journalist's occupational identification is the extent of their formal and informal social ties with other journalists. In the Baltic countries, issues of journalists' professional identity became central to the agenda when the first Congresses of editors, authors and literati occurred in St. Petersburg in 1905, Riga in 1909 and Tallinn in 1909. However, another decade or so passed before journalism was defined as an independent profession. The first journalists' organization in the Baltic countries was set up in Latvia in 1917 (*The Latvian Association of Writers and Journalists*). The *Estonian Journalists' Association* was founded in 1919 and the *Lithuanian Union of Writers and Journalists* in 1922.

In the early 1920s, the Estonian press became actively involved in the political life of the country. This did not, however, cause a conflict between the independence of the press and its loyalty to Estonia. Estonian journalism had served national aspirations since the first newspapers of the national movement in the late 1850s appeared.

During the struggle for an independent statehood and civic society from 1918 to the late 1920s, many well-known journalists became politicians. Thus, the unanimous support to the nation-state in the early 1920s was quite natural. The State did not restrict the freedom of the press until 1933. Journalists had access to information sources; they were free to criticize anything and anybody in society. In the 1921 congress, the journalists' association set as an underlying principle that the press should contribute to instilling in citizens a sense of duty to their country and improve the understanding of national independence. Journalism became interwoven with politics also on the level of individuals. On the other hand, it made it difficult for journalists to distinguish between partisan and independent journalism. Politicians manipulated several less experienced journalists and used them in political power games.

The crises of parliamentary democracy in Lithuania in 1926 and Latvia and Estonia in the early 1930s led to the establishment of authoritarian political regimes. The consequences for the independence and freedom of the press were devastating. Numerous restrictions were posed on journalism, including the requirement for applying to the authorities for establishing new periodical publications. In 1934, the Estonian Government established the Propaganda Service (later named the State Propaganda Service) to function as a propaganda ministry channelling and controlling the content of the press. The Press Law of 1938 legalized all the restrictions and regulations that had been imposed on the press since the early 1930s. The Banned section now listed 14 items, most of which served to prevent the press from criticizing State authorities and their practices. The law stipulated that newspapers should maintain a positive content and a constructive form, showing the Government's policies in a favorable light (Lauk 1993:125). Within the EJU, however, no opposition formed against the government media policy. The leadership consisted of people close to government circles and therefore, the EJU co-operated with the regime. The Union did not express collective disagreement with the 1938 press regulations and remained rather cautious in its public statements. In the 1930s, the EJU continued its international activities in the spirit of foreign political interests of Estonia.

An important concept in the Baltic countries' foreign policy was the so-called *Baltic Union*, the military-political alliance with the closest neighbor countries in the Baltic region. This alliance should have included the Baltic States, Finland and Poland. Therefore, the most active international communication of the EJU was also directed towards these countries. The first meeting of the journalists from the Baltic countries in Kaunas 1921 decided to form a Baltic press union that could later be joined also by Poland and Finland. The meeting was attended by 13 people from Lithuania, 10 from Latvia, and 7 from Estonia. Participants approved two resolutions – one on collaboration among Baltic journalists and the convening of a congress, and the other on closer relations among the Baltic States in political, economic and military terms. International contacts were also promoted by travel to other countries. Latvian journalists visited Lithuania in 1921, 1930 and 1931, Poland in 1922 (together with Finnish and Estonian colleagues), Germany in 1926 and 1934, Finland in 1927, and the Soviet Union in 1934. In 1936, a group of journalists from all three Baltic countries visited Prague, where they negotiated the establishment of a press alliance among the Baltic States and Czechoslovakia. From there, the journalists joined colleagues from Finland on a trip to Hungary.

To promote the idea of the Baltic press union, so-called friendly alliances were created between Estonian and Latvian and Estonian and Lithuanian journalists unions (in 1928 and 1931). In 1931, the Lithuanian and Latvian journalists' organizations created a similar alliance (Lauk 1993: 138). In the next year, an Assembly of Latvian, Estonian and Lithuanian journalists' unions took place in Riga. The Riga Assembly adopted a resolution for establishing the *Baltic Press Association (Baltic Press Entente*) and to work out its statutes. Newspaper coverage of the event clearly focused on the new organization's role in shaping a 'unified Baltic public opinion' and furthering political co-operation in the Baltic countries. The first conference of the *Baltic Press Entente* was organized in Tallinn in June 1933. The statutes were adopted and the foundation treaty signed by the representatives of all three countries. Each country created a National Committee to represent the *Entente*. The chairmen of the National Committees formed the Board of the *Entente*. In addition, two committees – the cultural committee and the journalistic committee – were appointed. In the following years, these committees initiated some cultural exchanges and visits of journalists among the member countries. In October 1935, the national committees of the three Baltic countries, which were focusing on a *Press Entente* met and, according to the minutes of their meeting, decided that there must be more intensive co-operation, including the publication of mutually favorable articles. Delegates at the meeting also insisted that solidarity among Baltic journalists was of great importance.[7]

The *Baltic Press Entente*, however, never became a genuine mobilizer of public opinion. Crises in the domestic policies of the member countries did not favor the activities of the organization. At the beginning of the same year, a conflict had occurred between the Estonian National Committee of the Entente and Munters, the Latvian Foreign Minister. The Estonian National Committee declared its withdrawal, but later cancelled it. The Ministers of Foreign Affairs often interfered in journalistic contacts between the countries. The restrictive regulations in all three countries and the tightening control over the press by the authorities deprived the press of any initiative. After its sixth conference in Kaunas in 1938, the organization became inactive. An attempt to revive activities was made in 1940, when the *Baltic Press Entente* held its seventh plenary conference. Delegates called for the hiring of press attachés at all Baltic embassies. They also welcomed the publication of the newspaper *Baltic Times* in Estonia and *Correspondence Baltique* in Latvia, both of which were the brainchild of the *Entente*. There was also a discussion of a broader meeting of Baltic journalists in 1940 and the eighth plenary conference in February 1941 in Tallinn. The Soviet occupation in June 1940 cancelled all of those plans (Treijs 1994: 361–363).

The Fatal End of the Baltic Journalists' Associations

Development of journalism as profession in the Baltic countries was ruined by the Soviet occupation in 1940 and World War II. The Soviet authorities shut down the Latvian Press Association and all

7 State Historical Archives of Latvia, 3758/1/570a/3–16, pp. 18–20.

other literary organizations in October 1940. The Soviet Latvian Association of Writers and Journalists was established instead (later it became the Soviet Latvian Writers Association).

The Soviets did not close the Estonian Journalists' Union as they did with most of the organizations of the Independence period, but smoothly reorganized it into a Soviet type trade union. To be legitimate, the organization had to carry out the reorganization formally on its own. Therefore, at the extraordinary general meeting in July 1940, the EJU 'unanimously' withdrew from the IFJ and joined the Central Association of Trade Unions. At the extraordinary general meeting on August 18, 1940 the whole Board of the EJU withdrew and a new Board was elected on which the communists had a majority (Lauk & Pallas 2008). There were not many voluntary collaborators with the new regime among the 'old guard' of journalists. The Soviet authorities did not trust journalists who had worked in the 'bourgeois' press and sacked most of them. Journalists who had been involved in politics during Independence were treated as especially dangerous enemies. The Soviet authorities executed 37 journalists in 1940. In June 1941 – as punishment for their 'anti-Soviet activities' – many journalists were deported to Siberia and never returned. Several journalists were also deported to concentration camps by the Nazis during the consequent German occupation, and died there. There is still no information about the fate of 211 journalists who disappeared during 1940–1946. In this way, the profession was ruined. Editorial offices were staffed with people who were loyal to the Soviet authorities but more often than not had no journalistic experience whatsoever. Many of them could not even write correct Estonian.

The Lithuanian Journalist Union was immediately closed down after the Soviet take-over in 1940. Journalists who did not agree to collaborate were executed or deported to Siberia. Nazi authorities also imposed strict control over the local press in 1941–1944. A few prominent journalists were sent to concentration camps. After WWII, most of the influential journalists fled Lithuania from the returning Soviet regime. In 1946, the Lithuanian Journalist Union was re-established in Germany, at the Hanau refugee camp, with over 200 members. In 1953, the union was renewed in New York and included 300 members in 1973 (Raguotis 1992:17). Those who stayed in the country either had to submit to the Soviet ideology and serve the totalitarian regime or became involved into anti-Soviet resistance.

Conclusions

The development of journalism as a cultural institution in late 18th and 19th centuries plaid a key role in the emergence of the national consciousness and the nation-state in the Baltics. The national press served as a platform of cultural public sphere for emerging civil society. Journalists became important public figures in all Baltic countries of the period. For instance, most of the signatories of the Lithuanian independence declaration that was signed in 1918 were either editors, journalists or contributors, including Jonas Basanavicius, editor of *Ausra*. The Prime minister of Estonia was an editor of the national daily. The fact that journalists were working together with the political elite, often supporting the state authorities, and construction of nation-states was typical for all three countries. Journalism as an occupation in the Baltic nations started to take shape in the last decades of the 19th century. In Latvia and Estonia, many developments occurred in parallel due to similarities in their political and cultural histories. Both countries started to develop into nations in the middle of the 19th century but had never had their own state. Both nations were ruled by the same foreign rulers; their intelligentsia, who began publishing national newspapers, started to develop only in the second half of the 19th century. In both countries, the literacy rate was high and printing technology relatively largely spread, which formed the conditions for the emergence and development of the press. By the last decade of the 19th century a critical mass of journalists emerged who clearly expressed their aspirations to be the representatives of an occupation. About 50–60 years passed from the appearance of the first full time editor to the establishing of Latvian and Estonian journalists' associations in 1917 and 1919, respectively.

The cultural, political and economic situation of Lithuania, on the other hand, was less favorable for its press, which could not develop in the country because of the ban on publishing in the Lithuanian language from 1864 to 1904. In addition, the literacy rate and economic conditions that were necessary to make journalism a massive phenomenon were lacking. Therefore, Lithuanian journalism developed as a diaspora press outside the country's territory in the U.S. and Lithuania Minor. The first journalists' organization was also established in the U.S.; somewhat earlier than in Estonia and Latvia because of more favorable conditions.

From the beginning of the 20th century onwards, journalism in the Baltic nations developed along similar routes. Journalists strove for legitimization of the developing occupation: setting up professional associations, discussing the occupational standards and defining the professional values, trying to improve journalists' education and seeking control over recruitment of newcomers. On the other hand, the associations functioned as trade unions – holding wage negotiations, pressed for collective employment agreements (in which only Latvian journalists succeeded) and taking care of journalists' social guarantees.

All the Baltic journalists' associations were also involved in politics both through individuals (several high political figures were former journalists) and through their journalistic activities. During the 1920s and 1930s the activities of the journalists' associations were largely directed towards supporting their countries' foreign political interests, first of all to develop Baltic public opinion and strategic alliance of Baltic Entente. Unfortunately, this political project was unsuccessful for many reasons.

During the authoritarian regimes, journalism and journalists were under the strict control of the State authorities and the associations collaborated with them. Legal steps towards more regulation of press were taken because of external threats mainly coming from the Soviet Union.

The beginning of WWII and the consequent Soviet occupation in the summer of 1940 were disastrous for journalism and journalists in the Baltic countries. The free press and the generation of experienced journalists of the Independent Republics of Latvia, Estonia and Lithuania were destroyed and replaced with the Soviet press system.

References

Andrews, George Reid (1994), 'Comparative History.' In: Stearns, Peter, N. (ed.), *Encyclopedia of social history*. New York: Garland Publishing, pp. 162–166.

Baerug, Richard (ed.) (2005), *The Baltic Media World*. Riga: Flera.

Balcytiene, Aukse (2006), *Mass Media in Lithuania: Changes, Development, and Journalism Culture*. European Journalism Review Series 8. Berlin: Vistas.

Bulota, Jonas (1992), 'Periodines Spaudos Raida Lietuvoje' (Development of the Periodical Press in Lithuania). Uztupas, Vilius (ed.), *Zurnalisto zinynas [Journalist's Manual]*. Kaunas: Vilius.

Dooley, Patricia L. (1997), *Taking Their Political Place. Journalists and the Making of an Occupation*. Westport, Connecticut, London: Greenwood Press.

Gudaitis, Leonas (2001), *Zurnalistikos mokslas ir mokymas Lietuvoje 1922–1943 metais [Journalism Science and Education in Lithuania, 1922–1943]*. Kaunas: Vytautas Magnus University Press.

Hallin, Daniel and Paolo Mancini (2004), *Comparing Media Systems: Three Models of Media and Politics*. Cambridge: Cambridge University Press.

Hanitzsch, Thomas (2005), 'Comparing Journalism Cross-Culturally. Defining the Core Concepts for Empirical Inquiry.' In: *Conference Papers – International Communication Association. Annual Meeting 2005*. New York, NY, pp. 1–30.

Harro, Halliki (2001), *Changing Journalistic Conventions in the Press. Empirical Studies on Daily Newspapers under Different Political Conditions in 20th century Estonia*. Oslo: Faculty of Arts, University of Oslo.

Høyer, Svennik (1995), *Pressen mellom teknologyi og samfunn. Norske og internasjonale perspektiver på pressehistorien fra Gutenberg til vår tid* [The Press between Technology and Society. Norwegian and International Perspectives on Press History from Gutenberg to the Present Time]. Oslo: Universitetsforlaget.

Koszyk, Kurt (1966), *Deutsche Presse im 19. Jahrhundert. Geschichte den deutschen Presse*. Teil II. Berlin: Colloquium Verlag.

Lauk, Epp, Inta Brikse, Jonas Bulota, Ainars Dimants, Sergejs Kruks, Bronius Raguotis, Richards Treijs, Rems Trofimovs (1993), 'A Retrospective Look at the Development of the Media in the Baltics.' In: pp. 41–118.

Lauk, Epp (1993), 'Journalism in the Republic of Estonia during the 1920s and 1930s.' In: Høyer, Svennik, Epp Lauk, and Peeter Vihalemm (eds), *Towards a Civic Society. The Baltic Media's Long Road to Freedom. Perspectives on History, Ethnicity and Journalism*. Tartu: Baltic Association for Media Research/Nota Baltica Ltd., pp. 119–139.

Lauk, Epp (1995), 'Eesti ajakirjanike kutsealane organiseerumine. Eesti Ajakirjanikkude Liit (1919-1940) ja selle tegevus.' [Professional Organization of Estonian Journalists. Estonian Journalists' Union And Its Activities] *Opetatud Eesti Seltsi aastaraamat. Annales Litterarum Societatis Esthonicae 1988–1993*. Tartu: Opetatud Eesti Selts, pp. 206–246.

Lauk, Epp (2000), 'Eesti ajakirjanduse arengujooni XX sajandi esimesel poolel' [Trends of the Development of Estonian Journalism in the First Half of the

20th Century]. In: Lauk, Epp, Maret Mälk and Anu Pallas (eds), *Peatükke Eesti ajakirjanduse ajaloost 1900–1940 [Chapters of the History of Estonian Journalism 1900–1940]*. Tartu Ülikooli Kirjastus: Tartu, pp. 9–42.

Lauk, Epp and Anu Pallas (2008), 'Early Development of Estonian Journalism as Profession (from late 18th Century to 1940),' *Acta Historica Tallinnensia*, 12 (2) (*In print*).

Leitans, Ans et al. (1875), *Ans Leitana dzive, darbi un mirsana. Nelaikim par pieminu no vina draugiem pasniegta latviesu tautai [The Life, Work and Death of Ans Leitans. In Commemoration of the Late Man From His Friends, Presented to the Latvian Nation]*. Riga: Ernst Plates.

Nygård, Toivo (1987), 'Poliittisten vastakohtaisuuksien jyrkentyminen sanomalehdistössä. Sanomalehden toimittaminen' [Sharpening of the political antagonisms in the press]. In: *Suomen Lehdistön Historia II. Suurlakosta Talvisotaan.* [*History of Finnish Press II. From the Great Strike to the Winter War*]. Kustannuskiila Oy, Kuopio, pp. 92.-122.

Pallas, Anu (2000), *Harrastusest elukutseks: Eesti ajakirjanikkonna kujunemine aastail 1878–1940.* Magistritöö. [From Hobby to Profession: Formation of the occupation of journalism in Estonia from 1878 to 1940. Master's thesis]. University of Tartu, Department of Journalism and Communication.

Raguotis, Bronius (1992), 'Zurnalistu rengimas Lietuvoje' [Journalists' Training in Lithuania]. In: Uztupas, Vilius. (ed.), *Zurnalisto zinynas [Journalist's Mannual]*. Kaunas: Vilius.

Schudson, Michael (1995), *The Power of News*. Cambridge, Massachusetts, London, England: Harvard University Press.

Schudson, Michael (2003), *Sociology of News*. New York: W.W.Norton & Company.

Tilly, Charles (1984), *Big Structures, Large Processes, Huge Comparisons*. New York: Russell Sage Foundation.

Tommila, Päiviö (1988), 'Yhdestä lehdestä sanomalehedistöksi. 1809-1859. Toimittajat ja toimitustyö' [From one Newspaper to the Press. 1809-1859. Editors and Journalistic Work]. In: *Suomen Lehdistön Historia 1. Sanomalehdistön vaiheet vuoteen 1905* [*History of the Finnish Press I. Development of the press until 1905*]. Kuopio: Kustannuskiila, pp. 196–207.

Tosh, John (2006), *The Pursuit of History*. 4th ed. Harlow: Pearson Longman.

Treijs, Rihards (ed.) (1994), *Latvijas Republikas prese: 1918–1940. [Press of Republic of Latvia]*. Riga: Zvaigzne ABC.

Vihalemm, Peeter (ed.) (2002), *Baltic Media in Transition*. Tartu: Tartu University Press.

Weibull, Lennart (1997), 'The Need for Comparative Approaches. Some Perspectives on the Possibilities for Media History Research on a Nordic Level.' In: Salokangas, Raimo, James Schwoch and Kalle Virtapohja (eds), *Writing Media Histories: Nordic Views*. Jyväskylä: University of Jyväskylä, pp. 57–65.

Zelce, Vita (2007), 'The Establishment and Early Activities of the Weekly "Majas Viesis" in the Second Half of the 1850s.' Latvijas Arhivi, 1, pp. 137–160.

Zelce, Vita (1994), "19. gadsimta latviesu preses petnieciba. Rezultati un dazas izpetes problemas" [Investigation of the Latvian Press in the 19th Century. Results and Problems]. *Latvijas Vestures Instituta Zurnals*, 2, pp. 27–39.

Zelce, Vita (2009), *Latviesu avizniecība: Laikraksti sava laikmeta un sabiedrība (1822–1865) [Latvian Newspapers in the Context of Their Times (1822–1865)]*. Riga: Zinatne.

Part IV:
History, Memory, and Self-Perception

Robert van Voren

Lost History
Memories of pre-War Podbrodz-Pabrade in Lithuania

Foreword

The weather must have been quite similar, at the end of June 1941, when Nazi Germany invaded Soviet occupied Lithuania. I am driving to Pabrade 67 years later, searching for remnants of the town's Jewish past. The blue sky is partially clouded, the temperature is well above twenty degrees Celsius and the forest smells of summer. Endless stretches of forest intermitted with agricultural lands and the occasional lake guide me to the town. Birds whistle and, stemming from a country that is overcrowded, I enjoy the serenity, the endless stretches without human interference and the fact that forests are still forests and have not been reduced to parks. When entering the town I am greeted by the inevitable Soviet apartment blocks and a bit further down the road the Lithuanian Center for Asylum Seekers, with walls covered with barbed wire and a disputable reputation.

Pabrade, Podbrodz, was one of the larger Jewish shtetls in Lithuania, a rather poor yet thriving community with a population of some 650 families, about 3,000 people, earning its living mainly through an extensive wood industry and a smaller meat processing industry. Located 45 kilometers from the Jerusalem of Lithuania, Vilna (Vilnius), on the road to the even bigger Jewish community of Svintsyan (Svencionys) and next to the beautifully meandering river Zhemyane (Zheimena), it was for many Jews a holiday resort, and during the summer months the population would earn additional income by catering for the vacationers. Originally located in Poland, it had become part of Lithuania after Poland had been carved up by the Nazi Germans and Soviets on basis of their Molotov-Ribbentrop Pact of 1939.

In 1940 it changed hands again, now becoming part of the Soviet Union after Lithuania 'voluntarily' gave up its independence. Part of the Lithuanian Jewish population welcomed the Soviet Red Army, some because they believed in the slogans of equality for all, others out of fear that otherwise the country could be occupied by Nazi Germany with far worse consequences for them. This caused considerable resentment among part of the Lithuanian population. Especially those who before Soviet occupation already expressed strong anti-Semitic feelings used this as a pretext for more vigorous anti-Semitic activity. As a result tension between the two communities increased and reached their peak during the months before the German invasion on June 22, when the Soviet regime introduced terror in full force. Mass deportations of Lithuanians started just a week before the German invasion. Resulting anti-Soviet sentiments were easily translated into increased anti-Semitism, even though the percentage of Jews deported to Siberia was relatively higher than that of Lithuanians and Poles.

In spite of this political turmoil, there is no indication that the relations among the almost exclusively Jewish and Polish communities in the town of Podbrodz were more tense than usual. And even though anti-Semitism was probably more prevalent here as well, the violent eruptions that took place in some communities further to the West seem to have bypassed this shtetl and were mostly 'imported' by anti-Semitic activists and students from places like Vilna, who came to Podbrodz with the sole purpose to create trouble.

Extermination

However, the situation spun completely out of control during the summer and fall of 1941. The power vacuum between the departing Soviets and the invading Nazi Germans somehow triggered a disastrous explosion of anti-Semitism. Everywhere in the country, ordinary Lithuanians put Nazi policy into practice, sometimes even before being asked by the invading Nazi forces. In Kaunas thousands of Jews were killed, hundreds of them were beaten to death with clubs and iron rods at Lietukis Garage and brutally murdered in the Jewish district of Vilijampole, without any direct involvement of Germans. In the Eastern part of Lithuania, which was covered with Jewish towns, shtetls and villages, the Lithuanian, Polish and Byelorussian inhabitants turned against their Jewish neighbors with whom they had been living for many centuries. In particular, Lithuanian anti-Communist partisans, who had been fighting the Soviet authorities, played a vicious role and participated actively in many of the killings that would follow. In towns with hardly any Lithuanian community, Lithuanian anti-Communist partisans from elsewhere assumed a leading role in the mass murder of Jews. Some Lithuanians were so zealous in their killing spree that German officers complained and asked them to slow down.

Between August and December 1941 more than one hundred thirty thousand Jews were killed. In the region around Podbrodz and Sventsyan many thousands were rounded up, taken to pre-selected places in the forest and murdered. On September 1, all Jews in Podbrodz were first forced to move to a temporary ghetto between Boyarel and Arnion streets, west of the river Zhemyane. On September 27 approximately 300 of them were taken down Maluno Street to the shooting range Poligon further west of the town, and brutally murdered. A larger group was kept in Army barracks for period of ten days, living under terrible circumstances, and subsequently taken to the forest West of Novy Svencyan (Svencioneliai). There they were, together with almost eight thousand other Jews from the region, mowed down with machine guns and finished off by Lithuanian partisans, while the Germans stood by watching. The shootings continued for several days; the mountains of decomposing corpses covered with only a thin layer of sand made the earth move for more than a week.

Almost all of the remaining Podbrodz Jews were killed shortly after. Some were buried in mass graves; others were left to be devoured by the wolves. The Jewish community of Podbrodz ceased to exist, and the same counted for all of the other communities in the region. The Germans did not even have to make much effort to convince the occupied Lithuanians that Jews should disappear from the face of the earth.

Photo 1. The Pabrade monument Polygon

Why?

Nobody will ever give a definite and final answer to the question why things turned so bad that more than 80 percent of the Lithuanian Jews were exterminated. The Soviet occupation of 1940–1941 clearly increased the already latently present anti-Semitism, in particular because many equaled Bolsheviks and Jews, a view very much stimulated by the propaganda of the Germans and their allies among the Lithuanians. But this is only a partial explanation. Lithuania and The Netherlands are both on the top of the list of percentages of murdered Jews in European countries. In The Netherlands it took the country more than thirty years to look at its past in a more honest fashion and acknowledge that the Dutch population had not only consisted of heroes, and that in fact a sizeable part of the population had accepted the German authorities as the will of God, and that therefore in their view resistance was out of the question. Even worse, it was a Dutch senior civil servant who created the internal passport for the Dutch, which turned out to be so difficult to falsify that the Germans were thrilled; they took the man to Berlin to meet Hitler and be honored. This internal passport became a crucial tool in separating the Jews from the Dutch, and in laying the grounds for their deportation to Auschwitz, Sobibor and other extermination camps. Amsterdam had, like Vilnius, a large Jewish community of approximately 80,000 thousand persons, and only a few thousand returned from the camps, only to find out that nobody was waiting for them and that all their possessions had been nicely taken away by their former neighbors.

But there is a difference between The Netherlands and Lithuania. The Netherlands is covered by museums, memorials and monuments to remind the population of what happened to their Jewish compatriots. Every year during the evening of February 25, a large gathering of young and old people stand in front of the old synagogue in the former Jewish ghetto of Amsterdam, commemorating the February strike of 1941, when workers in the city refused to go out to work in protest against the first deportation of 425 Jewish men on February 22, 1941. This event is generally seen as the start of the *Endlösung*, the extermination of the Dutch Jews. And every year on May 4, at 20.00 P.M., the country comes to a standstill when one minute of silence is observed commemorating all the victims of the Second World War, including the larger part of the Dutch Jews. Children in school are taught about what happened, also about who participated in the deportations and who was standing by without interfering. There is no way a citizen in The Netherlands cannot know what happened.

When visiting Pabrade by myself in June 2008, I can find no trace of its Jewish past. Nothing reminds of its former inhabitants, not a museum, a monument or even a plaque on a wall. The only plaque I find commemorates the Lithuanians who were incarcerated in a building in the period 1944–1949 by the Soviet rulers. There is absolutely nothing left, it is as if the Jewish shtetl of Podbrodz never existed. I leave the town discouraged, full of sadness and dismay over this insensitivity to its troublesome past.

Only during a later visit in September 2008 am I more lucky, when the last remaining Jew in Pabrade takes me around and shows the places he tries to preserve: the remnants of the Jewish cemetery north of the town, the monument at the shooting range Poligon in the forest, the modest monuments at the other places where Jews were mass murdered, three of which near Pabrade alone. The monuments are hidden among the trees or in the fields, exactly the way this painful part of Lithuanian history is kept hidden away, and only thanks to foreign donors they were erected. No Lithuanian government has felt the need to take responsibility for this, nor have they felt the obligation to attend the annual commemoration in the forest near Svencioneliai, where the 8,000 murdered Jews are remembered. In 1994, September 23 was declared the National Memorial Day for the Genocide of Lithuanian Jews, and officially it has been commemorated every year since. However, the commemorations go by almost unnoticed, as much hidden away as the monuments themselves.

No Past, no Future

A country that has no past has no future. It can never learn from its past mistakes and develop measures that help prevent a repetition in future. A country that passively but purposely distorts its past and pretends to its citizens that they were only victims of occupying forces and not collaborators of occupying regimes, makes the same mistake, if not worse. It puts itself above the law, creates heroes of its population when they were not and does nothing to avoid a repetition in future. Lithuania continues to have a serious problem in dealing with its past, not only its willing participation in the mass murder of its Jewish population but also, later, in collaborating with the Soviet regime.

When telling people that thousands of people were murdered, it says very little. It remains vague, untouchable; it is only numbers and not human beings. The Netherlands is still coming to grips with the murder of eight thousand Muslim men in Srebrenica in 1995.

This Muslim enclave in Bosnia was protected by Dutch UN forces and occupied by the Serbian Bosnian Army led by General Ratko Mladic. Under the eyes of the impotent Dutch soldiers all the men and boys were led away and slaughtered, eight thousand of them, just as many as the Jews that were killed at Novy Sventsyan. Many Dutch veterans are now suffering from post-traumatic stress, and the country is still trying to understand how 'we' could stand by and watch how thousands of innocent men and boys were killed. But even in his case, when it is only thirteen years ago, the numbers become unimportant, it makes hardly any difference whether there were five or eight thousand victims. It only makes a difference when you see the names, the life stories, the photos of those who were killed. Then they come to life, they speak to you, they cry out asking you not to forget.

So imagine how it is 67 years later, when the names, photos and life stories are almost completely gone. The neighbors are gone, who stood by in terror, who watched the deportations and who heard the shootings in the forest. Fifty years of German and Soviet occupation followed, and the memory of those who formed half of the population of Podbrodz faded away. The only way to bring this back is by telling the story of individual members of the Jewish community, people who survived the war or managed to get away in time, and lived their lives in safety elsewhere. Their stories can bring Podbrodz back to life and restore the lost history of Pabrade.

The Story of Joe (Yossele) Narotzky

These memoirs came to me by sheer coincidence, if one believes in such a thing as coincidence. In the course of my work I developed joint projects with a South African expert, and during one conversation he told me his ancestors came from Poland, 'near a town called Wilno or Vilna.' I told him it was Vilnius, the capital of Lithuania, where I have been living for the past nine years. He was intrigued, and promised to find out more about the past history of his family.

Photo 2. Narotzky with Van Voren, February 2009

To my surprise and happiness he soon informed me that his uncle had written memoirs of his life in Lithuania, and at a next meeting he handed me a copy. The same evening I read them, and they left me stunned. It was the story of a young man who, together with his family, emigrated from what is now Lithuania but was then still Poland, just in time to escape the war and almost certain death in the forests north of Pabrade. It lively described daily life in the shtetl, and when reading it I became immersed into a life that ceased to exist.

Indeed, when reading the manuscript there is no way one can avoid this feeling of a world abruptly and violently ended. At the beginning the writer sums up the families he knew or was related to, carefully pointing out who managed to survive the war and who perished in the Holocaust. Not surprisingly, most people mentioned perished, including part of the author's family.

The memoirs of Joe Narotzky are not literature, yet they are a powerful monument to those who lived in Jewish Lithuania and those who are now purposely forgotten. These memoirs bring some of them back to life. I carefully edited them, and here and there I altered the sequence to improve the flow of the story, but when reading it you can hear Joe Narotzky speak, and you can envisage Podbrodz the way it must have been.

Joe Narotzky[1]

Memories of Podbrodz (Pabrade)

Introduction

It was a cold winter day in December, when a red-haired shy boy, Welvel Narotzky, aged 24, got married to Mirel Steingold, aged 22.[2] Welvel was the son of Yankel and Ita Narotzky and Ephraim Yosef Steingold. The marriage took place in Podbrodz (Pabrade); the Narotzkys came to Podbrodz as war refugees from a village called Piechonke.[3] Welvel met his bride in Novo Sventsyan (Svencioneliai) and originally came from Kluschan.[4]

The difference in that marriage and a lot of other marriages of those days was that it was a love affair, and not a shidduch[5], which most of the marriages of that day were. It was interesting, the way they met. Welvel's train used to go past the back of Mirel's house, and she used to admire him, with his bright red hair. On Purim[6], she wrapped a mon kuchen[7] that she had baked and threw it to him as the train went past. On his return journey, Welvel threw a stone to Mirel, wrapped in a letter, in which he proposed to her. He always used to joke that the mon kuchen was his downfall.

1 Joseph (Yossele) Narotzky, born September 3, 1919.
2 Welvel Narotzky, born 1894 in Smorgon, now in Belarus; Mirel Steingold, born 1896. The marriage probably took place in 1918 or 1919.
3 This must have been at the end of the First World War, when a considerable number of Jews fled Russia and settled in Poland.
4 Kluchan, now in Belarus.
5 Pre-arranged marriage.
6 The most important Jewish holiday that commemorates the Jews' salvation from the Persian prime minister Haman's plot to annihilate them.
7 A cookie.

My Parents

Welvel and Mirel are my late parents, about whom I have decided to write, and also about the shtetl Podbrodz where we lived up to the time we all came to South Africa.

My father Welvel was considered a learned boy, because although times were hard, Welvel had learned the Talmud[8] up to the age of 18, which was considered quite unusual in those days.

My mother, Mirel, was the daughter of Beile Steingold, the real Aishet Chayil[9] of the whole district, respected by both Jews and non-Jews. Bobba[10] Beila was well known as a very learned woman. All the Meshullochim[11] and visiting Rabbis used to stay at her house when passing through the town. After she became a widow she ran a bakery to support her children. When she became a widow two of her nine children were self-supporting. Her husband, Ephraim Yosef, was only 42 years of age when he died. He had been paralyzed during the latter part of his life. My mother Mirel said she did not remember a father who was well. She was only 14 years old when he died and couldn't remember seeing him walking. There were two sisters younger than my mother, Minna of 12, and Channah of 10. Her mother Beile also supported a bachelor brother who couldn't make a living himself.

Back to Welvel: For his wedding he bought himself a second-hand army coat. It was all he could afford, but without it it would have been too cold to get married. They got married on the 5th candle of Chanukah[12]. Naturally, there was no honeymoon.

8 The Aural Torah. Commentary to the Torah, the Jewish Holy Script, which was written only much later and forms the basic compendium of Jewish law and thought.

9 Aishet Chayil is a special tribute to the Jewish woman. This song, written by King Solomon, sings the praises of the 'woman of valor,' extolling her for her loves and labors and the light she brings to the Jewish home. The expression is used here to explain that the author's mother was a very good wife to his father.

10 Booba means grandmother.

11 Itinerant collectors.

12 Festival of lights. It lasts eight days (and every day a candle is lit in a special Chanukah Candler, and is usually around Christmas. It celebrates the Maccabees' recapture of the second Temple from the Syrian Greeks.

Photo 3. The grandfather of Joe Narotzky, Podbrodz, date unknown

Welvel had his own horse and cart for transport business. What he did those days was bring loads of goods for the local shopkeepers of Podbrodz from the bigger town of Vilna, which was 59 kilometers away. While on his way to Vilna, he could carry fresh fish from the lake or fruit in summer to the Vilna Market and from all that he made a meager living. He didn't have the transport business for very long, as he got a job with his brother-in-law, Chaim Mottel Steingold, in the timber business. Chaim Mottel was the husband of Chaye, Mirel's eldest sister. They lived in Vilna and were much better off than Welvel and Mirel. Chaim Mottel gave the job to Welvel because of his honesty.

The way the timber business worked in those days was usually as follows: the merchant would buy a piece of forest, have workers to cut the trees, and then cut the trees into timber. A bigger merchant from Vilna would then buy the cut timber from him and sell it for building material or export it to Germany.

The earliest days of my memory date back to when I was almost three years old and my little brother Itzinke died of meningitis. He was 9 months old at the time. My mother took him to Vilna by train, trying to save him, but they could do nothing for him. About two years after that my sister Marsha was born.[13] I also remember that

13 Marsha Narotzky was born on May 8, 1924.

day. I was with my grandparents, when my Dad came to fetch me. He said to me, 'Yossele, we must go home now, because we've got a little girl, a sister for you.'

Our House

We lived at that time in a street called Swienciamer Gas[14]. Our house was the last in the street. Although I was very young at the time, I remember the house very well. My mother ran a bakery in the house that Marsha and I grew up in. She also had a confectionary in town. She had a baker and confectioner to make up the stocks for the shop while my Dad was working at his timber job.

In the middle of the wooden house here was a big built-in oven made out of bricks. In front of the oven was a dining room with a dining table and chairs. At the back of the big oven was the bakery, and also the kitchen where the kitchen utensils were kept. On the left-hand side was the bedroom. There was only one bedroom, and on the right hand side of the dining room and the bakery/kitchen combination was a summer bedroom, where we used to move during the months of June and July, when it was too hot in the bakery house to sleep in. However, it was lovely and warm in winter. Almost the whole front of the house had a big wooden stoep[15]. It was quite an old house at the time.

On the left side of the house, and partially in front of the winter bedroom, we had a little garden with 6 or 7 cherry trees. Everything was fenced with a wooden fence. One summer, I remember we had a huge crop of cherries, we took them off the trees in bucket loads – you can imagine how much jam Mommy made to have with Russian tea, especially in winter when the samovar was standing in the middle of the table in the dining room. We drank a lot of Russian

14 Now Svencioniu gatve.

15 Afrikaans for porch. Stoep is an originally Dutch word and means 'sidewalk.' Bobba Beila were married, they still had another two or three children after his paralysis.

tea. There was also a yard at the back and we had our own well for water. There was a stable for a horse, and the cart was standing in the yard. Right next to the yard, on the right hand side, was a piece of ground, I am sure it was more than an acre in size. The toilet was in the yard. There was no such thing as a bathroom in the house. There was no sewage. We had to bring a bucket of water from the well for the household requirements.

The Family of Grandmother *Bobba* Beila

As I said, Bobba Beila had nine children. Actually she had ten, but the tenth one died as a baby. Although her husband Ephraim Yosef was paralyzed from an early age, only a few years after he and

The eldest son, Nochum Yankel, and his wife, Auntie Fanya, lived in Riga. I only saw Uncle Nochum Yankel once, but I never saw Auntie Fanya. I've never ever seen a photo of her. They managed to survive the Holocaust.

The second son, Chloine Mendel, and his wife Tzirrel, sent their eldest son Joe to South Africa. Their daughter Zahava went to Israel. They lived in a small town called Krzywitzky[16] with three other children. They lost their lives in the Holocaust.

The third child was a daughter Chaya. She was married to Chaim Mottel, also Steingold, because he was the first cousin. They lived in Vilna. In about 1934 they moved to Riga. They had two sons and a daughter. They all died in the Holocaust.

The fourth child was a daughter, Reizel. She married Rephoel Trachtenberg, a baker. He had his bakery in his house and aunt Reizel ran the shop in town. She was short and fat. She did a great favor to our family by saving my sister Marsha from drowning, when she stepped down into a deep hole while swimming in the river and Reizel was there to pull her out. Uncle Rophoel was a small and thin man, weighing about 50 kilos, but he was a machine by

16 Current name unclear.

himself, capable of doing more work than two machines. He was fast like lightning and could work through the night, baking rolls, beigels, cinnamon buns, French bread, challah[17], white bread, brown bread and black bread. The bread was baked in big loaves and sold during the same day. Where he got his energy from, I don't know. He made a small-town living, but he wasn't rich. Aunt Reizel died before war broke out from blood poisoning from a rusty nail. There were no antibiotics in those days. Uncle Rephoel and two sons died in the Holocaust, and their daughter Rivka survived the concentration camp. She married in Germany when the war ended, to someone called Miechyk, who also survived the concentration camp. They then went to America and settled in Chicago.

Their fifth child was a daughter, Pere Hinde. She married a Rabbi, but she died shortly after their marriage. They had no children. He remarried shortly after her death.

Uncle Zalman was the sixth child. He married Keile Silverman. They had four children, and they lived in South America. We were very close to Uncle Zalman's family.

My mother, Mirel, was their seventh child.

The eighth child was a daughter named Minna. She was married to Hessel Gordon. He was the richest man in Novo Sventsyan.[18] They had three children. The whole family perished in the Holocaust.

The ninth child was a daughter named Channa. She married Moshe Feinberg. She inherited Bobba Beila's house and bakery. Chana was 30 years of age when she got married. Shortly before the war broke out they went to settle in Israel. They were the parents of Bella Pickman and the late Sholem Feinberg.

Bobba Beila had six daughters and one house. She promised the house to each son-in-law, but gave it to none, only to be inherited by the youngest daughter Channa after Bobba Beila's death.

17 A braided loaf baked in honor of Shabbat.

18 Now Svencioneliai.

Zaida Yankel and Bobba Ita's Family

Their eldest child was a daughter, Chaya Rivka. She was nearly 40 when she married a younger man, who was good for nothing. He left her about a year after their marriage, and they later divorced.

Their second child was a daughter named Razel. She remained a spinster. The eldest two daughters perished in the Holocaust in Podbrodz.

Their third child was my father, Welvel.

Their fourth child was a daughter, Meitke. She married Dovid Kopelowitz and lived in Krzywicz[19]. It was a shidduch made by Uncle Chloine. Meitke had one son. They all died in the Holocaust.

Their fifth child was a son, Zelik. His wife name was Zelda. They had no children. Both died in the Holocaust.

Their sixth child was a son, Itzka. He died at the age of 18.

Their seventh child was Uncle Boruch, who married Sora Riva. They had three children. One died in the Holocaust. Uncle Boruch and Auntie Sora Riva and one son survived the Holocaust and went to live in Israel. They had a son, Moishe, in Israel.

Unlike Bobba Beila, who had six daughters and got them all married, Zaida Yankel had less luck with his three daughters. The younger one of three daughters, Meitke, managed to get a husband, but Zaida Yankel had to give his son-in-law bills for 'Nadan'[20] because he had no cash. After the wedding Meitke got hold of those bills and brought them back to her father.

19 Current name unclear.
20 A dowry.

Podbrodz

Podbrodz was inhabited by 300 Jewish families and 350 Polish families[21]. There were two rivers passing through the centre of Podbrodz. The small river, the Dubinks[22], merged into the larger one, the Zhemyane[23], and there were three wooden bridges. The name Podbrodz in Yiddish was Podbrodze. In Polish Pod means 'under' and Brodzie means 'beard' or 'under the beard.' The story goes that Napoleon passed through Podbrodz and when his soldiers crossed the river Zhemyane, the water reached them till under the beard, and that is where the name came from. There were two Shuls[24] in Podbrodz. One was an old wooden Shul. It looked quite old, it could have been about a hundred years old[25]. There was a new Shul built of bricks, and that Shul was built about five years before we left for South Africa.[26] It took about two years to build it, on account of the shortage of funds. Podbrodz had seven streets. Every street was named after an adjoining town – like Vilna Street, Swienciany Street – except the main street in the centre of the town that was called Pilsudski Street[27], named after the Polish hero and Prime Minister, Marshall Pilsudski. There were three double story buildings in the main street. The others were just wooden houses with shops attached to them – shops in front and living quarters behind. There was even some empty ground in the main street where things grew, so the ground in the main street couldn't have been expensive.

On a market day the shops in the Market Street, Vilna Street, were more busy than the shops in Pilsudski Street. Monday was market day in Podbrodz and nearly everybody in Podbrodz depended on

21 According to a Podbrodz survivor living in the United States, Irving Engelson, there were also a Tatar family, a Kereile family and a few Polonized Lithuanian families living in the town.

22 Now called the Dubingiu upe (river).

23 Now called Zheimena.

24 Jewish synagogues.

25 This synagogue was standing at the beginning of Boyarel street.

26 This synagogue was standing on the Eastern bank of the river Zhemyane and was destroyed after the war by flooding.

27 Now Gaspariskiu gatve.

that market. Every Monday morning early, nearly all the smallholders from the adjoining villages brought their produce by horse and cart to sell at the market. They placed their carts in rows for the full length of the market. They unspanned their horses and stood them next to their carts and their horses fed there while the market was in progress.

There was a large variety of goods available on those carts, for example vegetables, fruits, eggs, butter, live chickens, turkeys, wool, mushrooms, dry beans, and many other things - all things that weren't sold in shops in those days. They could only be bought at the market. In turn, the smallholders bought in town what they required, like groceries, paraffin. It could have been a padlock, a piece of glass or grease for their wheels. They could certainly also spend a good deal of money on alcohol, and the local cafes would benefit too until the wagons would start moving in the direction of home.

There used to be stalls at the market. Gypsies would come and tell you your fortune for a few grozsy[28]; even magicians and fire-eaters would show their skill for just a few grozsy. 39 Zloty was a pre-war pound sterling, and 100 grozsy was 1 zloty.

Then there used to be the Jewish dealers who used to go to all the markets. Monday it was Podbrodz. Novo Sventsyan had markets twice a week. It was a bigger town, and I think the markets there were on Tuesdays and Fridays. The dealers who used to buy at the markets had certain outlets for those articles and they used to make a few zloty. I remember one of the things they used to sell was pig's hair (chazer hor). I don't know for what purpose it was required. They would carry their wares in their hands. They used the train for their transport. These Jewish dealers would have their meals at Bobba Ita's house.

In the afternoons before catching their train, the Jewish dealers played cards. They hardly ever had to pay for their train journeys. They already knew the conductors well and they used to 'schmuchel'[29]. Occasionally they would get caught and pay a fine.

28 As the region was part of Poland in those days Polish currency was used.
29 Yiddish for 'cutting a deal.'

On a Monday there was also a horse market, but the horse market usually finished earlier than the general market. The horse market was separate from the general market. It was on one – [the Eastern] – side of the river, while the general market was on the other side of the river. There were horse dealers who were experts in their profession. A smallholder who would bring a horse to the market, not knowing why his horse was sick and didn't eat and was thin, would sell it to the dealer for almost nothing and the dealer would fatten it up in a couple of weeks beyond recognition, and re-sell it at a good price, thus making a good living out of horses.

The Bod or Bathhouse

The Bod was the property of the Jewish Community of Podbrodz, or the Podbrodzer Kehile, and the Kehile used to lease out the Bod to the highest bidder for 12 months. It wasn't terribly profitable to lease the Bod and therefore the price the Kehile used to get for it was only 200 zlotys for the 12 months. The man who used to lease the Bod was called 'Der bedder' and he had a hard job boiling enough water for everybody. The Mikva[30] was a separate room in the Bod. Men and women went to the Bod on different days because there was not enough room for both sexes on the same day. The men used to bath on Fridays and the women on Thursdays. The soldiers that were stationed in Podbrodz[31], 1,000 men strong, used to go to the Bod on a different day and paid a special rate. Winter and autumn was a busier time for the Bod because in summer most people used to get to the rivers to wash, but the elderly people went to the Bod both in summer and winter. On Friday mornings people went to the Bod with dishes, towels and clean washing. The busier people used to go later and take less time, but some elderly men used to stay in

30 Mikva, or mikvah, is a ritual bath designed for the purpose of ritual immersion in Judaism.

31 Their military base was where the Center for Asylum Seekers is now located.

the Bod nearly all day or the same price. There was also a type of sauna, or you could have a bit of a steam bath for the same price by throwing a dish of water on the hot stones and that used to let off a lot of steam. So for a few groszy, one could enjoy oneself.

Another practice in the Bod was also mainly practiced by elderly people: they would take turns to whip each other, or as it was called in Yiddish 'besimmen.' One person would lie down flat on his stomach and his friend would besim his back and then they'd change over.

There was no sewage in Podbrodz, but the Bod had pipes and taps. I don't remember exactly how it worked, but I think the water was pumped from the river into the boilers and the boilers would be heated, and then the pipes would transport the water from the boilers to the Bod.

The Holiday Resort

Podbrodz was a dacha place, or a small holiday resort, due to its position on the edge of the forest and the two rivers that flowed through the town. Podbrodz was the best holiday resort in the whole district. About 60 'dachniks'[32] would converge on Podbrodz during the summer and the school holidays. The dachniks nearly all came from Vilna.

A dachnik family would hire a dacha for the summer. They used to get away from the big town for the summer season to enjoy themselves for about six weeks in the country. The men normally didn't stay with their families in the dachas but would go for business or their profession to Vilna and used to come to Podbrodz for the weekend to be with their wives and children. The Podbrodz population benefited from the dachniks mainly by catering for them.

The dachniks were wealthier than the Podbrodz residents, and bought only the freshest and the best produce. Strawberries and

32 Renter of a dacha.

cream was a favorite delicacy among the dachniks – something most of the Podbrodz inhabitants couldn't dream of.

One year, in 1928, my parents sent Marsha and me to a dacha. When I was a little boy I wasn't a strong child, and no matter how busy my mother was running a bakery in order to make a living, she had to take special care of me. One day my mother took me to a doctor in Vilna to see if he could do anything to improve my physical condition. The doctor told my mother that I was a weak child and needed lots of care. My mother, being a pessimist, thought my health was worse than it really was. She thought that she was going to lose me quite soon. She told me later that she sometimes would look at me and cry, because she thought I wouldn't last very long. But to go to a dacha was out of the question. Who could afford such a luxury? And who had time for such luxury? But when I was in second or third grade at school my mother and father decided to send Marsha and me to a dacha, together with the Jewish maid we had, Dode. When they finally made up their mind to send us, the school holidays were already finished and my Dad had to go to my school and ask my teacher special permission to allow me to go. Marsha wasn't at school yet, or she may have been in first grade. The place chosen for our dacha was Geladnie.[33] That was the station where my Dad kept his timber. My teacher gave my Dad special permission, telling him not to worry, as I would easily catch up with my schooling.

There were only four houses in Geladnie. We moved into one of them. This particular place was a dacha because it was away from everywhere and everything, so that we couldn't run around or do sports, and maybe we could gain a few pounds in weight.

My Dad would be in Geladnie during the whole week, but we hardly saw him because he was busy with his timber business. H stayed in another house, something like a boarding house where all the timber dealers stayed. He showed me his timber business. I think that month was the loneliest month in my childhood, and I was glad when the month was over and I could get back to Podbrodz and to school.

I remember one incident when we ran out of food in Geladnie and one of my aunts had to make a special trip there to bring us

33 A village near Pabrade.

some provisions. What a dachniks we were, to have almost reached the edge of starvation, and to be the only two children in Geladnie, and not have a soul to play with! That is a dacha for you!

My School

I was about seven years old when I started school. It was a Hebrew School and we paid for our education and for our own books. It was in Krol's Building on the first floor of a doublestory brick building right in the centre of Podbrodz. Had I chosen to go to the Polish school, education would have been free. When I first started school I could already do a little reading and writing, because my parents had hired a private lady teacher for about six month who coached me. Her name was Fanny Krol, and she was a half-sister to the owner of the building where the school was situated.

Photo 4. Joe Narotzky at school,
front row, fourth from right with white blouse

We lived in the last house in Swienciany Street[34]. The school was in the centre of town, so it was close to one kilometer for me to walk in each direction.

The school was not situated for very long in Krol's building. It moved to the last house in Kameliszky Street[35] into a house called Kamin's House. Generally, the school was roomier, but it was further away. I had to walk the full length of Swiencany Street and then turn into Melisaky Street[36] and walk its full length back, and for a little boy like me at that time, it was rather a long walk each way.

In winter I would wear a heavy coat and carry a lot of books on my shoulder in a shoulder container. I was very frightened of dogs in those days because we didn't have a dog at home.

The school at Kamin's House was a wooden house. It was situated there for about a year, after which the school moved into another house in Kameliszky Street, about halfway down the street. We didn't stay there long either. Then the Jewish community of Podbrodz bought a house in Kiesimer Street[37], right next door to my aunt Bobba Ita and my uncle Zeida Yankel. It only had four rooms and a teacher's office. I don't know how everybody fitted into that house. What I remember is that two classes of children occupied each room. Marsha started going to that school too.

Some time later we sold our house in Swienciany Street and we moved into the centre of town in Pilsudski Street, and from then on it was a pleasure because the school was only about ten minutes walk from home. Occasionally I slept over at Bobba Ita's house, and that was right next door to the school.

34 Now Svencioniu gatve.
35 Now Stotes gatve.
36 Current name unclear.
37 Current name unclear.

Photo 5. Joe Narotzky, eighth from right in the back row, Masha fourth from left in the front row

Tarbut[38]

Tarbut was a Hebrew and Zionist organization where Hebrew teachers were trained to teach in Hebrew schools. They only spoke Hebrew to us. Polish teachers, also Jewish, spoke Polish to us and our Yiddish was only spoken to our parents at home, so by going to a Tarbut School right up to seventh grade I became fairly fluent in Hebrew. There were a few teachers in our school who were not trained by Tarbut.

One teacher's name was Shukstulsky. He completed Hebrew High School in Vilna and was fairly fluent in Hebrew. He was a big fellow, about 28 years old and married, with a little boy of about

38 The Tarbut movement was a network of secular, Hebrew-language schools in parts of Poland, Romania and Lithuania. Its existence was primarily between World War I and Two, although some schools affiliated with the movement continue to operate today.

3 or 4 years old. He was quite strict with his pupils. He had a loud mouth and we were frightened of him. His teaching left a lot to be desired.

He used to give us marks and had made up a lot of his own secret signs so that we wouldn't understand what they stood for. He had such a lot of these signs that he finally didn't remember himself what they meant and he became completely mixed up with our marks. I recall once answering my oral questions very well. He had me down for a very bad mark, but he gave me a chance to re-answer and my mark came back to the top again. This time he marked it correctly.

On Monday, Market Day, Mr Shukstulsky would stay away from school from about 10 AM. He would go and help a widowed lady who had a chemist's shop and sold patent medicines. There was another chemist in Podbrodz that made up prescriptions and nothing else. These two chemists differed completely. Eventually the parent's committee who ran our school fired Mr Shukstulsky and placed a proper Tarbut teacher in his place.

We then had a teacher by the name of Mr Kopelowitz. He was about 45 years old and had two daughters and a little boy. He taught us religious subjects: Chumash and Tanach[39]. He couldn't speak Polish at all. If someone spoke Polish to him, he answered the person in Russian, which is quite similar. Mr Kopelowitz was so excellent in his subject that he knew the Chumash and Tanach by heart. If you opened a page in any Chumash or any Tanach and read two or three words for him, he was able to tell you what was written further. He was also able to tell you what Tanach or Chumash it was, the name of the Perek and the number of the Pasuk[40]. But unfortunately his teaching career didn't last for very long. He contracted yellow jaundice, which was fatal at that time, and he died within a day or two after his wife. Mr Kopelowitz was not a Tarbut teacher either. We then had an elderly teacher who we used to call the Rabbi. He wasn't a proper Rabbi, but he taught us Gemora[41], Tanach, and he

39 Chumash is one of the Hebrew names for the *Five Books of Moses,* also known as the Torah. The Tanach is the Bible used in Judaism.

40 Perek is chapter, Pasuk is phrase.

41 Part of the Talmud.

lower classes to read in the Siddur[42] and Chumash. He was in his 60's and was very poorly paid. He used to earn only about 30 zloty a month. He was a widower, and lived with his son, a tailor.

The Rabbi's name was Rabbi Ziml Itzik, and most of the week he could only afford to eat black bread, potatoes, sour milk and herrings. It was quite pitiful. During the school holidays he used to go to the dachas to give private lessons in religious subjects to the dachniks. He subsequently told us that at the dachas the parents of his pupils would offer him lunch. Sometimes he accepted the offer and enjoyed a decent meal that he couldn't have at home. Sometimes he would refuse, saying he wasn't hungry, because he felt it wasn't nice to keep on accepting, but in fact he was starving. He would tell us also that he couldn't believe how well the rich people ate. That's how poor he was.

The payment of school fees gave difficulties to ninety percent of the parents. The great majority of the parents were poor, and some pupils would come to school with torn shoes, but the parents made every effort to send them to the Hebrew Tarbut School. The majority of pupils were in arrears with the school fees, and it occasionally happened that most of the pupils were sent home to fetch their school fees, as the teachers depended on those few zloty as their livelihood. A teacher whose income was, let's say, 150 zloty a month, some months only received 100 or 120 zloty. The children were from big families, and could never get straight with their payments. Not every pupil paid the same amount of school fees. They were supposed to pay according to what they could afford, and it sometimes happened that pupil who couldn't pay Tarbut school fees had to leave and go to the Polish School, which was free of charge.

Almost each pupil possessed one pair of shoes, and when that pair of shoes needed repair, that pupil would stay away from school while his shoes were being repaired. A friend of mine once borrowed a pair of my shoes, because he wanted to have his photo taken, and his shoes were not good enough for that purpose.

42 Prayer book.

The Fire Brigade

The Fire Brigade was a voluntary organization in Podbrodz. The town couldn't afford a full-time paid Fire Brigade, and there was actually no need for a full-time one, so young men, both Jewish and Polish, were voluntary firemen.

In the centre of Podbrodz was the fire brigade hall, which was used to put on theatrical shows, and later used for silent films, and then talkies[43].

For putting out fires, the Fire Brigade had about 10 or 12 long wooden barrels, mounted on carts. Each cart would be spanned to a horse. The carts were always full of water. There were one or two pumps with long pipes attached to each pump and during a fire the pumps pumped water out of the barrels onto the object that was burning. However it had to be done by hand, and that was a hard job, because each pump had to be operated by two people.

When it was known that there was a fire somewhere, a big bell like a Church-bell was rung and all horses in the nearest vicinity and in the street had to be brought as soon as possible to the fire brigade. Anyone who refused was given a fine.

The houses of Podbrodz were nearly all made of wood and were all prone to fire, as the ovens were all inside the houses and were using wood. The danger was great, yet in my lifetime in Podbrodz, as far as I remember; there was only one fire in which the fire brigade failed to save the house. The house was near the river and the army came to help. They made up a chain with buckets, but all that was in vain. In another fire that broke out in a forest not far from Podbrodz everybody ran to the scene and threw sand on the fire and helped to extinguish it.

43 Films with sound.

The Jewish Theatre

There were three halls with stages in Podbrodz in which theatre plays could be staged. The biggest one of the three was the Fire Brigade Hall, which was made of bricks. The other two were wooden and all three were not much more than 4 walls, a roof and a stage.

The last one to be built was the Jewish Library Hall. It was situated on the same ground as the Hebrew school. The seats in the halls consisted of hard, wooden benches that could be moved or taken away. There were no change rooms at the back and the make-up was done on the stage before the act, or behind the stage. The curtains were also of poor quality.

Photo 6. Members of the Jewish Theatre from Vilna in Podbrodz

I don't remember how many dramatic societies there were in Podbrodz, probably one or two. A Jewish play was held approximately every three or four months. Some of the acting was quite well done, although those taking part were not professionals. It was usually done for charity. The price of the seats was reasonable. It was about 2 zloty in front, 1 zloty in the centre and half a zloty at the back.

All furniture needed for the stage had to be borrowed from Podbrodz inhabitants. The attendance was always good, and there were no reserved seats. Even young children liked watching the performances, but they could not afford the seats, so they used any opportunity to sneak in, and some of the kids waited outside the theatre to help or go for messages, after which they were allowed in.

In those days the theatre was the biggest source of entertainment. In Vilna there were two full time Yiddish Theatres with professional actors, who could sing and perform like experts. A lot of people from Podbrodz who had business in Vilna would go to the theatre when they had the opportunity.

An incident worth mentioning is that my Uncle Chaim Mottel Steingold once went to one of the theatres in Vilna with a few friends and relations. He hired the entire front bench. He was a big show-off. Another incident worth mentioning is about a certain Mr Dovid Krol, who came to Podbrodz from an even smaller town. When he went to the theatre, instead of facing the stage between acts, he faced the doors. When asked why he was sitting the wrong way, he said it wasn't nice to sit with his back to the audience.

Industry in Podbrodz

Before I left for South Africa in 1934, there were four industries in Podbrodz: a saw mill for timber, called Tartak in Polish; a small power station for electricity supply; a mill for the smallholders to mill their corn, etc., which was built long before I was born; and a mineral factory, which belonged to a certain Chaim Villian. The power station was built in about 1929 and the sawmill in about 1932.

All the industries employed very few workers. There were a lot of workers available from Podbrodz and adjoining villages, and very few could be absorbed. There were a few in the public services, a few on the railways, and that was all. Poles could also belong to the police force and the permanent army force.[44]

44 Jews were not allowed to work in public service according to a decision of the Polish government.

Anti-Semitism

Jews were allowed to work in industry so there were a few working at the saw mill and a few at the power station, but no Jews were accepted in public service, at the railways, at the police or in the armed forces. The Jews had to make their living mostly as tradesmen, shopkeepers and dealers in whatever they could. Poland was poor and times were hard, so life in the 1930s in Poland was difficult.

Most of the Poles loved alcohol, so most of their money was spent on alcohol. As a result their wives had to be around at pay-time, or else the pay would go in the wrong direction. The Jews were better able to make use of their income, and although many earned less than the Poles, they were better off. The resulting jealously brought about anti-Semitism.

In the Vilna University there were proportionately more Jewish students to Polish students. The Polish Students Organization, called Endecks, demanded quotas, that the percentage of Jewish students at the university should be based on the percentage of the Jewish population.[45] They also divided the class into two sections, for the Jews to sit separately.

In about 1933 Polish students from Vilna made some various demonstrations against the Jews, who they hated. They broke windows in Jewish shops and held anti-semitic meetings. It was soon after Hitler came to power, but they had no chance of doing anything serious on account of the large Jewish population in Vilna. One of the meetings was dispersed by an organized group of Jews. One of the student leaders named Wlotzlavsky ran away and hid in a toilet. A Jewish fellow caught him there and hit him so hard that he died. Since then, the Polish Endeck students held demonstrations every year on the day of Wlotslavsky's death.

There was talk of self-defense to be organized in Podbrodz, as a Pogrom was expected when Polish students were seen walking into the main bottle store of Podbrodz. (You could recognize students

45 The Polish National Democrats (the nationalists, Endeks, or Endecks) believed that Poland's Jews were an inimical factor in Polish life owing to the non-assimilated state of most of them, along with their dominance of the economy.

by the caps they wore). As no bottle stores could be owned by Jews, that's where they went, but nothing came of it. Perhaps the reason was that the owner of the bottle store, Grunievitz, had a Jewish mistress.

Shabbat

At least ninety percent of all shops in Podbrodz were owned by Jews. In Podbrodz all business came to a standstill on Friday afternoons. In summer they closed a bit later because it got dark after 9 o'clock and in winter it got dark before 3 PM. The men were coming home from the Bod to get dressed for Shul. They had their clean underwear on at the Bod already. The women would prepare the Sabbath meal. For Shabbat lunch they used to make a cholent[46], which was made up of meat and beans or barley, or tzimmes and kugel,[47] and cow's heel, etc. The meal was put in the oven on Friday afternoon, and would simmer through the night. It was ready to be eaten after Shul for the main Sabbath meal. The Sabbath main meal was always better than the rest of the week. A typical meal started with gefilte fish[48], then soup, then cholent, then stewed fruit or pudding. Challah was always baked for every Shabbat meal. If there were any Jewish families in Podbrodz who could not afford challah it would be provided by other families, and on Sabbath nobody went hungry. Jewish beggars who were in Podbrodz during Sabbath would be absorbed into Jewish homes to have good meals. After the meals nearly everybody needed to lie down to recover.

46 Cholent is a stewed dish enjoyed by Jews of all backgrounds on Shabbat afternoon.
47 Traditional Jewish dishes usually prepared for Rosh Hasannah, the Jewish New Year.
48 *Gefilte fish* are poached fish patties or balls made from a mixture of ground deboned fish, mostly carp.

Photo 7. Podbrodz synagogue - date unknown

Then there was the Shabbos Goy[49] who came down during Shabbat afternoon to make the samovar for a glass of tea or some other work. He used to get a piece of challah and a piece of gefilte fish, and sometimes there was somewhere half a zloty lying for him because money was not allowed to be touched on the Sabbath.

In summer on Shabbat, when the weather was nice, some people would go and lie down in the forest and relax.

On a Sunday officially all shops were closed, but one could buy anything at any of the Jewish shops. One only had to knock on the door, and one was let in, or else the owner of the shop sat outside waiting for customers, holding the keys in his hand.

49 The Shabbos Goy is an individual who regularly assists a Jewish individual or organization by performing certain acts for them on the Jewish Sabbath which are forbidden to Jews within Jewish law.

Tax Paying

Taxes in Poland were heavy. The Jews were mostly business people, and as most of the shopkeepers were poor and didn't keep books, the tax was estimated and they were made to pay beyond their means.

The Jewish people had to pay their taxes, let's say, within three months. The majority of them couldn't pay them, so the taxmen used to come and mark their belongings by putting tickets on the furniture and anything of value in the house. For example, if the house owner had two suits, and the taxman considered one to be enough, he could mark the other one. Certain things were considered necessities and could not be marked. They were then given, let's say, 60 days within which payments had to be made, or else those things were taken away to be sold. Each item was valued at a certain price and once it was taken away, it became the property of the Receiver of Revenue. Yet there was always a plan to overcome this. When the taxman was expected at the house, the house was found with a padlock hanging on the front door – the people were inside with the curtains down, watching the taxman and making themselves unavailable should he happen to look in through the window. Sometimes it couldn't be helped, and the furniture was taken away, as the owner couldn't find the money to settle the bill. An auction sale would then be held by the taxman. The victim who had lost his furniture would get a friend of his to buy back his furniture at the auction sale, usually for about half the price.

Armed Forces

Poland had a big army to support, and the government also paid the clergy. Podbrodz had one Church and one Minister, who was also an Army Captain. In Podbrodz there were a thousand cavalrymen stationed, plus a lot of permanent force officers and higher-ranking officers, and some more commissioned officers. They were all well paid, considering the way of life at that time. A sergeant in the armed forces earned nearly twice as much as a Hebrew teacher. The higher ranking officers lived in one area of the own. Whenever an officer rode through the main street on his horse, he had his own private soldier following him on another horse. The size of the army, one could see, was beyond the means of the country's finances, but it had to be paid for.

Army Wystzigi, or a type of army sports, were held once a year in Podbrodz sports ground. They were held on a Sunday in summer by the army unit that was stationed in Podbrodz and most of the people of the town turned out to watch them. It was free entry. The soldiers that were stationed in Podbrodz were all horsemen. It was a cavalry unit of a thousand men and they performed some fine feats on horses, besides many other sports. Prizes were awarded to the best performers.

I remember one incident. A wooden pole was put in the ground that was made very smooth. On top of the pole was tied a polony and a bottle of vodka, and the person who could climb to the top could take the polony and the vodka. A few soldiers had tried and couldn't even climb halfway and they gave up. Eventually one soldier, after a struggle, managed to get to the top and he got his prize. After he got down to the ground with his prize in his hands, another soldier came up to the pole and in half a minute he got to the top. There was no polony or vodka left for him, but he was rewarded with 5 zloty for his wonderful performance.

Unusual Professions in Podbrodz

In Podbrodz there were some occupations in the 1930's that we don't hear of anymore today. There was a man named Motte der Taiber (Motte the deaf man), he was an elderly man and was a woodchopper. In Podbrodz in those days one could buy a wagon of wood for the oven for a few zloty. Motte der Taiber would cut the wood up with a saw into more or less even lengths, and then chopped it up. Because coal was not being sold in bags, you had your coal when the wood burnt out. Everybody laid in a stock of wood in summer for the winter, and Motte der Taiber took more or less a day to cut and chop it. He charged about 2 to 3 zloty for it.

Then there was the glazier. When you had a broken window, you called him. He came to take the measurements, and then went home to cut the glass and put it in the window. That was all he did for a living. There was no pre-cut glass.

There was Tevke der Gazetchik, the only Jewish newspaperman in Podbrodz. He got his Jewish newspapers delivered to him from Vilna by train. He fetched the newspapers himself at the station and made his distributions. The Jewish newspapers were obtainable in other shops, but were only distributed by Tevke.

Other Professions

There was only one watchmaker in Podbrodz. His name was Hillel Ber Lubotzky. He couldn't make a living from his watch making as there weren't enough people wearing watches, so he had a place to bake matzos[50] and that kept Lubotzky busy the month before Pesach.[51]

There were two professional photographers in Podbrodz. The Jewish one was Chaim Lumewsky. He was a little man with a large hunchback. He had one of those wooden cameras mounted on a tripod. It took time for him to establish his camera into position to take photos. He was kept quite busy and he was one of the few better off people in Podbrodz. He married a girl about 20 years younger than himself. There was also a Polish photographer who

50 Matzos, or Matza, is a cracker-like flatbread made of white plain flour and water. The dough is pricked in several places and not allowed to rise before or during baking, thereby producing a hard, flat bread.

51 Pesach is a Jewish holy day and festival commemorating God sparing the Jews when He killed the first born of Egypt.

took photos mostly of soldiers that were stationed in Podbrodz. He did his business mainly on a Sunday when the soldiers had their holiday. The soldiers were far from home and had photos taken to be sent home.

There were a few bootmakers in Podbrodz. They made shoes to measure, as well as repairing shoes. They measured your feet in length and width and drew an impression of your foot. Very often the shoes didn't fit the wearer and they had to sell it to some other person, who was waiting for such an opportunity to obtain a pair of shoes cheaper. Ready-made shoes or manufactured shoes were available in shoe shops in Vilna.

There was one Polish bootmaker in Podbrodz who lived in a backyard, and he had his workshop at home. He had one wish in life and that was to be able to eat challah and butter with milk to his heart's content.

There were a few Jewish tailors in Podbrodz, who cut suits and coats to measure. Coats with sheepskin on the inside were a more specialized job. One couldn't buy ready-made suits or coats in those days in Podbrodz, but they were available in shops in Vilna.

In Vilna there were professional poultry pluckers, but in Podbrodz everyone plucked his own poultry.

In Vilna there was an occupation called a trigger. In Yiddish or in English it would mean a carrier who for a nominal fee would carry anything for you, even things that were quite heavy. Some of them operated at the railway station.

There were two blacksmiths in Podbrodz. They were both busy putting shoes on horses and repairing trollies, etc. There was only one sheet metal worker. There were no plumbers in Podbrodz, as there was no sewage.

There was one dentist in Podbrodz, a lady dentist. During the summer a lady dentist came to the dachas to do the dental work. She had a drill and treadle for filling teeth, and was that painful! Pulling teeth was done without anesthetics those days. I don't remember any dentist specialists in those days.

There were two or three horse and trolley taxis in Podbrodz. They used to wait at the station for every train arrival in order to try and get passengers. It was an occupation, because the railway station was one kilometer away from the centre of the town and to some places it was one-and-a-half kilometers. Unfortunately, sometimes the taxis went empty because most people couldn't afford that luxury and walked. The taxi owners charged only 2 zloty per customer. It was a poor man's occupation, because the horses had good appetites.

There were a few butchers in Podbrodz. A butcher's life in Podbrodz wasn't exactly easy. The butcher often bought a live calf or sheep at the market. Occasionally he had to go to one of the villages near Podbrodz to buy an ox or a cow from one of the smallholders. He would then tie the cow or ox to the back of his trolley and come back home at a slow pace. He would then take the animal to the abattoirs where the shochet[52] killed it. The butcher then had to do everything himself. He had to cut up the animals in the shop. He treibered[53] it, and the hind part was sold to the non-Jews. He then cut up the forequarter and hung the meat up on hooks. He also had a block and chopper and a balancing scale. There were no cash registers in Podbrodz by the time I left for South Africa in 1934. In butcheries there were no bandsaws yet either, and no automatic scales, or fridges of any sort. When the butcher finished selling his meat, he had to buy new livestock. Butchers in Podbrodz sold no poultry at all.

52 Ritual slaughterer of mammals and birds according to Jewish dietary laws.

53 A special way of preparing the animal for consumption. After the animal has been thoroughly inspected, there are still steps that have to be taken before the animal can be sold as kosher. The Torah prohibits the eating of certain fats and organs, such as the kidneys and intestines, so they must be removed from the animal. These fats are typically known as 'Chelev.' Chelev prohibition only applies to domesticated animals, such as cows and sheep. For wild animals, such as deer, this prohibition is not applicable. There is also a biblical prohibition against eating the sciatic nerve (Gid Hanasheh) so that too, must be removed. The removal of the Chelev and the Gid Hanasheh is considered complicated and tedious, and even more specialized training is necessary to perform the act properly. While the small amounts of Chelev in the front half of the animal are relatively easy to remove, the back half of the animal is far more complicated, and it is where the sciatic nerve is located. In countries such as America, where there exist a large non-kosher meat market, the hindquarters of the animal (where many of these forbidden meats are located) is sold to non-Jews so as to simplify the process. On the other hand, in countries like Israel, specially trained men are hired to prepare the hindquarters for sale as kosher.

There were also shepherds in Podbrodz. The job was available during the months of May, June and July, when there was grazing ground for the cows. There were some Jewish and Polish families who kept cows in the stables next to the house for milk. The shepherd used to come early in the morning and collect the cows and takes them to the grazing ground outside the town, he looked after them for the whole day. For each cow he was paid about 29 grozsy a day. He had a name for each cow. From what I can remember, the shepherd used to cut out whistles from tree branches and sit and whistle or play the harmonica for himself and his cows. In the evening he took them home again.

Cleaning the toilets was also an occupation in Podbrodz. There was no sewage, the toilets were built outside. An elderly woman had to empty the contents of the buckets from the toilets and bury the contents. She was paid about 50 grozsy. Toilets paper was unknown then, newspaper was used.

In an adjoining town to Podbrodz, there was a couple who decided to supplement their incomes by making home-made beer in a barrel. Before starting the venture, they decided that the business should be strictly cash and no credit whatsoever. They charged 1 zloty per glass of beer. When the beer was ready, the husband poured himself a glass of beer and drank it and paid his wife 1 zloty. She then poured herself a glass of beer and drank it and gave 1 zloty to her husband. They continued that process and paid each other cash – they both liked beer. It wasn't long before the barrel was empty and they only had the same 1 zloty that they started with. Only then they realized that the business wasn't paying.

When my Dad left for South Africa[54] he didn't make enough to support the family in Podbrodz, so my mother tried to keep the family going by having a cafe. In Podbrodz it was called Kaviarnia. It was a difficult task to earn a living from the Kaviarnia. She was allowed to sell beer to sit-down customers. On the quiet she used to sell vodka to sit-down customers. The three of us lived in a room next to the cafe and we ate in the cafe to save the expenses of running a house. At least my mother managed to keep the three of us going.

54 The author's father left for South Africa in 1929, see later in these memoirs.

She had one customer whose name was Meckiewitch. He used to come every morning and drink a quarter of a bottle of vodka which didn't touch his lips. He had a small thing to eat after a drink, and that was his breakfast.

Photo 8. The kawiarna of the author's mother.
Joseph Narotzky on the right, Masha on the left

As I mentioned before, to the average Pole the most important commodity was his bottle of vodka. Most of them couldn't afford to buy it in the bottle store, especially in the villages. To own a bottle store in Poland was a special privilege, which very few people were allowed. In Podbrodz there were two bottle stores. In the villages around there were some home brewers of that precious liquid which they could produce at about a quarter of the price. When caught, it meant jail – but that didn't stop them. There were informers who were paid for informing, but if an informer was found out, it could mean murder.

A Café Incident

A confectionery in Podbrodz was a place where you could sell rolls, beigels, cakes, bread, fried herring, fried fish, smoked fish, etc. A Jewish man happened to be in Podbrodz for business. He came to one of the confectioners and ordered a piece of fried fish with two beigels. He was served his fish and beigels, but he owner noticed that he wasn't eating it, but instead he bent down and was whispering to the fish. The owner said to him, 'I see you are talking to the piece of fish.' He thought maybe the man was mad. His answer was, 'An uncle of mine drowned some time ago, so I asked the fish if he had perhaps met my uncle.' The owner asked what answer the fish gave him. 'The fish told me that he has been a long time out of the water.' That was a sarcastic way of telling the owner that the fish wasn't fresh.

Nicknames

There were a lot of people in Podbrodz who had nicknames. For example: Peene die mufte. Mufte means a muff.[55] It originated when once Peene was going somewhere and he forgot his muff. (Muffs were worn then by men and women). His wife ran out as he was boarding his lift and shouted, 'Peene die Mufte, Peene die Mufte,' and that name stuck to him since then.

There was a man called 'Faive der ligner' (Faive the liar). That name speaks for itself. One of his stories was that he baked 20 kg of matzos for Pesach. When Pesach was over, he was left with 40 kg. Everybody used to bake more matzos than was used.

There was a poor family in Podbrodz called Soloveitzik. The three Soloveitzik children had poor appetites. There were two boys

55 A muff is a sort of case open on both sides and made out of fur, in which one could put ones hands in order to keep them warm.

and a girl. Their mother struggled to make them eat. When the three children sat round the table, their mother used this method to feed them:

> *Berelle a chap* (Berelle a catch)
> *Meishelle a zup*
> *Feigelle a pick.*

I don't know how anyone got to know this mother's way of feeding the children, but when they got bigger and they came to school each child already had a name. Those names stuck, and they couldn't get rid of them.

There was a family who carried the name Hoz (hare), right down to the third generation. At our school the grandson was called Hoz purely by inheriting it from generation to generation.

There was a Polish man in Podbrodz who walked straight. His surname was Barzdo, and the reason was because Barzdo was never seen sober. He was always referred to as Barzdo der Shikerer.

There was a man in Podbrodz called Moshe Patzieche. Patzieche in English means joy. I don't know the reason for his name. As a young man Moshe had to have an appendix removed. He was taken into hospital and just before the operation, he escaped and for many years his appendix never troubled him, until one day, in about 1933, we heard that Moshe Patzieche died of appendicitis. He was in his 40's. If he hadn't run away at the time, perhaps he would have had more years to live, or perhaps just as well he was spared from falling into Hitler's hands to be murdered.

Another appendix case that occurred in Podbrodz was after we came to South Africa. It was written to us in one of the letters we received from Podbrodz. There was a man in Podbrodz whose name was Michl Bavarsky. He was about 31 years old. He had a leather shop, and he was a very good friend of my Uncle Zelik Narotzky.He was newly married and had a little boy of about two years old. He was healthy and strong and well off, according to Podbrodz standards. One day he decided he didn't need his appendix, he thought it was an unnecessary evil and he wanted to have it out. He went to Vilna, made arrangements with his doctor and was admitted into hospital for the operation. The anesthetist applied the anesthetic but he wouldn't fall asleep. The doctor said that the patient was as strong as an ox, so the anesthetist applied much more chloroform than was necessary, and he never woke up from the operation.

Our Zionist camps

I was about 11 years old when we went with the 'Hashomer'[56] for our first camp. It was a place called Zatoka[57] about 6 kms from Podbrodz. He hired half a house from a smallholder. There were about 20 of us. We were the youngest section of the Hashomer. We walked the seven kms to Zatoka with rucksacks on our shoulders

We had a big room that was sectioned off into two by a big curtain to separate the boys and girls. We slept on straw mattresses, bags stuffed with straw.

During the day we swam, played games, had lectures, and cooked our own food. A boy of about 18 or 19 was in charge of the camp. We had a glorious time.

Zatoka was a village of about 5 houses. It is about half a kilometer from Bezdany[58] Railway Station. Bezdany is the famous station where the Polish hero, Marshall Pilsudski, then Prime Minister of Poland, made his historical raid. Before 1914, when Poland was under Tzarist Russia, a group of Poles under the leadership of Pilsudski

56 Hashomer Hatzair, the initial Zionist youth movement, was founded in Eastern Europe on the eve of the First World War. Many Jewish youth, affected by the process of modernization that had begun among Eastern European Jews, sought a means of maintaining their Jewish identity and culture outside the stifling barriers of the shtetl and of Orthodox Jewish life. On the other hand, they were troubled by the crumbling of the foundations of society around them and by the growing anti-Semitism that threatened their very existence. In its early stages the movement was strongly influenced by the Scout Movement organized by Baden-Powell and it embraced scouting as a basic principle to teach ghetto youth self-reliance, outdoor life and a love and knowledge of nature. Another important influence upon them was the Wandervoegel movement in Germany, which emphasized youth's independence and creativity.

57 Now called Santaka.

58 Now Bezdonys.

made a raid on a Russia train and got away with a fortune of money. That raid was regarded as famous in the history of Poland.

The following year I went to another camp, again about 20 of us. This time we went to a place called Szpinska, about 4 kilometers from Podbrodz. The smaller river that flows through Podbrodz starts from Lake Szpinska.[59] We stayed in a house of a local smallholder. He had a bit more ground than the average smallholder and was considered rich according to the standards of those days.

The camp was very similar to the previous year, except that one Sunday I was the lucky one to receive a lot of visitors. My Uncles Zelik and Boruch and my Aunts from Podbodz visited our camp. They brought cakes and biscuits for me. I gave all the cakes and biscuits to our camp chief, which he kept back for the day we walked home. We stopped about halfway from Podbrodz and we all had a party on the cakes and biscuits that my aunt and uncles had brought for me. I was highly praised by our chief for not being greedy, for sharing it with all the other campers.

Photo 9. A family outing. Joe Narotzky in the back, with a white shirt under his jacket

59 Probably this refers to Lake Spingla.

Matzo Baking

In Podbrodz there was no ready packed Matzo in boxes. Each family baked their own matzos. It all started about a month before Pesach and finished about a week before Pesach.

There were two houses in Podbrodz that were hired out for Matzo baking, with the right kind of ovens. During those three weeks, young and old were busy with matzos baking. Everybody helped each other. It was all done in the evenings. The minimum any family baked was 20 kgs. The matzos were rolled by hand with rolling pins. They were round. Every family had a special large basket to pack their matzos. There were some families who baked as much as 120 kgs. Some of the matzos were broken up for matzos meal and matzos farfel[60] in a thing called a steisel[61].

The Lodovmar

In Podbrodz there were no fridges of any sort, but there was a means of keeping food cool during summer. In June and July it was quite hot and for that the lodovmar was used. Lodovmar in Polish means an Ice House, which was prepared in winter for summer. It was a square area deep in the ground. It was about one-and-a-half meters deep and that was filled up to ground level with blocks of ice, which were chopped out or the frozen river. The house had four walls about a meter high about the ground and a roof. The front had a door that was locked. That was where the food was kept. The ice melted slowly during summer. As the ice melted, the flow of the lodovmar became lower and a ladder had to be used to go down for bringing food in or taking some out. Not too many families possessed a lovodmar.

60 Farfel is a cooked grain product.
61 A special pan.

Banks, Phones, Mail …

The Jewish shopkeepers in Podbrodz had to give credit, because their Polish customers didn't have cash enough, so they had to wait for the end of the month to get paid. However, that wasn't easy because when the customer got his pay, his wife was on his neck and his other creditors were also after his meager wages. There usually wasn't enough to go round. And if the wife and the creditors would not be around to intercept, there would be something else that could get first preference: that was his alcohol.

The Gemillus Chesed was an 'Interest-Free' Money Lending Organization. The funds for the Gemillus Chesed were donated, a lot of it from shnoddering[62] in Shul on Shabbat. All needy people could borrow a lump sum and pay it off on a weekly basis, free of interest, and when the money was paid back, another loan was obtainable.

Nobody in Podbrodz owned phones. One could make a call to someone who did own phone at the post office, which was a kilometer from the centre of the town. (for instance Uncle Chaim Mottel Steingold, who lived in Vilna, had his own phone at home). One had to go to the Post Office to book a call for a certain time and come again at that time to make the call. Calls were very seldom made. We used to send a letter once a week to my Dad in South Africa. I would walk one kilometer to the Post Office to buy a stamp for the letter. It was about 25 groszy. I never ever bought two stamps – I always walked a kilometer to the post office and a kilometer back to buy one stamp only.

There was a man in Podbrodz who walked to the station every day. His name was Kollie and he was a watchmaker by trade. He walked to the railway station every day to synchronize his watch with the station watch, that is about all he had to do. He married in his late thirties to a girl of the same age. She had a brother in America who sent money every month. There was no work in Podbrodz for Kollie in watchmaking, so he had to do something. Would you like to know what his wife was like? Plain ugly!

62 collecting

Preparing for the Winter

Quite a few preparations had to be made before winter. One of them was to put an extra or double window in every window frame. They were especially there for the purpose of keeping the house warm during the very heavy frosts that reached 35 degrees below Celsius. Occasionally it reached minus 40 degrees. Each window fitted well into a certain frame. They were glued on the inside of the room against the window frame with a wide and very sticky paper. A few decorations were put between the two windows.

Cabbage and cucumbers were pickled in barrels for the whole winter. Potatoes were buried in a hole in the ground. A lot of people grew their own potatoes, so they had enough for summer and winter. Sufficient wood was put away in a storage next to the house for the whole winter. Using coal for heating was unknown in Podbrodz, but in Vilna mainly coal was used. The reason is that Podbrodz had forests all around.

Bobba Ita used to knit woolen socks and gloves for the men. She had her own spinning wheel. She first spun the wool with the spinning wheel and the spindle at the bottom. It looked to me at the time like a highly skilled job to get the wool spun to the same thickness. Her wool was never dyed so her gloves and socks were always one color – light grey.

Podbrodz was in the snow a paradise for skiers, and for sledge riders, as Podbrodz was full of hills, a lot of them outside the town. We children took advantage of the situation. I used to be a keen skier.

There was another thing that I saw done in winter that I wouldn't like to do myself: there were two young Jewish men in Podbrodz. When the river started freezing and the ice reached already about two feet, they would jump from the ice into the water and swim.

I remember I also jumped in water once, clothes and all. There was a fight going on in a yard and I wanted to see what was going on, so I ran to have a look. It was either Rosh Hashanah or Sukkot, and I wore a new suit. Someone accidentally gave me a push and I fell into the mud with my new suit. Can you imagine my mother when she saw me!

Transport was a big problem between seasons. I know so well about it, because our family was engaged in transport. When they traveled with horse and cart to another town, and the first snow came, it was very difficult to get home. One needed a sledge for the transport. On the other hand, when one went with horse and sledge and the snows suddenly melted, one couldn't bring the sledge back without snow on the roads. But the snows normally didn't melt that fast, so it very seldom happened.

In winter it started getting dark at 3 pm in the afternoon. In summer it started getting light at 3 am in the morning, and it started getting dark at nine in the evening. You couldn't get o bed early in summer. In winter, during a full moon, when the countryside was white with snow, you could almost a read a paper or a book at night.

My Friend Ruvke Mirsky

In 1927, when I was in second grade, I had a friend Ruvke Mirsky. He went to America, either in 1929 or 1930. He was very clever in arithmetic, but a bit of a storyteller. He was about a year older than me. I believed all his stories. At the time I didn't understand such a thing as telling lies, so I thought that whatever he told me was true.

He told me that he flew an airplane (in those days there were no passenger planes), and that the airplane was of pure gold, and I sat with an open mouth believing him. Ruvke at the age of eight could already solve arithmetic problems that I didn't know how to start working out. Perhaps that's why I had so much trust in him. Some years ago I heard that Ruvke became a great professor or scientist in America, one of the greatest.

Novelties

In around 1930 a Jewish man in Podbrodz had his first radio. I remember seeing bare machinery, without a cabinet, with a pair of earphones. The man charged half a zloty to listen for half an hour. It was a great wonder to all of us to know that sound was transmitted without wires. I was dying to listen to this new miracle, and so were other boys and girls, but I couldn't afford the money. About six months or a year later Uncle Zelik Narotzky got himself a radio and I listened to it free of charge, and shortly after that it was no novelty as more and more people got radios.

Then there came the first lorry in Podbrodz. Three Jewish men bought in partnership a second hand lorry for transport. They were two brothers, Glass, and a man called Rautenberg. They earned very little from transporting with horses and trolleys. Before long the lorry was standing on brocks. I can't remember the reason, whether it was on account of government taxation or overheads, or the fact that they had to employ a driver.

Tropical fruit, like watermelon and grapes, were eaten once a year, on Rosh Hashanah[63] for Shehechiyanu.[64] Each person of the family received about two grapes or a tiny piece of watermelon. It was imported and very expensive, and that is all the great majority of people could afford. Fruit like pineapples, peaches, apricots and guavas I never saw until came to South Africa. The first time I saw bananas was on our way to South Africa, when our train stopped at station in Italy and bananas were brought up on to the station platform. We looked at them and we didn't know what they were. When we saw people buying them, somebody told us they were bananas. We couldn't afford the pleasure of tasting one of them.

My Dad was already in South Africa when I first saw a black man in Podbrodz. He was a driver of a panel van and he came out to Podbrodz promoting a certain make of floor polish. He came into our Kaviarna to eat. A crowd of boys and girls came to see what he

63 Rosh Hashanah: (literally 'head of the year'); the Jewish New Year holiday.
64 Shehechiyanu is a blessing in Judaism that thanks God for sustaining your live so that you could experience this moment of joy.

looked like. We had all heard of black people living in South Africa, but here we saw one in reality. I was the lucky one, because it was in our café that he ate. He spoke Polish. His earnings were 1000 zloty a month. That was an unusually high wage in those days, a small fortune. Hardly anybody earned that even in a year.

The Floods

One year in Podbrodz, when my Dad was already in South Africa, we had floods in Podbrodz. There were also floods in Vilna and other towns that had rivers. I was about 11 years old at the time. It was an unusual sight for me to see the two rivers of Podbrodz burst their banks. The water almost reached the walking level of the bridge, which was normally so high above it. The bathhouse was up to its windows in water and some gardens were flooded. The town itself wasn't under water as the banks of the river were higher where the houses were built.

The reason for the flood was that spring came too suddenly. It became warm too quickly and the snows and ice melted too fast, instead of usually melting slowly and freezing again by melting bit by bit. It didn't harm anybody, but this was unusual and fascinating for us youngsters.[65]

Eating Fat Meat

The poorest people would eat lean meat when they could afford it. The poor people used to buy an ox-head and feast on it. Others would buy the kidneys or a cow heel etc.. The 'better-off' people bought the fat meat at the butcher shops. My Dad used to eat very fat mutton

65 Apparently a similar flooding in the 1950s swept away the stone synagogue on the bank of the river.

with sauerkraut soup and enjoy it. We didn't even know at that time what cholesterol was. We understood that fat meat was healthy.

The Magician

Once a magician came to our school and performed his magic. It was a terrific show and all the children wondered how such things could be done. At the end of the show he showed us and explained all his tools of magic. It was so easy after he explained everything.

Another kind of magic was once told by a Chassid[66] who was telling about the magic his Rabbi could perform. He said his Rabbi came to a place where he saw a young man and woman dancing together. He considered that a great sin and became very angry. He immediately put a curse on the building that they were dancing in, that it should collapse immediately. The Chassidim[67] immediately next to him begged him, Please, Rabbi, let it stand. 'All right, let it stand,' the Rabbi was kind enough to say. That building is still standing to this day. Isn't it a great miracle?

Cigarette Offer to Zaida Yinkel

My grandfather Zaida Yankel Narotzky was a very Frumer Yid[68]. He used to smoke cigarettes but couldn't afford anything expensive, so he used to smoke the cheap stuff. There was a big difference in price between the cheap and the expensive cigarettes. Once someone offered Zaida Yankel an expensive cigarette. He took it, thanks, he

66 A member of the Chassidic community. The movement originated in Eastern Europe (what is now Belarus and Ukraine) in the 18th century.

67 Plural for chassid.

68 A pious and heroic Jew.

said, with a twinkle in his eye, I'll have to leave an enjoyable article like that for the Sabbath.

We had a Polish elderly woman who worked in our café as a servant. She smoked, but she couldn't afford to buy cigarettes at all. She used to take all the stompies[69] from the ashtrays in the café and break them up back into tobacco (these cigarettes had no filters) and roll it in newspaper, so she had her own cigarettes.

Bobba Mirel's Uncle

Bobba Mirel had an uncle who was a shadchan, a matchmaker[70]. He was a widower. He had to do other work for a living too, because he couldn't make ends meet from his matchmaking. He was once asked why he couldn't find a match for himself. The answer was: 'a doctor can't cure his own illness, but has to go to another doctor.'

Bobba Mirel's uncles were Chassidim, and most Chassidim liked a schnapps. This uncle of hers, at a party after a schnapps, said to a friend: 'I'll bet you a drink that you can't write a word with seven letters L in it.' After a bit of thinking, the friend said he couldn't, and asked what it was. 'Bemachalaklakot.' 'But that word only has 2 L's!': 'So I lost,' was the answer – 'in the meantime we will have a drink!'

Is This also a Jewish Tragedy?

There was a shogets in Podbrodz named Edek Matzkievitz. He was a small shogets but a big Anti-Semite. He liked to start fights with all the Jewish boys whenever he could. He was only 13. 'Jews go to Palestine' was one of his favorite slogans to shout. One day he heard

69 Cigarette butts.
70 A marriage broker

that his mother ran away with a Jewish barber from Podbrodz. He then calmed down, because someone told him he should also go to Palestine.

Panie Buck

Panie Buck meant 'Mr Buck' in Polish. He called himself that. He was one of the poor people who came to Podbrodz begging with other beggars. Somebody must have felt sorry for him and gave him a better shirt than the one he wore. He took off his old shirt and threw it away. It was a sight to see the lice were walking freely on his old shirt like ants, by the hundreds. Lice were available in Podbrodz, but this was a record.

Suicides

I remember some suicides in Podbrodz. The first one was while we were still in Podbrodz, and the second one after we left for South Africa. The first was a girl named Rose Shapiro. She took poison and killed herself. She had a boyfriend, his name was Welfke, the late Rabbi's son. They were both getting on in years and he hadn't had a job for years. Most of the young men of Podbrodz were out of work, and as she saw no future in her relationship, she took her life.

The second suicide was by a girl named Louisa Epstein. Her father was the richest Jew in Podbrodz. Louisa was a balebatisher[71] daughter, and she didn't work. There was no work to be found. There were no offices in Podbrodz, only government offices, and no Jew could get a job in any of them.[72] Louisa used to sit all day

71 A balebatisher is a man of middle-class respectability, who would never would resort to manual labor unless he had no other alternative.

72 As noted before, Jews were not allowed to work in public service.

and see to her nails, her face, her hair and her clothes. She was quite pretty and well dressed. Her parents could afford to give her good clothes. She used to crochet a bit. She could also play the mandolin. No young man in Podbrodz was good enough for her. I presume life was too monotonous for her. She poured paraffin over herself, set herself alight and jumped out of her father's building into the street and died.

My Dad's Miniature Writing

It was about 1928, or a year before Dad left for South Africa, that Dad read in the newspaper that someone wrote small writing on a post-card. He got interested in it and beat the record by writing the whole of Shir HaShirim[73] on a postcard. But soon somebody beat that and Dad thought he could do even better. That is when he wrote Tanach Mishlei, the whole Book of Proverbs, 7746 words on one post-card. I presume it was a world record – his name and photo was in a Vilna newspaper. He gave the postcard to the museum in Vilna. He then realized that his talents must not only go to the museum, so he wrote a post-card for himself as well. I remember when he wrote a postcard. He used to get up at 3.30 in the morning and do his writings. It took a lot of patience to write the Tanach Proverbs twice in miniature writing.

I am the present proud possessor of that postcard, and I hope to pass it on to my son.

73 Song of the Song of King Salomon.

Dad's Decision to Emigrate

In 1929 my Dad decided to emigrate. It was just as well his decision was made in 1929, because in 1930 all the gates for immigrants were suddenly closed throughout the world. He could see no future living in Poland, although a year before he had made a few hundred dollars in his timber business. It was considered a lot of money at that time.

He wrote a letter to Uncle Zalman Steingold in Messina, South Africa, and asked him to send him papers, because he wanted to immigrate to South Africa. Uncle Zalman wrote a letter back to him and discouraged him at first, as he had a hard time himself in Messina. Those days it was in the midst of a great depression. Messina has a hot climate. He wrote a letter back to Dad telling him that he must not think that South Africa, and especially Messina, was such an easy place to make a living, and that there are a lot of poor people in South Africa who were struggling. But Dad made his decision, his mind was set on going, so he wrote a letter back. Uncle Zalman was Dad's brother-in-law, Mommy's brother. He came to Messina himself in about 1925, through the efforts of his own brothers-in-law, Auntie Kalie's three brothers, the Silvermans.

'Dear Zalman,' he wrote in his letter, 'under no circumstances am I going to stay in Poland. If you can't send me papers, I will try to go to Argentina in Brazil, or Uruguay, or any place, as long as I can leave Poland. I have enough money for my fare.'

A letter came back from my Uncle Zalman: 'Dear Welvel, if you are that keen on going, I am not going to discourage you. I am sending out papers right away.' Immigration papers followed by return mail.

Parting with his father and mother, brothers and sisters, wife and children was difficult, but he went like a shot – nothing could stop him.

When he got to South Africa to Messina, he first took a job with Uncle Zalman's brother-in-law, Sam Silverman, as a shop assistant for ten pound a month, all inclusive. Only then did he realize that Uncle Zalman had said the truth – for going from the cold climate

Photo 10 . L. to r. Joe Narotzky, his sister Masha and his mother Mirel

of Northern Poland to the heat of Messina wasn't a pleasure. In Podbrodz he was considered 'a Yid a balebos'[74], with his own home and business. Here he was just nothing, working for ten pounds a month, away from his family, from his social circle and all the relations, while he had been making good money in the timber business. There wasn't even a Shul in Messina. But come what may, he decided to stick it out, although the black man was no match for his old social circle.

74 'Master of the house.'

He saved every penny he earned and within a year he saved another hundred pounds to add to the hundred pounds he had brought with him from Poland. He didn't have to send money to his family, because Mommy managed in Podbrodz on her own incomes, though poor.

About a year or so after his arrival, he packed his suitcase and off he went to Johannesburg. He arrived in Doornfontein, a purely Jewish locality, with about two hundred pounds in his pocket. He first took a job in a shop, but was looking out to go on his own. Some problems arose between him and his boss. His boss underpaid him. Dad didn't even know that he was being underpaid. When he realized what was going on, he nearly took his boss to court, but he didn't. He had heard that there was an outfitting shop for sale in Jeppe, and he decided to buy it. He knew that there were no fireworks there, but he thought it would be better than it was.

I was about ten years old at the time. Dad used to send me some used postage stamps which I was collecting. I was so proud of my collection. It was a craze in Podbrodz at that time. I was glad Dad was in South Africa. I was too young to realize the hardships he went through.

Within a short while Dad lost every penny he possessed in that business. Starting again from scratch, he started buying and selling empty wooden boxes, going around with a horse and cart. But he wasn't able to make a living. Only then did he start thinking going back to Poland. He wrote letters back home that he was thinking of coming back to Podbrodz. His father wrote back to him to go back to Podbrodz, but the timber business that had been going quite well went down the drain and nobody could make a living anymore at that time. A little later the timber business picked up, his old partner was going better again, and Dad decided to go back to Podbrodz.

He bought his ship ticket, booked his train ticket to Cape Town, packed his suitcase, and phoned for a taxi to take him to the station, but he left the possibility open to come back to South Africa, he still had no confidence in Poland.

The minutes were ticking past, as he was waiting for the taxi to come, about an hour later (he was boarding at the time in a house in Bertrams, owned by a woman called Rochel Levin) two old friends walked into the house and saw him sitting and waiting with his

Photo 11 – Joe Narotzky in the early 1930s

suitcase, ready to leave. They were very surprised. He told them that he had no option but to do back to Poland. The two of them thought he was mad. 'Don't do a stupid thing like that! Under no circumstances you must go back to Poland. Don't give up. There is a dairy up for sale, or try hawking, but don't go back to Poland. Don't be mad.' He listened to them and cancelled the taxi. He also cancelled the train ticket, and lost a certain percentage from cancelling his boat ticket.

I suppose, the Eibershte[75] watched over our family and took us out of Hitler's hands – we were meant to live, thank God.

Dad bought a second-hand lorry on terms and he went out hawking with fruits. Things were by no means easy, but about a year

75 The Allmighty.

later, a year after Hitler came to power in 1934, we arrived in South Africa.

I wrote to my Zaida and Bobba, aunts and uncles, about our whole journey to South Africa. My description of our journey went from house to house. Everybody was so interested to read about it.

We arrived in Cape Town on the ship Duilio, which went on her maiden voyage after a journey of 15 days, and stayed 4 days at the port of Genoa, Italy. We came to some old friends in Cape Town, the Joffees, who we knew from Poland. Dad didn't even have the money for our ticket from Cape Town to Johannesburg. Mommy only had one pound note in her bag when we arrived in Cape Town. Dad took a loan from the Gemillus Chesed in Johannesburg and sent us fifteen pounds for our train ticket to come to Johannesburg.

The battle was still on, but Mommy helped him, and after a year, in 1935, we moved to Springs, where Mommy and Daddy opened a café and fruit shop. Things started improving from that time. That is when my little sister Bella was born.

My parents lived to see 10 grandchildren, and Dad lived to be 85 and see 3 great-grandchildren.

I am writing this little story covering lots of sad moments, but also with great pleasure that Bella and I are grandparents of seven grandchildren, and Marsha and Alf have their first granddaughter, thank G-d.

The grandchildren of Welvel and Mirel have attended, and some are still attending, universities, and Colin is studying to be a doctor. My sister, Bella, is expecting her first grandchild, P.G.

I have personally seen my mother and father's tears of sadness, but there were also tears of joy.

Joe Narotzky, November 1984

Post scriptum February 1993:
Joe and Bella now have eight grandchildren. (kein ayin hora) The oldest one, Marc, (Meier, named after Mirel) is studying at university. He is the son of Edith and Basil, who also have Kerryn and Brett. Helene and Eddy live in a Kibbutz in Israel and have three children, Daniela, Ari and Orli. Rodney

and Janine live in Benoni and have two sons: Warren (Ze'ev, named after Welvel) and Rael.

Marsha and Alf now have four grandchildren. (kein ayin hore) Janice is divorced and doesn't have children. Glenda and Mervyn live in Los Angeles and have two daughters, Lauren and Candice Meryl (named after Mirel). Melvyn and Callie live in Johannesburg and have two sons, Robert and Alex.

Bella and Sammy now have nine grandchildren. (kein ayin hore) Julian and Lauren live in Johannesburg and have three children, Shira-Lee, Akiva and Tamar. Andy and Jeremy live in Los Angeles and have two children, Joshua and Gab Miryam (named after Mirel). Colin and Joanne are both doctors, and are at present working in Saskatchewan, Canada, before they got on Aliyah to Israel. They have one son, Netanel. Sheldon and Yael are leaving next month for Israel. They have three children, Amiel, Liron and Amira (named after Mirel).

Dovid Katz

On Three Definitions

Genocide; Holocaust Denial; Holocaust Obfuscation

There is a discomforting indistinctness in contemporary European discourse on matters of state that relate to the Holocaust. One lurking danger is a murkiness emerging from imprecision in the use of language. There would be difference of opinion on when and where such inexactness is a political ruse to confuse the issue or cover for some 'unwanted' part of history, and when it is an unchecked trend bereft of ulterior motivation. Instances of the wilful first may in any event readily feed into the stream of the innocent second. The present paper argues for literalist constructions of 'genocide' and 'Holocaust Denial'. Moreover, the term 'Holocaust Obfuscation' is proposed as a cover term for a newly energized European movement to confuse, recombine or equalize phenomena that are empirically and conceptually unequal, in service of the effort to obscure, relativize, minimize or delete entirely 'the Holocaust as such' from European history and consciousness.

The author is a supporter of the Western (and internationally known) narrative of the Holocaust, and of the Survivor community, and rejects the current attempts at revisionism; but, he holds that opponents should not be labelled 'Deniers' if they do not deny the actual occurrence of the mass murders that collectively constitute the Holocaust. They may minimize, trivialize, justify, try to fault the victims for alleged wrongs, and exaggerate and misname other evils to achieve the desired 'equivalence'. Still, they are not 'Deniers'. In mainstream Western civilization, Holocaust Denial per se was dealt a mortal blow in April 2000 when the British Royal High Court of Justice ruled in favor of the eminent American historian Deborah Lipstadt. It was in those days, at the dawn of the new century, that a sophisticated replacement for Denial was being developed in what was soon to become the new east of the European Union. The phenomenon now merits a term to help understand the local ideas that underlie it; to distinguish between it and classical Denial; and to expose a disturbing trend in Europe that has not yet been subject to adequate scrutiny.

The Holocaust Obfuscation campaign in Europe has diffused westward from various elite circles of the new-accession European Union and NATO states that had suffered Soviet domination or outright annexation. The set of ideas emanates particularly but not exclusively from the Baltics. Critiques of the campaign should not be taken to reflect in any way on the noble, long-suffering, and hard-working peoples of these successful countries, which have made such enormous strides, and whose long litany of torment under the evil regimes of communism began, or was relaunched, in the mid 1940s, just as the fortunate western nations were celebrating postwar freedom and nearly boundless prospects for prosperity. Proper recognition in the West of all that communism inflicted on the peoples under Soviet domination remains a vital project that deserves fully-focused attention, rather than, as at present, incorporation into an assortment of wily Holocaust reductionist campaigns, which in the end do a grave disservice to the victims of all evil regimes.

Rooted in ultranationalist moods – and not infrequently incorporating racist and antisemitic undertones – Holocaust Obfuscation seeks to cover up or deflect attention from massive local participation in the Holocaust in the regions where that participation was proportionately the highest in Europe. It seeks, as it were, to wipe the stain from history; to find fault with its victims and survivors (for example linking them a priori to communism), in the interests of further 'equalization'; and, most alarmingly, to convince the rest of the world of a bogus 'equivalence' of Soviet and Nazi crimes under the banner of redefinition of genocide to encompass all evils. The result is deletion of the Holocaust as a distinct concept, term and category in European history. The movement has an array of names, including Double Genocide, Symmetry, the Evaluation of Equal Totalitarian Regimes, the Red-Brown (or 'red-equals-brown') movement. The nexus of antisemitism and today's Holocaust issues in Eastern Europe are explored in the seminal papers by Zuroff (2005) and Donskis (2006). Coming from substantially different scholarly traditions, both expose the interrelationship of failure to deal accurately with the Holocaust and local antisemitism (see also Donskis 2004, 2006). This paper goes to press just after the appearance of an outstanding essay by European philosopher Leonidas Donskis, an essay that is one of the most important on the subject in recent years. It has once and for all debunked the efforts to inflate the notion genocide to cover an array of evildoings (Donskis 2009b). It is huge credit to Lithuania that this contribution comes from a proud Lithuanian citizen of proud multicultural heritage, and one who has recently been elected to the European Parliament.

The fall of the totalitarian and repressive Soviet regime, and the rise of a number of democratic states that relatively rapidly earned their way into the European Union and the North Atlantic Treaty Organization, made way for the freedom of expression that allowed for numerous previously 'limited-discussion' topics, including the Holocaust, to be discussed openly. In Lithuania, a number of bold truth-tellers from the country's Lithuanian majority came forward to discover, reveal and teach what it was that had happened, that resulted in their country having the highest rate of genocide of the Jewish population of any country in Europe (a percentage in the mid nineties, leaving today's tiny remnant Jewish community close to extinction). Among others, Saulius Berzinis, Ruta Puisyte, Vaidotas Reivytis, Vytautas Toleikis, Liudas Truska, Linas Vildziunas and Rimantas Zirgulis have made important contributions during various periods within the last two decades (see e.g. Puisyte 1997; Morkus and Reivytis 2000, 2001). Vildziunas established an innovative and successful NGO, the House of Memory, whose accomplishments include nationwide projects with Lithuanian school pupils (Vildziunas 2002; 2003; 2007). Truska boldly exposed the record of distortion by various historians, and reported with remarkable courage and straightforwardness on the facts of the Holocaust in Lithuania (in English see e.g. Truska 2001). The path forward had been presaged in Soviet times by the eminent exile Lithuanian scholar and poet, Tomas Venclova of Yale University, writing in the United States in the 1970s (see now Venclova 1999).

As in the other Baltic states, however, such initiatives have been overwhelmed and not seldom replaced by state-sponsored efforts. These include government supported commissions on Nazi *and*

Soviet crimes. The plot lines are not identical in the three Baltic states but analogous patterning is evident. Scholars, dignitaries and international Holocaust organizations were persuaded to either join these efforts or support them, in order to promote 'Holocaust Studies' in each of these countries. Verily, some excellent research volumes were published and important activities undertaken, in education and in public commemoration. But those constructive phases, themselves haunted from the start by the presumption of 'equivalence' or at least 'parallelism', were a prelude a very different political agenda: to persuade the European Union to accept a revisionist Equal Genocides model of twentieth century history in which the Holocaust, in a macabre semantic hat trick, disappears and then reemerges as one of two equal genocides.

At local level, in the little-known state languages, Soviet crimes and antisemitically motivated vast exaggeration of Jewish participation in them are in fact promoted as being 'genocide' while the Holocaust is obscured, minimized or omitted altogether. The situation in Estonia has been studied by Stevick (2006). The following remarks will focus on Lithuania, where wholly unexpected events of recent years provide ample empirical reason, first for precision in conceptualizing the notions of Genocide and Holocaust Denial; and, just as importantly, to begin to conceptualize and deconstruct the now steamrolling Holocaust Obfuscation tendency. At this point in time, it needs to be understood more by its deeds, words and intentions than by any precise dictionary definition. Nevertheless, first attempts at definition, or as a point of departure, description, cannot no longer be shirked.

Within Lithuania, the noble initiatives of individual Lithuanian champions of historic truth were overrun and largely eliminated by the state's 'International Commission for the Evaluation of the Crimes of the Nazi and Soviet Occupation Regimes in Lithuania', established by presidential decree in 1998. The commission is housed in the Foreign Ministry, in effect leaving the state and politicians in charge of history when it comes to this subject. Independent minded historians could be left out in the cold. Younger talents could be forgiven for being concerned about their career prospects if their views should conflict with the state's de-facto commission of 'historic truth'. The commission's name is itself somewhat Orwellian: the effort to acquire legitimacy from 'international' sources for what needs to be acknowledged at national and local level; the circularity that incorporates the desired conclusion (parallelism) into the very name of the enquiry; and last but not least, the stated delimitation to crimes of 'occupation regimes', obscuring in the title not only the voluntary initiatives of local forces and individuals, but the sadly well documented outbreak of barbarity against Jewish civilians in dozens of locations in Lithuania in the time from the morning of Sunday 22 June 1941 onward, and even before Nazi German forces arrived or had taken control, an event that occurred in different localities at various dates and times during the ensuing week (see e.g. Arad 1976: 234–272; Gilbert 1987: 154–155, 234–235; Garfunkel et al 1984; Kwiet 1998: 11; Levin 1996; MacQueen 1998: 34–37; Porat 1996; Rubenstein and Altman 2008: 277–315; cf. now also Arad 2009, Sutton 2009).

This multilayered and habitually unchallenged misuse of language in the naming of commissions may become a useful example of the kind of Eurospeak that can sometimes be employed to manage discourse at the European Parliament and other institutions. Informally, diplomats have taken to calling the three Baltic commissions 'the Red-Brown commissions', an archetypal instance of replacing a long obfuscating name with a critically motivated short one, with the intentional ring of a touch of satire.

Over the years the commission in Lithuania published some excellent, though minimally distributed, volumes (e.g. Dieckmann and Suziedelis 2006). But then, the principal activity turned political, in partnership with the commissions of the other two Baltic states and like-minded politicians in other new-accession states. The political project generates declarations, resolutions and new laws in the European Union that would in fact delete the notion of the Holocaust and have it replaced by various formulations of Two Equal Genocides. Periodically and incrementally, the Vilnius-based commission 'contributes' to the European Union one or another 'point of equality' in the proposed equalization of nazism and communism (see e.g. Commission 2008 on the 'equality of victimhood').

The rest, as they say, is history. The commission, with the active help of top-tier Lithuanian statesmen, persuaded Yitzhak Arad, a prominent Israeli Holocaust scholar, himself a survivor and resistance hero, to join. He was subsequently, and absurdly, accused of war crimes by the antisemitic press, in 2006, based on passages cited and distorted from his own published memoir (Arad 1979), and soon thereafter 'investigated' by the state's prosecutor responsible for war crimes. To the present day the commission has not publicly condemned the defamation of its own founding member. When international pressure forced the suspension of 'part' of the 'investigation', state prosecutors issued a defamatory statement against the octogenarian anti-Nazi resistance hero (Prosecution Service of the Republic of Lithuania 2008).

In 2008, the antisemitic press clamored for the prosecutor to pursue two additional Holocaust survivors, Fania Yocheles Brantsovsky and Rachel Margolis. On 5 May 2008, in a lowpoint of modern Lithuanian history, armed plainclothes police came searching for the women at a Vilnius address, and later that month, prosecutors announced to the press (ridiculously) that their whereabouts could not be determined (e.g. Balsas.lt 2008). This calumny has not been corrected to this day. Brantsovsky (born 1922) is librarian of the Vilnius Yiddish Institute. Margolis (born in 1921), is a biologist and Holocaust historian who rediscovered and published the lost diary of a Polish Christian witness to the mass murders of Vilna Jewry at Ponar (now Paneriai outside Vilnius), and is unable to return to Lithuania because of fears of harassment from prosecutors. The diary subsequently appeared in English translation (Sakowicz 2005). None of the Holocaust survivors defamed has been charged or subpoenaed, as natural justice would demand. The strategy seems to be to send them to eternity as 'suspected war criminals' as part of the wider strategy of generating mendacious 'equal paper trails' of Nazi and Soviet crimes in service to the perfidious red-equals-brown movement. This is particularly untenable in Lithuania, where not a single Nazi war criminal has been punished (see Zuroff 2009b). These sad events have been reported and commented upon widely in the Western press (see e.g. Foxman 2009; Gersten and Perelman 2008; Ginaite 2008; Gloder 2008; Katz 2008; Keene State College 2009; Lucas 2008; Weitzman 2008; Zuroff 2008). Antony Polonsky has commented: 'The dispute certainly demonstrates how difficult it is both for the Lithuanian elite and for the public at large to come to terms with the painful legacy of Lithuanian complicity in the mass murder of the country's Jewish population' (Polonsky in press).

There have been protests internationally in response to actions by organs of the one state in the world that attempts to prosecute Holocaust survivors who are alive because they joined the anti-Nazi Soviet-led partisans. These survivors are recognized as heroes throughout the free world. Protests have included a number from the Congress of the United States (including Hodes, Wexler and Berman 2008). The Jewish Community of Lithuania responded with swift and gallant rejoinders (see Alperovich and Jafet 2009a; 2009b). The accused partisan veteran still resident in Vilnius, Ms. Brantsovsky, has been honored, among others, by the American, Austrian, British, and Irish embassies in Vilnius. Significantly, and sadly, the episode represents the first occasion since Soviet times that a citizen maligned by state organs is conspicuously honored by western nations in this part of the world.

The commission is only one part of the state sponsored 'Genocide Industry' in Lithuania. The Museum of Genocide Victims (popularly 'the Genocide Museum'), on Vilnius's main boulevard, deals in fact only with Soviet crimes (for a critique see e.g. Steele 2008). It includes blatantly antisemitic exhibits (for example, a postwar caricature of a Soviet jeep driven by Lenin, Stalin, and 'the Jew Yankl', with no comment on the racism, this coming *after* the Holocaust). A recent exhibit on the Ukrainian famine showed a woman telling visitors: 'In Auschwitz we were given some spinach and a little bread. War is terrible, but famine is even worse'. And, the Genocide and Resistance Research Centre of Lithuania, located at separate downtown premises, has minimal interest in the Holocaust; of the twenty or so books on display in its window, only one, produced locally, deals with the Holocaust. A popular tourist attraction in the countryside is 'Gruto parkas', popularly the 'Lenin Park', to which statues of Lenin and other Soviet leaders were removed to make for an educational theme park. Its signposting, provided by the Genocide Research Centre, also contains blatantly antisemitic material. In all these cases, the Holocaust is barely mentioned or not mentioned all; there is a condemnation of survivors who resisted, and an application of the word 'genocide' primarily or exclusively for Soviet crimes.

The upshot is, that when it comes to 'back home', it is primarily the Soviet Union and the antisemitically motivated 'sublimated deicide accusation' of overwhelming Jewish collusion that are labeled 'genocide'. The actual genocide that occurred in the country, the Holocaust, is ignored, trivialized or implicitly justified. What is inter alia ominous here is that instead of combating the basest folklore of justification of the Holocaust (documented repeatedly in formulations such as 'they were all NKVD [KGB], and got what they deserved'), such sentiment has been remolded by sophisticated scholars and politicians into a Eurospeak that aspires to become twenty-first century standard history - and law - of the European Union area.

Needless to say, the expenditure of a state's resources and powers in favor of one historical model can in fact intimidate individuals and non-governmental institutions alike into not expressing contrary views. The result is diminution of the public feeling of freedom of speech. At the time this paper is submitted (Sept. 2009), there is an unfortunate, and quite incredible piece of proposed legislation before the Lithuanian parliament. It proposes that those who deny or diminish the 'genocide committed by communism and fascism' - packaged together in the law's wording - in speech, in writing, in the media, via posts on the internet, or using other technologies of public access shall be punished 'by fine or limitation of freedom, arrest or imprisonment up to three years' (Lietuvos Respublikos Seimas 2009). Here too, Professor Leonidas Donskis has boldly stood up proudly for his country's integrity, and for the European liberal tradition of tolerance and free speech. He has rightly called such attempts the 'criminalization of debate' (see Donskis 2008b, 2009a). Even if they stand little chance of passing, such proposals have succeeded in stifling the extant free debate. Let such developments at least serve as a warning to the rest of the European Union about where the red-equals-brown movement is headed and what curtailment of freedom of expression it is causing at the local level.

It is unfortunate enough for any state to be expending its nation's precious resources on revisionist history with racist undertones. But in recent years, a number of 'genocide establishments' in new-accession states have campaigned with increasing success to impose the 'new paradigm' on the European Union generally. In January 2008, the 'Common Europe - Common History' group was announced in Tallinn by a press release complaining about the phrase 'Never Again' being, it is implied, unfairly monopolized by Holocaust survivors.

British MP John Mann rapidly saw through the ruse and told the Commons: 'On 22 January, in Tallinn, Estonia, five MEPs from five different countries met to launch a group called Common Europe – Common History. It has the same theme – the need for an equal evaluation of history. It is just a traditional form of prejudice, rewritten in a modern context. In essence, it is trying to equate communism and Judaism as one conspiracy and rewrite history from a nationalist point of view. Those are elected MEPs' (Mann 2008).

But there were few voices of dissent in Europe, and frankly few who even noticed the growing effort. In June 2008 the 'Prague Declaration' was proclaimed. Instead of using the opportunity to create new institutions to educate Europe on the evils of communism (and its possible future incarnations), which is of major importance, the undercurrent of the Baltic-origin 'equality' pervades the text. Its provisions include demands for communism to 'be dealt with, in the same way Nazi crimes were assessed by the Nuremberg Tribunal' and for European textbooks to be overhauled 'so that children could learn and be warned about communism and its crimes in the same way as they have been taught to assess the Nazi crimes' (see Prague Declaration 2008). This is a document about calling two very different things 'the same thing'.

The next major step in the obviously orchestrated progression was the 'Vilnius Declaration of the OSCE Parliamentary Assembly' of 29 June – 3 July 2009, into which the red-equals-brown movement inserted the language 'in the twentieth century European countries experienced two major totalitarian regimes, Nazi and Stalinist, which brought about genocide [....]' (OSCE 2009: 48). In addition, there was insertion into the document of support for a Europe-wide day of commemoration for both victims of communism and fascism, a day that would inevitably supplant Holocaust Memorial Day and serve to bolster the red-brown construction of European history. This followed on from a little-noticed European Parliament resolution to the same effect of 2 April 2009. There was a rapid response from Zuroff (2009a). Bauer (2009), taking the proposed combined day of remembrance as his point of departure, goes on to demonstrate the plain historic inaccuracy of the underlying communism-equals-fascism construct, particularly with respect to genocide.

There have, to be sure, been some isolated critiques in the press of these attempts to replace the Holocaust with a paradigm of two genocides (e.g. Katz 2009a; 2009b; 2009c; Steele 2009; Zuroff 2009a). By and large, however, the European Union and its Parliament, and the wider western alliance, have thus far not scrutinized the motivations or implications of these wordings, and at times, there has been a willingness to bend history to perceived current geopolitical dangers involving Russia's relations with her neighbors. States on Russia's periphery are perfectly justified in their historically based fears. They deserve solid western support for security and independence. These resolutions would best be replaced by new resolutions on the history, legacy and dangers of communism and its potential successors. The untenable equals sign does grave damage to these legitimate aspirations.

The abuse, intentional or unintentional, of terms and concepts, is at the heart of the murkiness now spreading across Europe on these issues. As noted at the outset, the inflation of the word 'genocide' has been boldly corrected by Donskis (2009b) in an essay that will outlive the current debates, and that will help in challenging other inflations bound to be attempted in the future.

'Genocide'

The term *genocide* was coined by Raphael Lemkin in his *Axis Rule* (Lemkin 1944). It first occurs in the preface to the book, itself dated 15 November 1943. In the section 'Genocide – A New Term and New Conception for Destruction of Nations' there is, to start with, a succinct and precise formulation: 'New conceptions require new terms. By "genocide" we mean the destruction of a nation or of an ethnic group' (Lemkin 1944: 79). In subsequent passages of the same chapter, however, rather lesser bars come into an increasingly casual discussion, for example: 'Generally speaking, genocide does not necessarily mean the immediate destruction of a nation, except when accomplished by mass killings of all members of a nation. It is intended rather to signify a coordinated plan of different actions aiming at the destruction of essential foundations of the life of national groups [...]' (ibid).

Lemkin's work, based in large measure on his study of the tragedies of the Armenians during World War I and the Jews during World War II, formed a basis for Resolution 260 (III) of the United Nations General Assembly, adopted on 9 December 1948, where Article 2 begins: 'In the present Convention, genocide means any of the following acts committed with intent to destroy, in whole or in part, a national, ethnical, racial or religious group, as such' followed by the acts so considered: (a) Killing members of the group; (b) Causing serious bodily or mental harm to members of the group; (c) Deliberately inflicting on the group conditions of life calculated to bring about its physical destruction in whole or in part; (d) Imposing measures intended to prevent births within the group; (e) Forcibly transferring children of the group to another group' (United Nations 1948).'

Murder of an individual or a number of individuals, as a symptom of enmity toward a group to which that individual is assumed to belong, is a horrific enough crime, but if 'genocide' is not to become a mere synonym for say 'a coordinated multiple murder spree', or even more precariously, a cover-term for crimes that do not even rise to murder (e.g. causing serious mental harm to members of a group with intent to harm a national, ethnic, racial, religious or political group; imprisonment; deportation; loss of status or career), then its definition must be restored to the primary, and not the secondary, Lemkenian sense.

The following proposal is meant to be a point of departure for discussion on twenty-first century usage of the term:

Genocide is the mass murder of as many people as possible on the basis of born national, ethnic, racial or religious identity as such; with intent to eliminate the targeted group entirely and internationally; without allowing the victims any option to change views, beliefs or allegiances to save themselves; and with large-scale accomplished fulfilment of the goal. Genocide leaves in its wake an extinct or nearly extinct group within the territory under the control of the perpetrators.

'Holocaust Denial'

The term *Holocaust Denial* arose from a lexical polygenesis, entailing numerous occurrences of strings of words such as 'denying that the Holocaust [or… 'murder of the Jewish population in countries under Nazi control'] actually occurred [in the degree accepted by history as factual]'. The concept of Holocaust (little d) denial is older than the Holocaust per se. There had been denial of what was being prepared and beginning to take shape; then, of what was happening, or had just happened; denial by perpetrators, witnesses and even faraway individuals, groups and national powers. The notion Holocaust [big D] Denial as a historic term can perhaps be dated to the time around the first actual formulations and publications by explicit propagators of Holocaust Denial after the war. These have been carefully chronicled by a number of researchers (especially Lipstadt 1993 and Shermer and Grobman 2009).

Holocaust Denial is by now a commonly known term. Its dissemination into larger popular culture may result in some measure from Deborah Lipstadt's *Denying the Holocaust* (Lipstadt 1993), which led to an internationally covered trial. British Holocaust Denier David Irving brought a lawsuit for libel against her (in London, in 1996, coming to trial on 11 January 2000). In her famous victory of 11 April 2000, the court was able to determine that Irving's falsification of the historical record was 'deliberate' and 'motivated by a desire to present events in a manner consistent with his own ideological beliefs even if that involved distortion and manipulation of historical evidence' (Gray 2000).

In *Denying the Holocaust,* Lipstadt devoted a chapter to the 'future course of Holocaust denial'. She provides multiple examples of a new kind of relativism that she correctly foresaw as potentially evolving out of Denial. Her documented examples include 'historians intent on obscuring the crucial contrasts between Stalinism and Nazism'. Lipstadt's words have proved to be potently prophetic. In fact, this particular tack has grown exponentially, from being a view of some historians to being the established policy of a number of European Union *states* that are able to mobilize the finance, administration and wherewithal of the state to propagate such views as accepted fact, and to cause to be marginalized or eliminated contrary opinions that lack such support and are readily miscast as somehow disloyal or 'unpatriotic' (or even 'pro-communist'). Lipstadt took note of other Holocaust-diminishing strategies, including what she calls 'yes, but' syndrome: 'Yes, there was a Holocaust, but the Nazis were only trying to defend themselves against their enemies. Yes, there was a Holocaust, but most Jews died of starvation and disease (as is the case in every war) or were killed as partisans and spies. Yes, there was a Holocaust, but the Jews' behavior brought it on them. Yes, there was a Holocaust, but it was essentially no different than an array of other conflagrations in which innocents were massacred' (Lipstadt 2005: 212, 215).

In 2007, Lipstadt followed up with the term *soft-core Holocaust Denial* to cover attempts to minimize the Holocaust (see Paul 2007). It is a perfectly adequate term as used by Professor Lipstadt herself. However, just as in the case of 'genocide', there is danger in letting loose a slipshod definition, when the wider scope that ensues, quite harmless 'in the safe pair of hands of the maker', is prone to abuse by the selfsame potential distorters of history whose devious work these terms were designed, or adapted, to combat in the first instance.

The definition of Holocaust Denial should be retained for those who deny that the documented murders of the victims occurred. The term is self-defining, and its compass is perhaps best not extended to 'soft' or 'hard' core or otherwise. In short:

Denial is denial.

'Holocaust Obfuscation'

In response to the unfolding of events in Lithuania that were briefly summarized above, the author proposed the term *Holocaust Obfuscation* in a February 2008 presentation at the Rothschild Foundation Europe's offices in London, followed by a March 2008 memo circulated to the US-based Board of the Friends of the Vilnius Yiddish Institute. The term was subsequently used in the BBC radio documentary of Tim Whewell, in the *Economist* by Edward Lucas, by Leonidas Donskis in his 'Hostages to an Ill-Begotten Theory' and by Steven F. Lawson in his 'Muddling the Holocaust in Lithuania' (Whewell 2008; Lucas 2008; Donskis 2008a; Lawson 2009).

'Holocaust Obfuscation' is proposed as adequate to the description of the range of efforts currently underway. Adoption of the notion Holocaust Obfuscation enables the retention of Holocaust Denial sensu stricto, for Denial of the Holocaust in the commonly understood sense of 'denying that something happened' which conceptually differs from 'agreeing that something happened but claiming that it was not a unique or singular or important event but one of a number of conceptually identical or analogous events', or, even for example, claiming that 'many of the victims had committed some grave evil'. The following text is offered as a point of departure for the unfolding chain of events and ideas, rather than for a broader theoretical range of eventualities.

Holocaust Obfuscation is the systematic effort to relativize, minimize, obscure, confuse or eliminate the Holocaust, as a distinct historic entity in European history, without necessarily denying any of the documented murders. By the early twenty-first century Holocaust Obfuscation evolved as a major trend of thought in some governmental, political, press, academic and other elite circles of some new-accession states in the east of the European Union. Its ideas have been packaged in a number of declarations and proposed laws aimed at eliciting compliance from Western nations and organizations of nations. The most frequent apparatus includes: inflation of the term genocide *to encompass a variety of Soviet crimes; the claim that Nazi and Soviet crimes were inherently equivalent; thereby leaving the Holocaust as a conceptual 'half' in the replacement paradigm. At the local level, variants of the model have included claims of overwhelming Jewish complicity in communism; claims that the murder of the Jewish populations in Eastern Europe was a reaction to alleged Jewish communism; claims that the miniscule percentage of Jews who survived by escaping to Soviet-supported partisan groups in the forests are a priori guilty of 'war crimes' (hence they may be investigated with neither evidence nor charges). The Holocaust Obfuscation movement frequently harbors antisemitic and racist undertones.*

References

Alperovich, Shimon and Jafet, Tobijas [Alperavicius, S. and Jafetas, T.] (2009a). 'An Open Letter', July 2009. At: http://www.genshoah.org/LithuaniaLetter0708.pdf.

Alperovich, Shimon and Jafet, Tobijas [Alperavicius, S. and Jafetas, T.] (2009b). 'An Open Letter', 28 August 2009. At: http://www.litjews.org/Default.aspx?Element=ViewArticle&ArticleID=1700&TopicID=2&Lang=EN.

Arad, Yitzhak (1976). 'The Final Solution in Lithuania in the Light of German Documentation'. In: *Yad Vashem Studies*, vol. 11, pp. 234–272.

Arad, Yitzhak (1979). *The Partisan. From the Valley of Death to Mount Zion*. New York: Holocaust Library.

Arad, Yitzhak (2009). *The Holocaust in the Soviet Union*. Jerusalem: Yad Vashem.

Balsas.lt (2008). 'Wiesenthalio centras kaltina Lietuvos teisesauga zydu diskreditavimu'. At: http://www.balsas.lt/naujiena/198144.

Bauer, Yehuda (2009). 'Memo to the ITF on Comparison between Nazi Germany and the Soviet Regime' [to be published].

Commission (2008). Commission presents Lithuania's suggestions for the evaluation of totalitarian regimes on the EU level. At: http://www.komisija.lt/en/naujiena.php?id=1215150457.

Dieckmann, Christoph and Suziedelis, Saulius, *The Persecution and Mass Murder of Lithuanian Jews during Summer and Fall of 1941. Sources and Analysis*, Vilnius, Margi rastai, 2006 [= vol. 3 of the International Commission's *The Crimes of the Totalitarian Regimes in Lithuanian. The Nazi Occupation*].

Donskis, Leonidas (2004). 'Preface'. In: Nikzentaitis et al 2004: pp. ix–xv.

Donskis, Leonidas (2006). 'Another Word for Uncertainty: Antisemitism in Modern Lithuania' in *NORDEUROPAForum* 1, 2006, pp. 7–26. Online version at: http://edoc.hu-berlin.de/nordeuropaforum/2006-1/donskis-leonidas-7/PDF/donskis.pdf.

Donskis, Leonidas (2008a). 'Hostages to an Ill-Begotten Theory'. In *Transitions Online* (TOL), 10 October 2008. At: http://www.tol.cz/look/TOL/article.tpl?IdLanguage=1&IdPublication=4&NrIssue=290&NrSection=2&NrArticle=20079&search=search&SearchKeywords=DONSKIS&SearchMode=on&SearchLevel=0.

Donskis, Leonidas (2008b). 'Savoku infliacija ir diskusiju kriminalizacija'. At: http://www.balsas.lt/naujiena/222320/savoku-infliacija-ir-diskusiju-kriminalizacija/rubrika:naujienos-lietuva-komentaraiiranalize-lietuva.

Donskis, Leonidas (2009a). 'Savoku infliacija ir diskusiju kriminalizacija'. In his: *Nepopuliarios izvalgos. Politikos komentarai ir ese* [Unpopular Insights: Political Commentaries and Essays]. Vilnius: Versus Aureus.

Donskis, Leonidas (2009b). 'The Inflation of Genocide'. At: http://www.europeanvoice.com/article/2009/07/the-inflation-of-genocide/65613.aspx. Earlier Lithuanian versions = Donskis 2008b; 2009a.

Foxman, Abraham (2009). 'Lithuania must stand up against Antisemitism'. In *Jewish Standard*, 13 March 2009. At: http://www.jstandard.com/index.php/content/item/lithuania_must_stand_up_against_anti-semitism/7235.

Garfunkel, L. et al (eds) (1984). *Yahadut Lita. IV: Hashoah, 1941-1945* [Lithuanian Jewry. IV: The Holocaust, 1941–1945], Tel Aviv: Association of Lithuanian Jews in Israel.

Gersten, Lana and Perelman, Marc (2008). 'Tensions mount over Lithuanian Probe'. In *The Forward*, 2 July 2008. At: http://www.forward.com/articles/13704/.

Gilbert, Martin (1987). *The Holocaust. The Jewish Tragedy*. London: Fontana (Harper Collins).

Ginaite, Sara (2008). '"Investigating" Jewish Partisans. The Protest of a Veteran Jewish Partisan'. At: http://jewishcurrents.blogspot.com/2008/08/disturbing-events-in-lithuania.html.

Gloger, Dana (2008). 'Holocaust Survivors Facing War Crimes Trials (Lithuania)'. In *The Jewish Chronicle*, 8 June 2008. At: http://www.freerepublic.com/focus/f-news/2027755/posts.

Gray, Charles (2000). Text of Mr. Justice Charles Gray's judgment, electronic edition: http://www.holocaustdenialontrial.org/trial/judgement.

Hodes, Paul and Wexler, Robert and Herman, Howard (2008). Letter from the Congress of the United States to the Prime Minister of Lithuania. At: http://www.genshoah.org/CongressForLJC080108.pdf.

Katz, Dovid (2008). 'Rokhl Margolis, 86, ken nit kumen in ir heymshtot Vilne, vayl zi hot gekemft kegn di natsis' in *Algemeyner Zhurnal*, 15 August 2008. At: http://www.dovidkatz.net/dovid/Lithuania/ROKHL_MARGOLIS-1.pdf and http://www.dovidkatz.net/dovid/Lithuania/ROKHL_MARGOLIS-2.pdf.

Katz, Dovid (2009a). 'Prague's Declaration of Disgrace'. In: *The Jewish Chronicle*, 21 May 2009. At: http://www.thejc.com/articles/prague%E2%80%99s-declaration-disgrace.

Katz, Dovid (2009b). 'Genocide Industry has Hidden Agenda'. In: *The Irish Times*, 30 May 2009. At: http://www.irishtimes.com/newspaper/opinion/2009/0530/1224247744866.html?via=mr.

Katz, Dovid (ed.) (2009c). *The Holocaust in the Baltics* (website). At: http://www.holocaustinthebaltics.com.

Keene State College (2009). 'Cohen Center Honors Dr. Rachel Margolis'. At: http://keeneweb.org/media/2009/04/09/cohen-center-honors-dr-rachel-margolis/.

Kwiet, Konrad (1998). 'Rehearsing for Murder: The Beginning of the Final Solution in Lithuania in June 1941' in *Holocaust and Genocide Studies* 12:1, pp. 3–26.

Lawson, Steven F. (2009). 'Muddling the Holocaust in Lithuania'. In *George Mason University's History News Network*, 26 January 2009. At: http://hnn.us/articles/59710.html.

Lemkin, Raphael (1944). *Axis Rule in Occupied Europe: Laws of Occupation. Analysis of Government. Proposals for Redress*. Washington, DC: Carnegie Endowment for International Peace.

Levin, Dov (ed.) (1996). *Pinkas hekehillot. Encyclopedia of Jewish Communities from their Foundation till after the Holocaust. Lithuania* [in Hebrew], Jerusalem: Yad Vashem.

Lietuvos Respublikos Seimas (2009). [Proposed law] XIP-664. At: http://www3.lrs.lt/pls/inter2/dokpaieska.showdoc_l?p_id=344389.

Lipstadt, Deborah (1993). *Denying the Holocaust*. New York: Free Press.

Lipstadt, Deborah (2005). *History on Trial. My Day in Court with a Holocaust Denier*. New York: Ecco / Harper Perennial.

[Lucas, Edward] (2008). 'Prosecution and Persecution. Lithuania must stop blaming the victims'. In: *The Economist*, 21 August 2008. At: http://www.economist.com/world/europe/displaystory.cfm?story_id=11958563.

MacQueen, Michael (1998). 'The Context of Mass Destruction: Agents and Prerequisites of the Holocaust in Lithuania' in *Holocaust and Genocide Studies* 12:1, pp. 27–48.

Mann, John (2008). Speech in the House of Commons, 31 January 2008. At: http://www.publications.parliament.uk/cgi-bin/newhtml_hl?DB=semukparl&STEMMER=en&WORDS=absurd&ALL=Absurd&ANY=&PHRASE=&CATEGORIES=&SIMPLE=&SPEAKER=&COLOUR=red&STYLE=s&ANCHOR=80131-0010.htm_spnew2&URL=/pa/cm200708/cmhansrd/cm080131/debtext/80131-0010.htm.

Morkus, Jonas and Reivytis, Vaidotas (2000). *Saulelydis Lietuvoje*, 2000, 110 minutes (4 parts).

Morkus, Jonas and Reivytis, Vaidotas (2001). *Saulelydis Lietuvoje: pazintis su Lietuvos zydu bei holokausto istorija*. Vilnius: Garnelis.

Nikzentaitis, Alvydas; Schreiner, Stefan; Darius Staliunas, Darius (eds) (2004), *The Vanished World of Lithuanian Jews. On the Boundary of Two Worlds. Identity, Freedom, and Moral Imagination in the Baltics*, Amsterdam & New York: Rodopi.

OSCE (2009). 'Vilnius Declaration of the OSCE Parliamentary Assembly and Resolutions Adopted at the Eighteenth Annual Session, Vilnius 29 June to 3 July 2009'. At: http://www.oscepa.org/images/stories/documents/activities/1.Annual%20Session/2009_Vilnius/Final_Vilnius_Declaration_ENG.pdf.

Palevsky, Elliott (2008). 'Open Letter to President Adamkus and Prime Minister Kirkilas' [signed by faculty and students of the Vilnius Summer Program in Yiddish Language and Literature at the Vilnius Yiddish Institute]. At: http://www.genshoah.org/LithuaniaLetter0808.pdf.

Paul, Jonny (2007). 'Holocaust Scholar Warns of New 'Soft-core' Denial'. In *Jerusalem Post*, 6 Feb. 2007.

Polonsky, Antony (in press). 'Jews in Russia, Ukraine, Belarus and Lithuania since 1991' in his *The Jews in Poland and Russia, volume 3, 1914 to the Present Day*.

Porat, Dina (1996). 'The Holocaust in Lithuania. Some Unique Aspects' in David Cesarani (ed.), *The Final Solution. Origins and Implementation*. New York, Routledge, 1996, pp. 159–174.

Prague Declaration on European Conscience and Communism. At: http://praguedeclaration.org/.

Prosecution Service of the Republic of Lithuania (2008). 'Part of the pre-trial investigation in respect of crimes committed by the Soviet partisan squad during the WWII and related to Yitzhak Arad was closed'. At: http://www.prokuraturos.lt/News/YizthakArad2/tabid/290/Default.aspx.

Puisyte, Ruta (1997). 'The Holocaust in Jurbarkas. The Mass Extermination of Jews in Jurbarkas in the Provinces of Lithuania during the German Nazi Occupation'. Vilnius University BA thesis. English translation. At: http://www.shtetlinks.jewishgen.org/yurburg/bathesis.html.

Rubenstein, Joshua and Altman, Ilya (eds) (2008). *The Unknown Black Book. The Holocaust in the German-Occupied Soviet Territories,* Introductions by Yitzhak Arad, Ilya Altman and Joshua Rubenstein. Translated by Christopher Morris and Joshua Rubenstein. Bloomington & Indianapolis: Indiana University Press in association with the United States Holocaust Memorial Museum.

Sakowicz, Kazimierz (2005). *Ponary Diary, 1941–1943. A Bystander's Account of a Mass Murder.* Edited by Yitzhak Arad, New Haven and London: Yale University Press.

Shermer, Michael and Alex Grobman, *Denying History: Who says the Holocaust Never Happened and Why do they Say it?* Berkeley: University of California Press.

Steele, Jonathan (2008). 'In the Jerusalem of the North, the Jewish Story is Forgotten'. In *The Guardian,* 20 June 2008. At: http://www.guardian.co.uk/commentisfree/2008/jun/20/secondworldwar.

Steele, Jonathan (2009). 'History is Much Too Important to be left to Politicians'. In *The Guardian,* 19 August 2009. At: http://www.guardian.co.uk/commentisfree/2009/aug/19/eu-parliament-soviet-nazi-history.

Stevick, E. Doyle (2006). 'The Politics of the Holocaust in Estonia: Historical Memory and Social Divisions in Estonian Education'. In: Stevick, E. D. and Levinson, B. A. U., *Reimagining Civic Education: How Diverse Societies Form Democratic Citizens,* Rowman and Littlefield, 2007, pp. 217–244.

Sutton, Karen (2009). *The Massacre of the Jews of Lithuania. Lithuanian Collaboration in the Final Solution, 1941–1944.* Jerusalem and New York: Gefen.

Truska, Liudas (2001). 'Contemporary Attitudes toward the Holocaust in Lithuania'. In: *Jews in Eastern Europe,* Hebrew University, Avraham Harman Institute of Contemporary Jewry, 2 (45), Fall 2001, pp. 5–26.

United Nations (1948). *Convention on the Prevention and Punishment of the Crime of Genocide.* Adopted by Resolution 260 (III) A of the United Nations General Assembly on 9 December 1948 (http://www.hrweb.org/legal/genocide.html; http://www.un.org/millennium/law/iv-1.htm & others).

Venclova, Tomas (1999). 'Jews and Lithuanians' in his *Forms of Hope,* Riverdale-on-Hudson, New York: Sheep Meadow Press, pp. 43–51 [earlier English version in *Cross Currents,* 1989; original version in Lithuanian, 1976].

Vildziunas, Linas (ed.) (2002). *Mano seneliu ir proseneliu kaimynai zydai: moksleiviu darbu konkursas* (sud. Linas Vildziunas). Vilnius: Holokausto ir zydu kulturos Lietuvoje studiju centras Atminties namai, Garnelis [*Our Grandparents' and Great-Grandparents' Jewish Neighbors: Student Writing Competition,* Vilnius: The House of Memory / Center for Studies and Commemoration of the Holocaust and Jewish Heritage in Lithuania, and Garnelis Press].

Vildziunas, Linas (ed.) (2003). *Mano seneliu ir proseneliu kaimynai zydai: antrasis moksleiviu darbu konkursas* (sud. Linas Vildziunas). Vilnius: Holokausto ir zydu kulturos Lietuvoje studiju centras Atminties namai, Garnelis [*Our Grandparents' and Great-Grandparents' Jewish Neighbors: Second Student Writing Competition.*

Vildziunas, Linas (ed.) (2007). *Mano seneliu ir proseneliu kaimynai zydai: moksleiviu darbu konkursas. Trecioji knyga*. Vilnius: Holokausto ir zydu kulturos Lietuvoje studiju centras Atminties namai, Garnelis [*Grandparents' and Great-Grandparents' Jewish Neighbors: Student Writing Competition. The Third Book*].

Weitzman, Mark (2008). 'Vilnius: Capital of Culture or Injustice'. In *The Jewish Week*, 20 August 2008. At: http://www.thejewishweek.com/viewArticle/c55_a13203/Editorial__Opinion/Opinion.html.

Whewell, Tim (2008). *Crossing Continents: Lithuania and the Battle for Memory*, BBC Radio 4, broadcast 17 July 2008 and 21 July 2008 at 2030 BST. At: (http://news.bbc.co.uk/player/nol/newsid_7530000/newsid_7533600/7533687.stm?bw=bb&mp=wm&news=1&bbcws=1).

Zuroff, Efraim (2005). 'Eastern Europe: Antisemitism in the Wake of Holocaust-Related Issues' in *Jewish Political Studies Review*, 17.1-2 (Spring 2005), pp. 63–79. Online version at: http://www.jcpa.org/phas/phas-zuroff-s05.htm.

Zuroff, Efraim (2007). 'Why the Expert Witness will not Face Scrutiny'. In: *The Jewish Chronicle*, 28 September 2007. At: http://www.operationlastchance.org/LITHUANIA_32-7.htm.

Zuroff, Efraim (2009a). 'A Combined Day of Commemoration for the Victims of Nazism and Communism?' in *The Jerusalem Post*, 12 July 2009. At: http://www.jpost.com/servlet/Satellite?cid=1246443787714&pagename=JPost%2FJPArticle%2FShowFull.

Zuroff, Efraim (2009b). *Operation Last Chance. One Man's Quest to Bring Nazis to Justice*. New York: Macmillan.

Leonidas Donskis

Nationalism and Patriotism Revisited: An East-Central European Perspective

> Nationalism is patriotism misliked and patriotism nationalism liked.
> (Bernard Yack, cited in Zygmunt Bauman, *Liquid Modernity)*

1. The Grandeur and Misery of Nationalism

In the eyes of antimodernists, whether conservative or radical, modernity is a liability. It is open to the charge of uprooting individuals and peoples, depriving them of a sense of history, tradition, fellowship, human relationship, and faith. Yet some scholars insist on the substantial difference between the two basic notions of nationhood and citizenship, a difference that shaped the political consciousness of Europe. They draw the dividing line between what they take as the French version of modern citizenship, or citizenship based on the principle of *jus soli* (the right of territory), and the German version of it that rests on the principle *jus sanguinis* (the right of family; see Brubaker, 1992, 1999; Greenfeld, 1992). Both concepts, lead to a kind of modern mystique, however.

Whereas the *jus soli* principle is instrumental in establishing a nearly mystical relationship between identity and territory, the latter being seen as shaping and determining the former, the *jus sanguinis* principle seeks an in-depth explanation of identity. In so doing, the proponents of the *jus sanguinis* logic try to derive such an explanation from the mysterious substance of history and from the depths of community – family, language, and culture. Although scholars tend to view the *jus soli* cultural logic, emphasizing its more or less liberal political and moral implications – and quite justifiably so, given the blood-and-soil mystique present in the *jus sanguinis* cultural logic – these principles have a sort of common denominator. The essence of both of them lies in the assumption that something exists before us, something that shapes us in terms of our belonging to something larger than ourselves; this can be pre-established designs of selfhood, such as history, language, culture, tradition, or collective identity.

The modern concepts of citizenship appear to rest on the metaphysics of secularized hierophany, or the manifestation of the sacred, to use the term employed by Mircea Eliade (see Eliade, 1961). Adding a pivotal qualification to Eliade's idea that, while pre-modern societies lived in a sacralized cosmos, modern societies live in a desacralized one (an assertion which, in its essence, is undeniably true), we might well suggest that the manifestation of the sacred survived into the modern world as secularized hierophany. Interestingly, the emergence of secularized hierophany is manifest in a derivative albeit reverse tendency overlooked by Eliade and other students of comparative religions in sacralization of some aspects of what unquestionably represents the realm of the profane, namely language, culture, history, and tradition.

Hence exists the propensity to accord some undertones of the sacred and religiosity to history and culture. The modern myth of spirituality as something that results from the principle of culture, the latter being contrasted to the principle of civilization with its skepticism, cynicism, spirit of science and technology, and lack of depth and creativity, is the outcome of this reversal. It was through this complementarity between the secularization of the sacred and the sacralization of the profane that language, history, and culture were all conceived of by modern philosophers as forces shaping individual and collective forms of human existence. Nationalism and other modern philosophies of history and culture became possible through this trajectory of consciousness. History with a capital H becomes a symbolic design within which modern individuals seek frames of meaning and concepts to explain themselves and the world around them, in the ordinary moments of their lives and in critical junctures of history. Culture with a capital C, for its part, has been transformed into a kind of self-sufficient, self-asserting, and unique monad of history, a self-contained and mysterious substance that generated creative energy, vitality, spirituality, and meaning of human existence. Hypostatized to the level of autonomous and independent existence, culture was eventually divorced from other faculties of human experience and provinces of the soul, which were ascribed to another pole, civilization.

Vytautas Kavolis defines nationalism in the following way:

> Nationalism is a conception of the cultural identity of a nation which becomes a mobilizing political program even when the nation is [...] in the process of being invented. National identity is what, unless it is either culturally put into question or politically endangered, does not need to be explicitly declared about one's sense of being more at home in one this-worldly community of participation and historical experience than in any other. The close alignment of culture with politics is perhaps the most general source of the dangers which nationalism has presented not only to the world, but to the members of the nations it sought to represent, to revive, or to 'build.' This alignment gives to nationalism a deeper, quasi-religious kind of power, an ability to overwhelm, which 'normal' political forces generally lack. It leads to the exploitation of culture by politics. (Kavolis, 1991, 134)

In his short, sharp, and precise formulations regarding the symbolic codes and the structures of meaning within nationalism, Kavolis reveals what other theories of nationalism are missing. Not only does Kavolis show the modernizing and liberal potential of nationalism, at the same time clearly pointing out its dubious and dangerous points that largely depend on the political, historical, and cultural context within which a given nation or community builds or revives itself, but he also shows the similarity between nationalism and other civilization-shaping movements, from romanticism to feminism. Kavolis succeeded where other students of nationalism failed. From the point of view of the link between theoretical sophistication and empirical evidence in viewing nationalism as a major civilization-shaping force, Kavolis far surpasses other theorists of nationalism.

> Democracy in particular benefits from loosening the connections between culture and politics [...] Like religion, national identity operates optimally in a democratic setting [...] In nineteenth-century Germany and Eastern Europe and the present-day Near East, nationalism tends toward the archaic. American nationalism and, to a lesser extent, mainstream French nationalism since the Revolution have been modernizing. The crucial issue in distinguishing modernizing from archaic nationalism is whether one derives society from individuals having 'human rights' or perceives individuals as embodiments of the 'collective soul' of the nation. (ibid., 134–135)

In his thorough analysis of the four types of nationalism (archaic, modernizing, antimodernistic, and postmodern), Kavolis describes Central and Eastern Europe as a laboratory of the diverse trajectories of the 'modernization of nationalisms.' 'In Central Europe, Hungarian nationalism has probably changed most since 1939, toward the modernistic model, Yugoslav nationalisms have changed least' (ibid., 135). Interestingly, the difference between conservative nationalism and liberal nationalism is still overlooked by the current social sciences and critical scholarship in general. As noted, liberal nationalism allows room for cosmopolitan stances and multiculturalism in politics and public discourse, as well as the modernizing critique of politics and culture it employs.

Whatever its guise, nationalism is inseparable from what we describe as 'national identity,' a phenomenon that 'was from the start, and remained for a long time, an *agonistic* notion and a battle cry' (Bauman, 2004, 21). In terms of power as a force to name the segments of reality and to translate our terms into social practices, legitimizing and institutionalizing the interpretation of ourselves and the world around us, modern identity has several faces. The trinity of modern secular power, deeply intertwined with identity politics, starts, in early modernity, with the old good rule *cuius regio, eius religio* (he who rules decides the religion). Then the time comes for the rule *cuius regio, eius lingua* (he who rules decides the language; see Plasseraud, 2000, 13–15); both pave the way for the rule *cuius regio, eius nation* (he who rules decides the nationality; see Bauman, 2004, 21).

However insightful, the authors of general theories of nationalism – in particular Ernest Gellner, Eric Hobsbawm, Anthony Smith, and Benedict Anderson – failed to take into account the importance of national cultures for the political and institutional settings for liberal democracy and the enormous modernizing potential of Central/East European nationalism. Finally, they overlooked the ethic of liberal nationalism and its implications for public discourse and social criticism. The merits of liberal nationalism in disclosing totalitarianism are too obvious to emphasize. It suffices to recall Czeslaw Milosz, Vaclav Havel, Milan Kundera, Tomas Venclova, and other eminent Central European critics of totalitarianism, ideocracy, xenophobia, and manipulative exchanges. George Orwell's piece of philosophical writing, his thoughtful essay 'Notes on Nationalism,' rather than his remarkable dystopias, gives us a clue to the origins of ideological and political fanaticism. Not having found a better word to describe this disturbing phenomenon of the twentieth century, Orwell employs 'nationalism,' which means here something radically different from what the scholars of nationalism, safely distanced from their subject and equipped with conventional wisdom, would have meant when discussing it.

By nationalism, Orwell means the habit of assuming that human beings can be easily classified like insects and that millions of people can be lightly and confidently labeled 'good' or 'bad.' Yet an even more important trait of nationalism is our habit of identifying with a single nation or other unit, no matter whether real or imagined, placing it beyond good and evil, and doing our utmost to advance its interests and to give it as much power and prestige as possible. Orwell also adds that nationalism should not be confused with patriotism. Although both words are used in so vague a manner that any definition is liable to be challenged, the difference between two opposing ideas calls for a sharp dividing line between nationalism and patriotism (see Orwell, 1970, 155).

Nationalism can easily be defended against Orwell's devastating criticism. For instance, what he describes as a propensity to place our object of devotion and affection beyond good and evil and to recognize no other duty than that of advancing our group or nation's interests concerns conservative and radical nationalism rather than liberal nationalism. Nationalism could be advocated by reminding ourselves of the myriad ways in which it manifests itself. Liberal nationalism, the initial phase of nationalism in the first half of the nineteenth century, could be taken as just another term for liberalism itself. Johann Gottfried von Herder's idea that every culture is a self-asserting, self-sufficient, unique, and irreplaceable collective individual cannot be conceived here otherwise than as another version, German or Central European, of liberalism. Liberal nationalism has always been, and continues to be, an interpretive and normative framework for the critical questioning of society and culture rather than a blind and deaf glorification of history. As a social and moral philosophy, liberal nationalism established a pattern of intellectual culture, whose essence lies in the modernizing critique of society and culture. Liberal and democratic nationalism sustains our modern intellectual and moral sensibilities.

How ironic that, by lightly discarding nationalism as a whole, Orwell dismisses his substantial contribution to the modern democratic world, namely, the struggle against totalitarianism. Yet he had not foreseen this sort of nationalism, whose merits in the struggle against totalitarianism were to mark the political history of twentieth century Central and Eastern Europe (see Donskis, 2002). Regrettably, in the second half of the nineteenth century, nationalism in Europe was increasingly defensive, mass-oriented, ideological, and doctrinal. It seems to have been because of the effect of Social Darwinism, and because of strong antimodernist reactions, which capitalized on the idea of the defense of the nation from external and internal enemies. In many cases, nationalism became primitive and 'zoological.'

However, this has not always been so. In the first half of the nineteenth century, Europe was full of liberal nationalists who maintained the ideas of universal brotherhood and sisterhood, human fellowship, moral reciprocity, commitment, and sympathetic understanding. They firmly believed that the fight for the independence and freedom of any country was a common cause. As Ernest Gellner noted, liberalism and nationalism, in the nineteenth century, were allies, even brothers; only later, would their paths diverge (see Gellner, 1996).

The epoch of the springtime of the peoples, and Herder's noble-spirited and generous philosophy of culture, is out of touch with what we can depict as the blood-and-soil, ethnic-cleansing brand of nationalism. If we are not to conflate National Socialism, as a global racist ideology and as a blueprint for a world order, with nationalism, then we have to admit that a widespread propensity to blame all evils of the twentieth century solely on nationalism is out of place. The ethics of liberal nationalism was instrumental in morally discrediting and, consequently, politically dismantling totalitarianism. Moreover, conservative nationalism played a crucial role in Communist countries, advocating such fundamental forms of human rights and dignity as freedom of speech, conscience, association, and the practice of religion and culture.

This is not to say that all forms of nationalism are compatible with the ideals of peace and democracy. As a para-ideology, nationalism proved adaptable to all principal modern ideologies, namely conservatism, liberalism, and socialism. This fact makes nationalism a vague phenomenon of modern politics and culture. As Orwell admits, every definition of nationalism is doomed to be incomplete. If so, every definition of nationalism is liable to be challenged.

One reason is that 'nationalism' cannot in principle function as an abstract and polysemantic term. By making it so, we deprive the term 'nationalism' of any sense. This is to say that we would make no sense by disconnecting nationalism from an ideological framework within which it comes to define identity, freedom, tradition, power, authority, virtue, and other key phenomena of politics and culture in whose name it speaks up.

At the same time, to detach nationalism from the concrete political setting in which it operates is an unpardonable mistake. In a liberal democracy, nationalism can be integrated into the liberal moral culture and thus accommodated in the pluralist setting. This is not exclusively the case. Even in a liberal democracy, nationalism can be adjusted to, or translated into, a set of racist and xenophobic sentiments, antimodernist reactions, or the illiberal systems of moralization, such as the culture of determinism. In undemocratic regimes, nationalism can be translated into any kind of predominant militant rhetoric or symbolic design of political and ideological partisanship. As a frame of reference for blood-and-soil mystique, nationalism can be incorporated into the general pattern of hatred and paranoia instigated by politically, ideologically, or religiously motivated hate groups, whatever their guise. To deal with nationalism without defining its ideological framework and political setting is either pointless or unfair.

How important the setting is within which nationalism comes into existence and operates we can learn from different patterns of nationalism, which are closely connected to a given society's traditions, religiosity, historical injuries, or moral traumas. As Ralph Fevre suggests, 'Nationalism is more of a reaction to the *threat* of over-rationalization than to its actual occurrence. Nationalism takes hold in more traditional and usually more religious societies. Indeed nationalism seems to complement religious feeling, especially fundamentalism' (Fevre, 2000, 151). Without its political setting and cultural context, nationalism becomes just a phantom of the imagination.

2. My Country, Right or Wrong

Orwell defined patriotism as a devotion to a particular place or a way of life, which we believe to be the best in the world but which we do not want to impose on anybody. In his view, patriotism is defensive by nature, both militarily and culturally. No decent patriot talks about his or her country or publicly celebrates its history and culture unless that country is attacked or insulted. Nationalism, on the contrary, is inseparable from the desire for power. Whereas patriots are attached to a particular place, its culture, dialect, and landscape, nationalists have no more abiding purpose than to secure more power and prestige for the nation or any other group or unit into which they have chosen to sink their individuality (see Orwell, 1970, 155–156).

Neither are things clear with patriotism. If the liberal facet of nationalism implies the critical questioning of society and culture, patriotism, in most cases, is an attachment to, and identification with, a country, its territory, history, landscape, language, and symbols of power. This attachment and identification can be devoid of any critical approach. The principle, 'my country, right or wrong,' may have always been the quintessence of patriotism. Whereas nationalists would criticize sharply any deviation from what they assume as the moral substance of the object of their devotion or commitment, patriots would insist that no fact or event could prevent them from keeping fidelity to their country.

As Aleksandras Shtromas, a Lithuanian émigré political scientist who foresaw the collapse of the Soviet Union, convincingly argued, ardent patriots of Russia were able to close one eye to the Soviet Union's criminal policies of expanding Russia's territory and advancing its interests (see Shtromas, 1994, 183–225). Moreover, they justified

Stalin's crimes precisely for the same reason. Imperial patriots had gone so far as to condemn as traitors those dissidents or former KGB officers who sided with the Soviet Union's ideological enemies, that is, the United States, Great Britain, and NATO. Things were absolutely different with nationalists who, according to Shtromas, drew a sharp dividing line between Russia and the Soviet Union. Not only liberal-democratic dissidents like the generous and noble-spirited Andrei Sakharov or the fearless humanist Sergei Kovalyov, but also the fiercely nationalistic Aleksandr Solzhenitsyn explicitly regarded the Soviet Union as a criminal state and the Soviet regime as a crime against Russia and humanity.

The dramatic encounter between nationalism and patriotism can be understood only by those who are able to empathize with those who were bound to choose between the Soviet Union as their state and the West, regarded by Soviet propaganda as the embodiment of evil. When you are forced to choose between a rogue state, which claims the exclusive rights of your only motherland, and the supposed enemy of your state, which defends the right cause and protects human rights, it is no longer a theoretical and hypothetical choice. Instead, it is an existential move that leads you to cross the point of no return. This raises another interesting question: Was Soviet identity compatible with Russian identity? Much energy has been spent over the past years arguing about the Soviet Union and its legacy in the academic, intellectual and cultural life of the former republics of the USSR. If we approach Soviet culture as a project and as a historical phenomenon from the perspective of our current situation and experience in the world, then we are in a position to grasp our cultural gains and losses, benefits and misfortunes over the past five decades.

It is tempting to describe Soviet culture to have been merely a political phantom that spoke in the name of culture, or an ideological ghost that served the establishment as a tool of sovietization. If we distinguish between genuine and forced internationalism, then we have to ask whether Soviet culture was just an ideological mask of Russian culture or a serious attempt to create something like a rival civilization, using the Russian language as a lingua franca of Eastern Europe and Russian culture as a great modern alternative, to the West. Was Soviet culture based on the grandeur and charms of an imperial culture that became a unifying force and a gravitation field in terms of arts, culture, and intellectual life? Every empire has its gravitational field due to a rich and cosmopolitan culture, the latter being part of imperialism. If this was the case with the British, Spanish, and French empires, why should things have been different in Tsarist Russia and the Soviet Union?

Much ink has been spilled arguing over the nature of the Soviet empire and whether it was an heir to Tsarist Russia or its irreconcilable foe and destroyer. Yet the fact remains that the USSR inherited and used the immensely rich classics and modern culture of Russia as the beautiful face of the empire as the symbolic center of its cultural policies and networks, and as the gravitational field to attract and educate the elites of non-Russian-speaking republics.

Yet a deep gulf exists between socialist realism in literature under Stalin and the people of the 1960s (*shestidesiatniki*) under Nikita S. Khrushchev and his reform policies. It is a long way from the ideological and political travesties of the 1950s to such great poets and writers of the 1960s as, for instance, Bulat Okudzhawa, Yevgeny Yevtushenko, Andrei Voznesensky, Vasily Aksionov, and Robert Rozhdestvensky. Or it suffices to recall such great figures in Russian or Soviet cinematography as Grigory Kozintsev who made superb Shakespearean productions, such as *Hamlet* (1964) and *King Lear* (1970), working with Lithuanian, Latvian, and Estonian actors and appointing his crew from many Soviet republics. Kozintsev appears to have been a perfect example of great culture permeated with genuine internationalism.

It is through these high points in literature, cinematography, theater, and academic music that we can raise the issue of the legacy of Soviet culture, trying to determine its role and place in the processes of political emancipation and relative liberalization of the regime. Was Soviet culture able to become in reality an alternative to the role that was ascribed to it by the regime? Was a Soviet patriot any better and morally superior to a Russian nationalist? Or was everything the other way around? Soviet culture seems to have revolved around the ambition of a nation of workers to create a new individual and an alternative civilization to the West. This endeavor failed, but left many unanswered questions in its wake. What was Soviet culture? Was it the same Russian culture, only ideologized to the extreme and transformed into a totalitarian project, or was it a completely new type of culture, erasing both history and traditions, and incompatible with anything that had existed before it? Perhaps it was simply an imperial culture seasoned with added radicalism due to Russia's path to modernization and totalitarian order, or was it a new destructive neologism, eliminating first of all Russia and then all the other nations and cultures that had fallen to its sphere of influence?

There is no single and clear answer to these questions. If Soviet culture was indeed completely incompatible with the traditions of Russian and European culture, the question arises, why did the Soviets then still show no tolerance for the truly revolutionary proletarian cultural movement, which, had it only been allowed to gain momentum, would have simply wiped out all of the literature of the Russian golden and silver ages, not to mention the classics and canon of the West. Something similar to the absolute triumph of proletarian-cultural logic occurred during the Chinese Cultural Revolution, when the old Confucian Chinese civilization and its cultural traditions were wiped away, like paint from a canvas, all in the name of revolutionary modernization. Later, the same Confucian cultural logic that had been pushed out the back door by the Communists came back in through the window and legitimized the Communist Party as the new managerial class, but that is another story.

Vladimir Lenin's and Anatoly Lunacharsky's tirades about the Soviet person, absorbing the very best that humanity has created and adding to this cultural golden fund the Soviet ideals of incomparable value, testifies to the compromise that this seemingly lethal heroism and death-worshipping culture has made in respect to the classics and the Western canon. It suffices to recall Lenin's open admiration for Leo Tolstoy's novels, Ludwig van Beethoven's sonatas, and the comparison of Tolstoy with a rock and the belief that there is nothing of greater beauty than Beethoven's *Appassionata*. If we compare these classical tastes and orientation toward the ideas of artists and philosopher-modernists of Western Europe, such as Theodor W. Adorno's evaluation of Beethoven's music as the aestheticization of the bourgeois world, and the reconciliation of that world with – to use Adorno's term – his affirmation, then Lenin in reality appears not as the great leader of the October Revolution and creator of the workers' nation, but rather, as a small-league bourgeoisie, a stranger to real radicalism, change on a worldwide scale and the spirit of creative experimentation.

In other words, this attempt by Lenin and other more highly educated Bolsheviks to reconcile totalitarianism and the cultural canon was most likely what the Nazis called cultural Bolshevism (*Kulturbolschewismus*), that is, the lack of radicalism and heroism when renouncing vital values and worshipping brute force. While this phenomenon was not the only evidence of the parasitic effect of Soviet totalitarianism at the cost of European traditions, and its inability to provide any suitable antithesis, it did, at the same time, save the Hermitage and other art galleries and libraries from physical destruction. Stalin, with his aesthetic tastes and evaluation of art-works, in no way reminds us of a leftist modernist (there were also right-leaning modernists – let us not forget the Italian Fascist artists). During the World War II, he was forced to rely on Sergei Eisenstein's film *Alexander Nevsky* to mobilize feelings of Russian patriotism, not to mention Eisenstein's other film *Ivan the Terrible*, in which Stalin undoubtedly recognized himself, symbolically incorporated into the tradition of Russian political might and the state's history. After Lenin's open renouncement of Tsarist Russia's imperial patriotism, such sentiments expressed by Stalin appear at the very least strange and can be evaluated as a covert return to traditions about the might of the old regime. This can also be likened to Stalin's predilection for nightly listenings to the arias of famous Ukrainian tenor Ivan Kozlovsky and other well-known opera singers of the time.

So what was Soviet culture after all, which was meant to create the new Soviet person? A feeling for history and reality must first be lost to determinedly state it was the sister of authentic modernism, and even less so the avant-garde. Wonderful Russian modernism, which had no equal at the time in Europe, apart from French and Viennese modernism, was literally murdered by the Bolsheviks. The emigration of Wassily (Vasily) Kandinsky, Kazimir Malevich, Marc Chagall, and Mark Rothko, and their transformation into Western artists not only had the effect of saving their artworks (perhaps also their lives) but also shows what Russia may have become in a modern cultural context had it not been subjected to a social and political catastrophe.

Soviet culture was a strange amalgam of propaganda, revolutionary rhetoric, socialist realism, the remains of classical and modern Russian culture, allegorical art and writing between the lines, that is, Aesopian language, in which, as described by Milan Kundera, political and ideological kitsch coexisted alongside talented artists and grandiose cultural expression. If the strangest feature of Soviet culture had to be identified, I would undoubtedly have to mention the following parallel yet nonconverging realities: Alexander Dovzhenko's Soviet propaganda kitsch film-studio productions and mass culture at one pole, and geniuses, such as Andrei Tarkovsky or Sergei Parajanov, at the other; Mikhail Shatrov's hopeless revolutionary plays about Lenin at one end of the spectrum, and at the other, Georgian theater director Robert Sturua, who innovatively brought Shakespeare's tragedies to the stage, and who on the occasion of its Moscow premiere, had to listen to a fraught Shatrov defend his own authored play. The existence of these parallel realities, allegedly representing the same Soviet culture, is in fact its greatest paradox.

A fractured and continually reasserting identity, always producing something different than what existed before, was typical among many participants in the Soviet project – at one stage, the continuity of great Russian culture and traditions was highlighted, concurrent with the advance of the new, that is, Soviet, whose cultural character was incompatible with the old monarchial Russian life, the oppression of other nations, and so on. Indeed, it remains unclear what held Soviet culture, if it ever existed, together. Was it the forcible and ideological 'alliance of nations,' or expressions of the sometimes authentic multinational Soviet Empire's internationalism?

When Kozintsev created his immortal film versions of Shakespeare's tragedies, he consciously invited actors from the Baltic countries, allowing them to speak Russian with an accent without dubbing voiceovers. Additionally, both films – *Hamlet* and *King Lear* – were filmed by the great Lithuanian cinematographer Jonas Gricius. Are all these mere coincidences? Perhaps the Russian master simply needed Western characters? Or maybe not. Instead it may have been his conscious desire to raise the status of his colleagues from other nations to take on the roles about which the cultural representatives of his own nation could only dream of. Or is it more the becoming of the Baltic nations as the Other in the consciousness and imagination of Russians? Baltic country actors appeared as Westerners but were the same as the rest. In fact, sometimes there was no love lost for the greater fatherland (even more specifically, they were lost between a state of *odi et amo* and tortured by a love-hate ambivalence), but all the same, they were not strangers.

Perhaps this is the root of the painful question directed toward Lithuanians, Latvians, and Estonians, often asked by simple Russians: Why do you dislike us so? More so, perhaps this is the origin of the most chauvinistic of today's Russian political groupings' hate for the small Baltic countries, founded on the belief that they betrayed the great nation's geopolitical interests and rejected its historical friendship? Of course, the memorable role of the Lithuanian film actor Donatas Banionis in Andrei Tarkovsky's *Solaris* as well as the impressive ensemble of Baltic cinema masters in Kozintsev's films reach the greatest heights of Russian culture and are not a typical case of Soviet culture. In Soviet films meant for mass consumption, actors from Lithuania and the other two Baltic countries were more often assigned to take on the roles of Nazi Germany's officers, or American CIA agents (in other words, historical and ideological enemies). It is no wonder that the recent Estonian documentary film *Nazis and Blondes* reveals an interesting phenomenon – the continual assignment of Nazi roles to Lithuanian, Latvian, and Estonian actors eventually allowed the regime to project the image of the Baltic countries as enemies and fascists. This provocative Estonian film has already received a strong reaction in Estonia but has undoubtedly raised a problem worthy of analysis in postcolonial studies.

So, Soviet culture has a mix of everything – the grandeur and universalism of Russian culture not extinguished during Soviet times, authentic internationalism (which appears to have vanished from contemporary Russian culture), as well as combative, yet fruitless propaganda, artworks of little value, caricatures of high art, and a deformed black-and-white social optical image of the world. Of one thing there is no doubt – this culture did not produce anything close to a new person. Just as it never became an effective alternative to the West. Soviet modernization (just like the no more and no less terrible and brutal Chinese modernization) created modernity without freedom, or, paraphrasing the catch-cry of the 1960's generation after Nikita Khrushchev's thaw policy, modernity without a human face. George Orwell's prophecy had come true, that all totalitarian revolutions are destined to become the longest road leading from one form of oppression and exploitation to the next. Or a transformation from one form of capitalism to another that is even more savage.

Yet the most beautiful aspect of Soviet culture, and probably the only beautiful and truly authentic thing in and about it, was the everyday cares, objects, nostalgia, and memories that survived and were fiercely defended in the films, plays and books from Russia and other nations, just as Winston Smith found in Orwell's *1984*. Such Soviet film directors as Eldar Riazanov, Georgi Daneliya, or Mark Zakharov, and their warm, humanistic films were nothing else than evidence of the longing for modernity with a human face. Most likely, the same could be said about the great moments of Lithuanian culture from the Soviet period. Whether Shtromas is right or wrong by making a highly provocative move and deliberately subverting the rules of the game, that is, by regarding nationalism as a good thing and patriotism as a bad thing, remains to be further discussed. In any case, it is difficult to describe this provocation other than as the best example of how patriotism becomes nationalism liked and nationalism (patriotism) disliked, or the other way around.

Interestingly, G. K. Chesterton made fun of the principle 'my country, right or wrong' perceived as sufficient proof of one's loyalty and attachment. He reacted to this pearl of wisdom in the following way: "My country, right or wrong' is a thing that no patriot would think of saying [...] It is like saying 'My mother, drunk or sober." In 1872, the general and senator Carl Schurtz, who was a German-born patriot and civil war hero of the United States, rephrased the words 'my country, right or wrong' in a rather plausible way. Having been told by somebody that this is 'my country, right or wrong,' Schurtz replied that he can repeat these words about his country, the great American Republic. And he added: *my country, right or wrong; if right, to be kept right; and if wrong, to be set right.*

Any form of government or political regime, in the perception of patriots, is an inalienable part of their country and as such has to be supported. Loyalty to government is as necessary as opposition to those who too critically judge it or those who do not wish it well, whether from within or from without. The dividing line between small-scale, timid, and apologetic patriotism, and imperial attachment to, and identification with, with the territory as a symbol of the crown or of majestic history, that is, *Landespatriotismus*, is not as sharp as Orwell imagined it. Both forms of patriotism rest on a vague territorial sentiment and a loosely bound idea of superiority of one country over the rest of the world. Both reject a critical perspective in viewing their country, which is perceived as an object of pride and of defense against those wishing it ill rather than as an embodiment of a link between moral imagination and social reality.

Imperial patriotism has a strong inclination toward a moral monopoly to control and define our sense of roots and our attachment to the place of our memory and primary self-identification. To append a pejorative connotation to the term, which signifies the same that you and your adversaries practice, and to project that connotation onto your adversary, is also an aspect of power. To name means to define and to define means to possess. Stable names solidly attached to the objects of reality allow us to identify and exercise our own or someone else's power. The rest of the world has to become us, an extension of our sociopolitical body, and a continuation of our forms of life.

Zygmunt Bauman, even though he admits that the differences between patriotism and nationalism tend in most cases to be rhetorical, offers a penetrating insight into their real, not to say ontological, difference. Whereas patriotism is related to the discourse of 'becoming,' nationalism is more about 'being.' Patriotism commits itself to the modern creed of the 'unfinishedness' and 'reformability' of human beings, thus keeping the call to close ranks along with the standing invitation to join the nation, no matter whether real or just imagined and declared. Nationalism, according to Bauman, stands much closer to the Calvinist version of salvation or St. Augustine's idea of free will:

> It puts little trust in choice – you are either 'one of us' or you are not, and in either case you can do little, perhaps nothing at all, to change it. In the nationalist narrative, 'belonging' is a fate, not a chosen destiny or a life project. (Bauman, 2008, 175)

However, Bauman reaches beyond rhetoric and goes to the root of the inclusion-exclusion issue pivotal in both patriotism and nationalism. Of the inclusion-exclusion dichotomy in social life, Bauman writes,

> This difference between patriotism and nationalism tends to reach beyond mere rhetoric into the realm of political practice. Following Claude Lévi-Strauss's terminology, we may say that the first formula is more likely to inspire 'anthropophagic' strategies ('eating up' the strangers so that they are assimilated by the body of the eater and become identical with its other cells, having lost their own distinctiveness), while the second associates more often than not with the 'anthropoemic' strategy of 'vomiting' and 'spitting out' those 'unfit to be us,' either isolating them by incarcerating them inside the visible walls of the ghettos or the invisible (though no less tangible for this reason) walls of cultural prohibitions, or by rounding them up, deporting them or forcing them to run away, as in the practice currently given the name of ethnic cleansing. (ibid., 175–176)

Yet when it comes to political rhetoric devoid of any philosophical reflection and critical questioning of oneself, everything ends up in a black-and-white optics of reality. We are patriots, but they are miserable nationalists. Within this identity paradigm, the large and powerful nations appear as movingly patriotic, whereas the small ones remain fiercely nationalistic. At this point, a patriot relates to a nationalist much in the same way as a hero relates to a suicidal and homicidal fanatic. It all depends on what side you are on, and who defines whom. The question is who has enough power and prestige to create plausible dichotomies and polarities. When we and our co-nationals or fellow citizens listening to our national anthem feel the lump in the throat, we find ourselves moved and united by our national spirit and collective memory. Yet when we observe this happening to our adversaries or foes, we use harsh words to express our disdain for chauvinistic hysteria of a backward people obsessed with their nationalism.

However astonishing it may sound, George Orwell applied the ethics of liberal nationalism to his social and cultural critique without being aware of this. In terms of far-reaching insight into modern sensitivity and its relationship with social reality, Orwell achieved incomparably more than he would have achieved writing in an easily predictable manner as just a fair-minded patriot of England, who passionately opposed jingoism and imperial patriotism. The point is that he found himself at odds with the banal and reactionary essence of jingoism because of his liberal nationalism. I realize that I am going against the current here. The idea that Orwell was a liberal nationalist may be perceived as a heresy, as a characteristically East-Central European obsession with the recent past of East-Central Europe, or else as an imposition of its realities on the rest of the world.

Liberal nationalism, as a moral and political paradigm, has little, if anything, to do with British intellectual and political culture. Only with difficulty could we imagine a more inhospitable and insensitive theoretical setting for the nationalist moral culture than Anglo American philosophy permeated by nominalism and by mistrust for what it takes as continental idiosyncrasies and wild political theories. This sort of epistemology and social philosophy regards nationalism as one more nebulous concept of notorious holism, that is, of taking a social whole rather than a separate individual as basic unit for social analysis. Holism prizes what it takes as social facts and phenomena, including collective sentiment and memory. For nominalism, which is just another term for methodological individualism, individuals, instead of a social whole made up by the relations between those individuals, constitute an identifiable and trustworthy social reality. True, the former imperial entities, such as Great Britain, France, Sweden, or Russia, are considerably more leaning to *Landespatriotismus*, patronizing politics, and to what they perceive as their civilizing mission than to that powerful ethical dimension of genuine internationalism, which is at the core of liberal nationalism. Hence, a great deal of moral provincialism and insensitivity to small countries and their cultures is inherent in politics of the former empires. We have good reason to believe that liberal nationalism, which is by no means irreconcilable with skeptical liberalism, is likely to have originated from the specifically East-Central European political realities and moral sensibilities.

Yet Orwell's political and moral stance may best be described as being liberal nationalism, which made him so remarkably close and emphatically sensitive to the tragedies of Central and Eastern Europe. The idea that Orwell's moral stance was much closer to liberal nationalism than to abstract, ideological, and doctrinal socialism sheds new light on his overall hostility to doctrinaire intellectuals, ideological true believers, and fanatics of all shades. Here and nowhere else lies the secret of Orwell's nearly magical appeal to East-

Central European intellectual and moral sensibilities. Noteworthy is that liberal nationalists tend to be the harshest critics of the sinister mystique, barbaric vocabulary, and ferocious politics of blood-and-soil nationalism. Recall such great Central and East European critics of illiberal nationalism as Czeslaw Milosz, Adam Michnik, Milan Kundera, Vaclav Havel, or Tomas Venclova (see Donskis, 2002). We do not have to call ourselves a nationalist to be one.

3. Disputing Loyalties, Dislocation of Identity, and Transferred Nationalism

Orwell did touch on the nerve of what we could call a dramatic encounter of disputing loyalties and conflicting values. He described with the stroke of genius what we could take as intrinsic conflicts that occur within the troubled moral imagination. For Orwell, 'nationalism' was a code word for a more disturbing and complex phenomenon. Whatever the term he employed, Orwell gave us an invaluable clue to the origin of modern ideological and political fanaticism as a form of hatred. Although mass movements and their interchangeability, doctrinal and mass-oriented politics, and exclusive ideologies may be more accurate terms to describe the target of Orwell's devastating critique, his concept of transferred and transposed nationalism provides a valuable perspective to view modern fanaticism.

It sheds new light on the modern moral imagination as the battleground of conflicting sets of concepts, values, ideas, stances, and objects of attachment. He stresses the modern uncertainties and ambiguities as a source of fanaticism. The implication is that transferred nationalism results from uncertainty about our primary identity and object of attachment. We do need an identity and an object of loyalty or attachment. If we are deprived of them, or if we are not at peace with what others passionately identify, we are inexorably doomed to forge their substitutes. In so doing, we are at risk of dangerously improvising or else fabricating an identity, which has no reference point in this-worldly reality and which extends an invitation to the realm of the troubled imagination. If we are not rooted in this-worldly reality in the sense of being an autonomous individual and of having a solid, resilient, and immutable identity, we will search for a substitute to somehow fill the gap. If we happen to have no attachment to our country, or if we are little appreciated in our culture, a dislocation of our human attachment and loyalty will inevitably take place. The paradox of nationalism, as a thought-and-action system capable of sustaining the modern intellectual and well-grounded moral sensibilities, occurs because its excess and absence can both end up in disaster.

Whereas excess of nationalism leads to moral provincialism and total insensitivity to those who do not belong to us, absence of nationalism results in disconnectedness from all recognizable, down-to-earth idioms of human loyalty and attachment. Nationalism, if it operates in a liberal-democratic setting, does protect us from ideological and political fanaticism, and myriad travesties of human attachment, loyalty, collective memory, and collective sentiment. Our attachment to our culture, language, and landscape is among fundamental human needs. If we lose the primary object of our love and attachment, or if we are deprived of it, we will transfer our loyalty. We will find a new object of attachment elsewhere. It can be another country to which we will attach an alternative, whether real or imaginary, a revolutionary political program, a dissenting religion, a rival civilization, or an opposing value-and-idea system.

No wonder that transferred nationalism is possible because of the instability and intensity of the nationalist's loyalties. The only thing that remains constant in the nationalists, according to Orwell, is their state of mind. The object of their feelings is changeable and may be imaginary. This sort of ideological fervor, nationalism, as Orwell would have it, can be transposed or reversed. Thus, former admirers of the United States can turn into the greatest skeptics and critics of that country, reserving their love and admiration for its newly found adversary, if not a rival civilization, namely, Russia. This happened to H. G. Wells, who moved from Americophilia to Americophobia, coupled with Russophilia. That several members of the Nazi Party were recruited from the German Communist Party when the Nazis came to power, and that the Communists were regarded a far lesser evil than the Social Democrats by the Nazis is a fact.

This was subtly interpreted by Eric Hoffer, who also placed much emphasis on what he termed the 'interchangeability of mass movements' (see Hoffer, 1963, 17–21). This is much the same phenomenon that Orwell described as transferred nationalism. In his masterpiece *The True Believer,* Hoffer showed convincingly how easily and naturally some Russian and East/Central European Jews moved from Communism to Zionism, and the other way around, or how complementary Communism and National Socialism were (see idem). A nearly perfect example of how it was possible to hold, in the epoch of manifesto ideologies and mass movements, two - one would think mutually exclusive - identities and sets of *Weltanschauung,* was provided by Isaiah Berlin who analyzed the case of Moses Hess, at one and the same time a Marxist and a Zionist (see Berlin, 2001, 213–251).

If people deny their primary linguistic and cultural identity, they have to forge a new one. If they feel that they have lost or not yet found their homeland, they will search for one somewhere else. If they abandon an earthly homeland as such, they are condemned to fabricate an ideology as a substitute for one. A most telling hint that Marx drops concerns the proletarians, who have no homeland by definition. Therefore, the proletarians' guiding principle and salvation come from the otherworldly reality, since they represent the home-free class with no attachment to bourgeois this-worldly values, rituals, and traditions. This ontological placelessness, cultural homelessness, and historical rootlessness logically lead to Marx's assertion that the proletarians have nothing to lose in this world. Instead, they have Communism as their real homeland. This is a modern travesty of early Christianity with its idea of the *populus christianus,* the people in Christ or a spiritual ensemble of human individuals who become so, insofar as they meet in Christ. Yet this is exactly what happens to people within whose minds and souls a dislocation of identity, attachment, and loyalty has taken place. An ideology may become a spiritual Motherland for those who have been deprived of safe attachment to recognizable this-worldly idioms of human connection. An exclusive political ideology or a radical ideological movement may come as a replacement of the lost sense of secure, this-worldly existence in a community of collective memory, shared sentiment, and symbolic participation.

However, we must not all be classified like flies, bees, or ants. We must not all be associated with, and attached to, a once-and-for-all defined culture and community. Modernity denies neither individual identity nor collective identity. A substantial difference between pre-modern and modern conditions is that identity transforms itself from a matter of ascription into achievement and free choice. Modernity attempts to free us from our inherited identity, one of the central and greatest, although unfulfilled, promises of the modern era. As Bauman notes:

> The modern project promised to free the individual from inherited identity. Yet it did not take a stand against identity as such, against having identity, against having a solid, resilient and immutable identity. It only transformed the identity from a matter of ascription into one of achievement, thus making it an individual task and the individual's responsibility. (Bauman, 1996, 62)

The modern individual can work out multiple, open-ended, and communicating identities. We can participate in several cultures or trajectories of consciousness, conceiving of them as complementary with regard to one another, and critically questioning our primary object of loyalty, attachment, and culture. This helps understand what has been suppressed in our culture, though it may be more developed in other cultures. A presupposition of human incompleteness and of the dialogue-based nature of human awareness and self-comprehension, the principle of the polylogue of identities and cultures, is the most valuable achievement of the modern condition. Kavolis stressed the crucial role of such a phenomenon as postmodern nationalism, which 'would allow for and recognize the human quality of *openness* and the cultural characteristic of translucence.' and which could best be described as 'a Milosz-like commitment to one's own nation permeated with a responsiveness to others, a sense of multiple, communicating identities' (Kavolis, 1991, 136).

Such a variety of inclusive and pluralist nationalism, whether we call it liberal or postmodern, is not a fiction. This sort of nationalism as an identity-building or identity-upholding strategy rests on the recognition of the fact of modern life that multiple and communicating identities do exist and that their reconciliation and interplay enable the existence of such dialogue-based and multidimensional modes of self-perception and self-comprehension as being an East-Central European or just a European. Without such a mode of self-comprehension, we would fail to understand key modern moral and political sensibilities.

For instance, Aleksandras Shtromas, an ardent patriot of Lithuania, regarded himself both a Jew and a Lithuanian. In addition, he was a man of Russian sensitivity who felt much at home in Russian culture. It suffices to mention that Shtromas was a native speaker of Lithuanian and Russian, and spoke to his father in Lithuanian and to his mother in Russian. Leonid Pinsky, a noted Russian scholar of Renaissance literature and Shakespeare, and Grigory Pomerantz, an eminent Russian philosopher and scholar of Oriental cultures, made a great impact on Shtromas. As a Soviet dissident active in Lithuania and Russia, Shtromas knew in person and cooperated with such great Soviet dissidents as Andrei Sakharov, Elena Bonner, Andrei Sinyavsky, Yuli Daniel, and Vladimir Bukovsky. Alexander Galich and Alexander Ginzburg were his close friends. Yet the attachment to Lithuania and Russia did not prevent Shtromas from becoming an enthusiast of Great Britain and the United States where he spent much of his time as an émigré scholar.

Or recall Vasily Sesemann, a towering figure in Lithuanian academic philosophy. Born in Finland, the son of a Swedish-speaking Finnish father and of a Russian-speaking German mother, he was brought up in Russia and then spent much time in Germany until he moved to Lithuania in the 1920s, accepting the full professorship in philosophy at Vytautas Magnus University in Kaunas, Lithuania. Exiled to Siberia in 1945, Sesemann survived the Soviet camp and returned to occupied Lithuania where he continued his research and lecturing at Vilnius University. Influenced by German neo-Kantians of the Marburg School and phenomenology, Sesemann stood close to the Russian Formalists and may have laid the theoretical foundations for semiotics (see Tarasti, 2006; Donskis, 2007). Fluent in Lithuanian, Russian, German, and Swedish, Vasily Sesemann (Wilhelm Sesemann in Finland and Vosylius Sezemanas in Lithuania) may well be described as a Finnish, Russian, German, and Lithuanian philosopher, and he, perhaps, merits the title of a great Baltic philosopher more than anybody else.

Throughout the twentieth century, Lithuania's self-image as the Athens of the North has peacefully coexisted with a moderate messianic construct, casting this small nation as an important bridge between East and West (the former often reduced to Slavic civilization or Russia). The concept of a synthesis of civilizations – East and West – was elaborated and promoted by the Lithuanian philosopher Stasys Salkauskis, particularly in *Sur les confins de deux mondes* (1919), the book on Lithuania Salkauskis wrote in French while he was living in Switzerland. An examination of several interwar Lithuanian philosophical texts reveals just how strongly Lithuanian philosophy was affected by nineteenth- and twentieth-century Russian philosophy.

Two key Lithuanian intellectuals – Stasys Salkauskis and Vincas Mykolaitis-Putinas – wrote their doctoral dissertations at the University of Fribourg in Switzerland (both in French), focusing on the prominent Russian religious philosopher Vladimir Soloviev (1853–1900). Salkauskis studied Soloviev's philosophy of religion, while Putinas analyzed the Russian thinker's aesthetics. Salkauskis's dissertation was titled *L'âme du monde dans la philosophie de Vl. Soloviev* (1920), and Putinas's was titled *L'Esthétique de Vladimir Soloviev* (1923). During that period, in addition to Soloviev, other Russian writers and thinkers – Nikolai Berdyaev, Fyodor Dostoevsky, Konstantin Leontyev, the Russian nihilists, among others, influenced many Lithuanian academics and public intellectuals. In addition to other influences of Russian culture on Lithuania, these thinkers' ideas can, in part, be seen as a principal source of Lithuanian messianism.

Roughly speaking, Salkauskis's vision of Lithuania as a bridge between the civilizations of East and West is nothing but another term for the specifically Russian notion of Eurasia, though this concept is usually reserved exclusively for Russia and its historic mission. A devout reader and follower of Soloviev, Salkauskis's concept of a synthesis of civilizations is merely a Lithuanian variation on a classic theme in nineteenth- and twentieth-century Russian social philosophy. 'Eurasianism,' both as a philosophical tendency and model of cultural or civilizational identity, was a central concept in Lev Karsavin's work and writing – he spent several decades lecturing in Lithuania and fundamentally influenced the development of a Lithuanian philosophy of culture and cultural history. In

1928, he was offered a professorship at Vytautas Magnus University in Kaunas, where he had arrived from Paris. An eminent Russian religious thinker and an erudite cultural historian, Karsavin soon became a fluent speaker of Lithuanian and established his reputation as one of the most brilliant lecturers at the University of Lithuania. His five-volume magnum opus, *Europos kulturos istorija* (*The Cultural History of Europe*, 1931–1937), written in Lithuanian and published in interwar Lithuania, is a work of European significance and has yet to be surpassed among Lithuanian contributions of the sort. When the Soviet Union repeatedly occupied Lithuania after World War II, Karsavin was exiled to the Komi ASSR, where he died in 1952. A man with several planes of identity and of multidimensional spiritual and moral existence, Karsavin converted to Roman Catholicism.

At the same time, Lithuania would be unthinkable without its magnificent Jewish legacy. Before the World War II, Lithuania was famous for its very large Jewish community. About 240,000 Jews lived in Lithuania; only 20,000 survived the Holocaust. The Lithuanian capital, Vilnius – occupied by Poland from 1920 to 1939 – was known around the world as the Jerusalem of the North, and many internationally eminent Jews lived in or were from Lithuania. Needless to say, the history of Jewish civilization would be unthinkable without Lithuania's Jews – the Litvaks. Suffice it to recall those who inscribed the names of the Litvaks and Lithuania on the cultural map of the twentieth-century world – the philosophers Emmanuel Lévinas and Aron Gurwitsch, the painters Chaïm Soutine (a close friend of Amedeo Modigliani in Paris), Pinkus Krémègne, Michel Kikoine, Marc Chagall (all these painters were related to Belarus and, in one way or another, to Lithuania – most importantly, all were Litvaks) and Neemija Arbitblatas, the sculptor Jacques Lipchitz, the violinist Jascha Heifetz, and the art critic Bernard Berenson. How can one describe Berenson other than as a Lithuanian-born Italian-British-American art critic or Chagall as a Belarusian-born Russian-French (and deeply Jewish) painter?

But the question remains why and how is Chagall, born in Vitebsk, described as a Belarusian- or Russian-born French painter and why and how is Soutine, born in Smilovichi, characterized as a Lithuanian-born French painter? Both towns, Vitebsk and Smilovichi, throughout the nineteenth century and in the beginning of the twentieth, belonged to that same Vilnius administrative area in Tsarist Russia. More than that, both towns are historically related to what once has been the Grand Duchy of Lithuania. Is not this difficulty to strictly define an artist with several planes of identity a symptom of the absurdity of the 'one language, one nation, and one culture' logic of mainstream nationalism? Or to 'categorize' far and away the greatest ethicist of the twentieth century Lévinas other than as a Lithuanian-born French philosopher deeply rooted in Russian and Jewish cultures? Do they all exclusively belong to Litvak or Yiddish legacy? Or should we identify them as Europeans who chose a country and a language of self-fulfillment? Do they tell a story about their culture, or is it the other way around?

We can continue the list of people who do not easily fall into the category in terms of identity or culture. The description 'British political theorist and historian of ideas' does not cover an immense territory of Sir Isaiah Berlin's identity as a Latvian-born and Russian-speaking person with his roots in East-European Jewish life. When we put Isaac Bashevis Singer into the category as a Polish-born American or Jewish writer, we miss the point by putting aside his Chasidic cultural substance and the world of the Yiddish language and literature as a primary source of his selfhood and moral imagination. The same applies to Martin Buber in relation to whom all ready-made labels stop working. True, Buber was an Israeli philosopher, but a significant part of his identity and background came from Austria and Germany. Having said that, we have to add that even the configuration of Austrian, German, Jewish, and Israeli symbolic meanings and cultural references would fail to do justice to Buber's identity, which was formed by his conscious attempt to bridge Western and Eastern European segments of Jewish identity by choosing Chasidic tales and legacy. How to interpret Buber's *I and Thou* without taking into account his idea of mapping Jewish religious experience and identity through a close link between the dialogue-based personalism and direct invocations of God that permeate Chasidic tales? Who is a Jew then if not someone who does not allow his or her words to come easily when defining him or herself and saying aloud who she or he is.

At this point, we have to agree with Orwell. To classify human beings as insects and to over-generalize entire nations as intrinsically good or bad makes no sense. Such pearls of conventional wisdom as describing Spaniards as natural-born aristocrats, Britons as hypocrites, or Germans as treacherous were conceived by Orwell as that same kind of divorce of loyalty and moral judgment, a symptom of modern consciousness, which he described as nationalism. As we have witnessed, a sinister propensity to equate much-hated modernity exclusively with the 'Jews' or with 'America,' which is one of the most dangerous follies of the modern troubled imagination, may lead to far more tragic consequences than stereotyping or the spread of exhausted clichés. You might suggest, however, that nothing is innocent in the age of intense collective hatred, that everything begins in political cartoons or literary forgeries and ends in the killing of innocent people.

4. Two Europes: Post-Imperialism and Small Nations

What exactly does post-imperialism mean here? One could call it a strange state of affairs between politics and international relations, when former empires deny their colonial history but maintain their great influence in their former satellite states, which, under the guise of political correctness and good taste, are called friendly nations and traditional allies. Besides, post-imperialism cannot be imagined without a paternalistic and protective attitude to smaller or economically and politically weaker countries.

The current European Union vision, as seen from the perspective of the exclusive club of France, Germany, and Great Britain, which also includes countries holding less power and influence (noted for not having de facto a decisive vote at critical moments), is a typical expression of post-imperialism or post-imperialist syndrome. There is however another possible future for Europe – a Europe where smaller states and nations would have the last word, when speaking about cultures or the details of community life hundreds of years in the making. That would be a Europe where Danes, the Flemish, Lithuanians, Latvians, Estonians, and Icelanders would play a role that is no smaller than the role played by the French, Germans, or British.

When the former president of France, Jacques Chirac accidentally said that the countries of Eastern Europe had missed their chance to keep quiet, he undoubtedly stripped bare a carefully disguised post-imperialist syndrome. It resulted in leaving a huge gulf between the two Europes, irrespective of what titles they are given. A post-imperialist syndrome can also exist in countries that have long ago lost the positions they once held in the international arena but still maintain a thinly disguised paternalistic, moralistic, and arrogant attitude to their former colonies or weaker neighbors. The British and French are too obvious to mention here – it suffices to remember the commonly expressed feelings of Swedish politicians toward Finland or the Baltic states.

Interestingly, the imperial sentiments of the Swedes, which up until now have not descended into a strange amalgam of Swedish socialism and monarchism, enshroud the veil of Sweden as a 'moral superpower' – they often assign themselves the reputation of being the most just and advanced country in the world, allowing Swedes to easily moralize all the other 'backward' countries. I shall never forget how, during a seminar in Stockholm, the outwardly respectable moderator, a former diplomat, started talking about the Baltic states as if they were countries whose mentalities and customs were difficult for Swedes to understand because everything was completely different there. The argument was that similar forums would aid in increasing their awareness. In other words, the territory of the Baltic states is *ubi leones*.

After this masterpiece of post-imperialist syndrome, a Finnish film director stood up and openly mocked the Swedish moderator, calling his ideas recidivistic, from the perspective of taking a colonialist approach to one's neighboring countries. This was not an isolated case – in Sweden, as well as Germany, the Baltic states are spoken of more often than the United States in the sense that to understand them, one must in the least take a course on Baltic anthropology, which would reveal incomprehensible codes of behavior, feelings, and thinking new to the West.

Post-imperialism is a mask or veil of power once held but now lost, of which there are attempts to remind a significantly changed world of the division of roles in the former theater of world politics. The post-imperialist syndrome is expressed not only through nostalgia, political rituals, or the hope of maintaining one's importance, but also through intellectual strategies that hope to deflect the origins of today's most painful problems away from oneself and address them to new political actors. In other words, place one's own historical mistakes on the shoulders of newcomers. For example, a typical element of the discourse on post-imperialist syndrome is throwing the shadow of doubt onto the appearance of smaller nations on the world political map – deliberately discrediting the current world order or the logic of emancipation that helped these very same smaller nations disentangle themselves from their respective empires and create modern states.

Nationalism is frequently described in pejorative terms not only by Americans – for example, the adjective 'suicidal' was appended to the word by President George Bush – but also by European scholars, though an obvious difference in emphasis and assessment remains between American and European academics. In fact, neither a highly enthusiastic point of view nor the demonization of nationalism can lead to an in-depth interpretation and analysis of the origins of this nineteenth- and twentieth-century phenomenon. Instead of attacking or attempting to justify nationalism, we should explore how it influences the social structure and symbolic organization of a given society or even civilization. For, in fact, nationalism has been and continues to be instrumental in (re)shaping modern consciousness and social reality. Such a fundamental change is worthy not of the reduction to which it is so often subjected, but rather of serious analytical attention and theoretical exploration.

Alexander J. Motyl had accurately analyzed the tendency to describe nationalism exclusively in pejorative terms. According to Motyl,

> Further complicating the definitional problem is that users of the term often ascribe to it an exclusively pejorative connotation. The adjectives that are frequently appended to the word – such as suicidal, irrational, hyper and emotional – reveal that nationalism is merely a code word for exaggerated national sentiment [...] Indeed, Conor Cruise O'Brien explicitly defines nationalism as 'a conglomerate of emotions. [...]' (So, too, I add, are love, hate and, alas, virtually everything else!) (Motyl, 1992, 309)

In simple terms, this is a way of frightening the world with the monster of nationalism, at the same time feeling remorse that the former world order has fallen apart, where the logics of identity were completely different, and where there was no alleged antagonism between nations. The dramas of the twentieth century are often explained by nationalism or its dangerous intrusion into the system of international relations and world politics. The sentiments of larger nations are presented as authentic patriotism, and the reaction it creates among smaller nations is presented as being suicidal nationalism.

First, an attempt to explain the twentieth century's social catastrophes without attributing them to the decline of empires, changed power constellations, and the total 'modernization' of the world, but, instead, attributing them to nationalism is at the very least unfair, and perhaps even foolish. The two world wars were not started by nationalism, but by collapsing empires, and the new regimes stepping into their place, which sought to occupy the former power positions and realize the same totalitarian projects, regimes guided by global Communist and racist Nazi ideologies. Second, empires have collapsed thanks to nationalism. It was due to the disintegration of the Russian Empire that Poland, Finland, and the Baltic states became independent – Finland at that stage was also considered a Baltic state. The British Empire was seriously shaken by the battles for Irish liberation, while the Mahatma Gandhi movement made a no less gentle impact. The last nail in the coffin of the French Empire was the war in Algeria.

This raises the simple question, where should our sympathies lie? With the nations who have liberated themselves from empires (sometimes these empires were quite liberal, such as the Austro-Hungarian Empire, but nonetheless empires) or with the fallen empires? Whose side are we on – of imperialism or freedom? The burden of white man or the emancipation of former colonies? Those secretly believing in the post-imperialistic factor of a mission that instills a civilized way of life or the legitimacy of new nations of the world. The belief that great powers stabilize the world and therefore should not be dismantled is truly absurd.

This logic led to the outbreak of both world wars and is most likely to ignite another if there is no timely reaction to declarations that the collapse of the Soviet Union was the greatest geopolitical catastrophe of the twentieth century. In fact, this statement by Vladimir Putin, former president and present prime minister of Russia, is different to the expression of post-imperialist syndrome in the countries of Western Europe - unlike Western politicians, Russia's president did not even try to disguise his way of speaking and thinking. What is being discussed is not a political facade, which needs to serve as a reminder of formerly held, but now lost, power, but the restoration of the Soviet Union and the former borders of the empire. The world may well be better off if Russia would only apply Western post-imperialism, especially the British version that allowed the English, with their trademark political humor and ability to laugh at their former pretences and grandeur, bid their imperial past farewell.

When the tragedy of the former Yugoslavia is mentioned and nationalism is offered as an explanation, it is hard to dismiss the thought that a helplessly superficial perspective of the problem is being taken. The Balkans was a time bomb set on delay immediately after the collapse of the Austro-Hungarian Empire. It is obvious that after World War II Josip Broz Tito only superficially brought this fragmented country together as a federation, thereby only conserving Pandora's Box, which was bound to open sooner or later.

Not nationalism but the delayed domino effect of the collapse of empires created massacres in places where the West could have and should have intervened in time but failed to do so. There is no more bloody a period in international politics than the first and last phases of an imperial cycle –their formation and collapse starts a long-term killing and destruction effect; yet in their periods of stability, they can undertake their 'civilizing mission' in the colonies and maintain a power-balance-based period of relative political stability. In this respect, are there not uncanny similarities between the massacres in Yugoslavia and Rwanda? In both cases, one group was favored at the cost of the other, thus sowing the seeds of their mutual deadly hatred: Belgian bureaucrats and administrators chose the Tutsis, not the Hutus, to work in the police force or as minor clerks. In both cases, the passivity of the West and mere waiting to see how it would all end was in itself a crime. And in both cases the empires finally collapsed and in their former colonies an artificial code of ethnic and political relations was introduced.

After these events, and in light of the increasing aggression in Russian politics, only cynics could state that the nationalism of small and weak nations is the greatest threat to Europe and the world. The real threat is the delayed collapse of old empires and the resulting formation of new hegemonic derivatives. I do not wish to make allusions, but it may well be that the real and most terrible effects of the disintegration of the Soviet Union will only be felt in the possibly not-too-distant future.

With sound reason, Aleksandras Shtromas, echoing Johann Gottfried von Herder, Immanuel Kant, and Ernest-Joseph Renan, defined nationalism in the following way:

> Insofar as a nation tries to establish itself in the world as an entity independent from another nation's rule and recognisable as a separate and equal partner by other nations and the world at large, that nation's nationalism is justified in the same way in which is justified the demand of the individual for the recognition and guarantee of his right not only to liberty but to life itself – *for a nation is a kind of collective personality which, differently from an individual human being, cannot survive without liberty even in sheer physical terms; it will, in the end, either get assimilated by the nation-state in which it lives … or it is going to be otherwise annihilated. In all other respects the rights of nations as collective personalities are akin to the human rights of individuals, too.* In today's world of nation-states, this translates itself, in the first place, into each nation's equal right to self-determination and sovereign statehood. Therefore, as long as nationalism is understood as 'primarily a political principle which holds that the political and the national unit should be congruent' [this is Ernest Gellner's definition], as long as it demands for each nation the equality of political condition, it is a healthy nationalism deserving in my view the wholehearted support of every fair-minded person and every free and democratic nation. (my emphasis) (Shtromas, 1994, 201–202)

Here we find ourselves in the world of modernity and ambivalence. Everything depends on the social and political context. Like marriage, nationalism can easily become a tool of oppression or emancipation, traditionalism or reform, subjugation or liberation. The life of a society and of its individual members is created by dipping into a chest of instruments that is not wide or deep. Everyone wears clothing, everyone needs food, everyone thirsts for intimacy and eroticism, and everyone seeks security and recognition. But precisely at this juncture we encounter the inevitable duality of social life: clothing can mean both the tramp's rags and a luxurious silk shirt; wealth can secure people's dignity and increase their freedom, but it can also lead to their debasement; organized and legitimate power is capable of greatly diminishing the level of depravity and violence in a society, but, at the same time, it can cause the death of many innocent people; sex can become an act of brutality, violation, and humiliation, but in other circumstances, it can liberate persons and make them happy. All of this comes about from that selfsame human material, from that same person's body and its means of self-realization.

Like the search for an identity, nationalism and patriotism come as a promise of self-comprehension and self-fulfillment in the world of ambivalence and ambiguity. Yet if we end up as a conservative nationalist opposed to a liberal patriot, or vice versa, we do not find the way out of this predicament. The split of our faculties of the soul and of our political and moral sensibilities remains as deep as it was before our attempts to make up our mind, choosing one of the modern paths to emancipation and authentic existence.

References

Bauman, Zygmunt. *Identity: Conversations with Benedetto Vecchi.* Cambridge, England: Polity, 2004.

—. 'Making and Unmaking of Strangers,' In *Stranger or Guest? Racism and Nationalism in Contemporary Europe,* edited by Sandro Fridlizius and Abby Peterson, pp. 59–79. Stockholm: Almqvist & Wiksell International, 1996.

Berlin, Isaiah. *Against the Current: Essays in the History of Ideas.* Edited and with a bibliography by Henry Hardy. With an introduction by Roger Hausheer. Princeton, NJ: Princeton University Press, 2001.

Brubaker, Rogers. *Citizenship and Nationhood in France and Germany.* London: Harvard University Press, 1992.

—. *Nationalism Reframed: Nationhood and the National Question in the New Europe.* Cambridge: Cambridge University Press, 1999.

Donskis, Leonidas. *Identity and Freedom: Mapping Nationalism and Social Criticism in Twentieth-Century Lithuania.* London: Routledge, 2002.

—. 'Editor's Introduction: Mapping Inter-War Lithuanian Philosophy.' In *Aesthetics,* by Vasily Sesemann. Edited and introduced by Leonidas Donskis, pp. xi–xxvi. Amsterdam: Rodopi, 2007.

Eliade, Mircea. *The Sacred and the Profane: The Nature of Religion.* New York: Harper & Row, 1961.

Fevre, Ralph W. *The Demoralization of Western Culture: Social Theory and the Dilemmas of Modern Living*. London: Continuum, 2000.
Gellner, Ernest. *Conditions of Liberty: Civil Society and its Rivals*. London: Penguin Books, 1996.
Greenfeld, Liah. *Nationalism: Five Roads to Modernity*. Cambridge, MA: Harvard University Press, 1992.
Hoffer, Eric. *The True Believer: Thoughts on the Nature of Mass Movements*. New York: Time, 1963.
Kavolis, Vytautas. 'Nationalism, Modernization, and the Polylogue of Civilizations,' *Comparative Civilizations Review* 25 (Fall 1991): pp. 124–143.
Motyl, Alexander J. 'The Modernity of Nationalism: Nations, States and Nation-States in the Contemporary World.' *Journal of International Affairs* 45, no. 2 (1992): pp. 307–323.
Orwell, George. 'Notes on Nationalism.' In *Decline of the English Murder and Other Essays, by* George Orwell, 155–179. Harmondsworth, Middlesex: Penguin Books, 1970.
Plasseraud, Yves. *L'identité*. Paris: Montchrestien, 2000.
Shtromas, Aleksandras. 'Ideological Politics and the Contemporary World: Have We Seen the Last of 'Isms'?' In *The End of 'Isms'? Reflections on the Fate of Ideological Politics after Communism's Collapse*, edited by Aleksandras Shtromas, pp. 183–225. Oxford: Blackwell, 1994.
Tarasti, Eero. 'Preface: Wilhelm Sesemann in the Context of Semiotics' In *Vasily Sesemann: Experience, Formalism, and the Question of Being*, by Thorsten Botz-Bornstein, vii–xiii. Amsterdam: Rodopi, 2006.

Contributors

AUKSE BALCYTIENE is Professor and Vice-Rector for Public Communication at Vytautas Magnus University in Kaunas, Lithuania.

VYTIS CIUBRINSKAS is Associate Professor of Anthropology, and Head of the Center for Social Anthropology at Vytautas Magnus University in Kaunas, Lithuania. He also is an Adjunct Associate Professor at Southern Illinois University in the USA.

LEONIDAS DONSKIS is a Member of the European Parliament and acts as a recurrent visiting professor of politics at Vytautas Magnus University in Kaunas, Lithuania. He also is an academic writer and editor.

GABRIELLE HOGAN-BRUN FCIL is Senior Research Fellow at the University of Bristol, England, and PD at the University of Basel, Switzerland.

KRISTINA JURAITE is Associate Professor of Public Communication at Vytautas Magnus University in Kaunas, Lithuania.

DOVID KATZ is Professor of Yiddish Language, Literature and Culture at Vilnius University, and Research Director at the Vilnius Yiddish Institute, Lithuania.

KAAREL KILVITS is Professor of Economic Policy, and Chair of the Department of Public Policy at Tallinn University of Technology, Estonia.

EPP LAUK is Professor of Journalism at the University of Jyväskylä (Department of Communication), Finland and at the University of Tartu (Institute of Journalism and Communication).

TATJANA MURAVSKA is Professor LU and Jean Monnet Professor in the Centre for European and Transition Studies at the University of Latvia in Riga, Latvia.

JOE NAROTZKY was born in the town of Podbrodz (now called Pabrade) in 1919, and emigrated to South Africa in 1934, where he lives in Springs, Johannesburg

IRINA NOVIKOVA is Professor in the Department of Culture and Literature, and Director of the Centre for Gender Studies at the University of Latvia in Riga, Latvia.

ROBERT VAN VOREN is a political scientist and human rights activist. He serves as Chief Executive of the Global Initiative on Psychiatry, an international foundation for mental health reform that led the campaign against the political abuse of psychiatry in the Soviet Union. Van Voren is Honorary Fellow of the British Royal College of Psychiatrists, Honorary Member of the Ukrainian Psychiatric Association, and was knighted by Queen Beatrix of The Netherlands in 2005 for his work as a human rights activist. He lives in The Netherlands and Lithuania.

VITA ZELCE is Associate Professor of Communication Studies at the University of Latvia in Riga, Latvia.

INTERDISCIPLINARY STUDIES ON CENTRAL AND EASTERN EUROPE

Edited by
Rolf Fieguth & Nicolas Hayoz

This new series focuses on the political, economic and cultural changes in Eastern, East-Central and South-Eastern Europe. It publishes scholarly papers presented at the "Eastern European Day" conferences held at the University of Fribourg. These annual conferences examine the various East European countries. Moreover, the series also presents a forum for other conferences held in Switzerland on topics related to Eastern Europe. It aims to reflect on what could be considered the rapprochement of the different branches of Swiss research on Eastern Europe (history, political science, philosophy, Slavic languages). The articles are written in English.

Band 1 Nicolas Hayoz, Andrej N. Lushnycky (eds)
Ukraine at a Crossroads.
269 pp. 2005.
ISBN 3-03910-468-3, US-ISBN 0-8204-7157-7

Band 2 Nicolas Hayoz, Leszek Jesień, Wim van Meurs (eds)
Enlarged EU – Enlarged Neighbourhood.
Perspectives of the European Neighbourhood Policy.
392 pp. 2005.
ISBN 3-03910-624-4, US-ISBN 0-8204-7167-4

Band 3 Nicolas Hayoz, Simon Hug (eds)
Tax Evasion, Trust, and State Capacities.
How good is Tax Moral in Central and Eastern Europe.
379 pp. 2007.
ISBN 978-3-03910-651-6, US-ISBN 978-0-8204-7168-6

Band 4 Andrej N. Lushnycky, Mykola Riabchuk (eds)
Ukraine on its Meandering Path Between East and West.
Interdisciplinary Studies on Central and Eastern Europe.
210 pp. 2009.
ISBN 978-3-03911-607-2

Band 5 Leonidas Donskis (ed.)
A Litmus Test Case of Modernity.
Examining Modern Sensibilities and the Public Domain in the Baltic States at the Turn of the Century.
314 pp. 2009.
ISBN 978-3-0343-0335-4

Band 6 Marta Dyczok, Oxana Gaman-Golutvina (eds)
Media, Democracy and Freedom.
The Post-Communist Experience.
246 pp. 2009.
ISBN 978-3-0343-0311-8

FSC
www.fsc.org
MIX
Papier | Fördert
gute Waldnutzung
FSC® C083411

Kolibri 360 GmbH
Ferdinand-Jühlke-Straße 7
99095 Erfurt, Deutschland
produktsicherheit@kolibri360.de